The Adjunct Professor's Complete Guide to Teaching College

Anthony D. Fredericks, Ed.D

INDIANAPOLIS, INDIANA

The Adjunct Professor's Complete Guide to Teaching College
Copyright © 2019 by Anthony D Fredericks, Ed.D

Published by Blue River Press
Indianapolis, Indiana
www.brpressbooks.com

Distributed by Cardinal Publishers Group
A Tom Doherty Company, Inc.
www.cardinalpub.com

All rights reserved under International and Pan-American Copyright Conventions.

No part of this book may be reproduced, stored in a database or other retrieval system, or transmitted in any form, by any means, including mechanical, photocopy, recording or otherwise, without the prior written permission of the publisher.

ISBN: 978-1-68157-133-1
LCCN: 2018943658
Cover and Book Design: Rick Korab, Korab Company Design
Cover Photos: Shutterstock
Editor: Dani McCormick

Printed in the United States of America

10 9 8 7 6 5 4 3 2 1 19 20 21 22 23 24 25 26 27 28

TABLE OF CONTENTS

Introduction	VI
Part One: Starting Out	**1**
Chapter 1: Help! I'm an Adjunct Professor!	3
Chapter 2: What They Never Told You in the Interview	15
Part Two: Preparing to Teach	**25**
Chapter 3: Best Practices: Seven Principles	27
Chapter 4: Designing a Course	39
Chapter 5: Selecting and Using Textbooks	51
Chapter 6: Designing a Course Syllabus	65
Part Three: Teaching College Students Successfully	**81**
Chapter 7: What College Students Want	83
Chapter 8: How College Students Learn	97
Chapter 9: The First Day; First Impressions	109
Chapter 10: Conducting a Class	125
Chapter 11: Effective Lectures = Effective Learning	139
Chapter 12: Teaching Large Classes	155
Chapter 13: Questions—Your Most Powerful Teaching Tool	169
Chapter 14: Discussions: The Right Way	189
Chapter 15: Collaborative and Cooperative Groups	203
Part Four: Challenges and Possibilities	**219**
Chapter 16: Problem Students (and their solution)	221
Chapter 17: Teaching Nontraditional Students	235
Chapter 18: Diverse Students; Diverse Populations	249
Chapter 19: Evaluation of Students	261
Chapter 20: Issues and Concerns	283
Part Five: Life as an Adjunct	**299**
Chapter 21: Evaluation of Teaching	301
Chapter 22: The Successful Adjunct Professor - You!	315
BONUS CHAPTER: How to Get an Adjunct Professor Position	327
Appendixes	341
Appendix A: Professional Resources	341
Appendix B: Sample Syllabi	342
Index	346
About the Author	354

INTRODUCTION

We have been touched by their compassion! We have been inspired by their dynamic presentations! We have been stimulated by their passion and their energy! Perhaps, we have been motivated to emulate their classroom behaviors in our quest to become college instructors.

I am sure that you, like me, have been affected by great professors who have pushed you into intellectual endeavors and scholastic pursuits that far exceeded your initial expectations. What combination of affect, knowledge, and process did those great professors create that made learning a passion—and their teaching a beacon for your entry into this grand and glorious profession? How did they make 300-person lectures intellectually stimulating? How did they turn an 8:00 a.m. class into an event you never missed? How did they take the driest of topics and inspire you to examine its every detail and subtle nuance?

I firmly believe that teaching—particularly teaching college—is not the simple transmission of data from one head to another. It's not what you have learned in your unique discipline or what you try to inject in students' heads that is important. Rather, good teaching is the creation and nurturing of a relationship. Teaching is not the pedantic delivery of information; rather teaching is only as successful as the learning it produces. Teaching occurs between people; it is a human endeavor—a partnership of discovery and intellect. I have long believed that education is a change process. Change someone's thinking, and they learn; dispense data to be memorized, and learning is quashed.

This book is an overview of what adjunct professors can do to create classrooms where learning is valued, productive, and personal. This is not a book of "shoulds," but rather a compendium of practical tips and innovative strategies offered by some of the most successful instructors in the country. It is a guidebook of suggestions (as opposed to absolutes) that can help you create interactive classes that value an exchange of ideas, an engagement of minds, and a celebration of the highest goals of learning. It is a book that will help you become—no matter what your discipline or field of endeavor—an adjunct professor who is both memorable as well as influential.

In this book, I'll discuss the practices and procedures that will change you—move you away from the stereotypical professor who dispenses knowledge while students dutifully record it in their notebooks or on their laptops. I'll introduce you to great minds and the processes they've incorporated into their college classes. I'll share the practices and procedures that will intellectually inform and engage students in incredible journeys of discovery and exploration. I'll provide you with the best ideas from the best minds. And, I'll talk about the practical ideas and innovative suggestions that will enhance every class and every course you teach.

Recently, while observing a colleague's class, a student asked her a penetrating question during an animated discussion. My friend thought for a moment and replied, "That's a good question. Let's see what we can do to discover the answer." For her, learning is an intellectual partnership—as I hope it will be for you and your students. This book is written to guide you on that most joyful of journeys—a journey, not of absolutes, but of possibilities.

After more than three decades of teaching college students (I'm now retired), I've come to one inescapable conclusion—no two students and no two courses are ever alike. There is as much diversity and variety in classes and the students that attend those classes as you'll find in a child's bag of Halloween candy. And I loved it! I discovered that each new class had its own unique personality, just as each student in those classes brought a distinctive set of expectations and learning behaviors to the classroom environment. That's both scary and exciting, and it truly means that no two days and no two semesters were ever the same! For me, teaching college students was one of the most incredible, challenging, and satisfying experiences of my life—and I loved it!

I wrote this book for several reasons. The most important was simply because there was a need for a down-to-earth, practical guide that would cut through all the theory and get right down to the essential ingredients of effective college teaching specifically for adjunct professors. Trust me, this is not a textbook overflowing with citations and research—rather it is a guidebook based on the best thinking espoused and practiced by some of the best college teachers. What you have in your hands is an all-inclusive guide that brings together cutting edge thinking and innovative teaching strategies that guarantee your success as a college instructor. There are no long-winded harangues, no boring presentations, and no faded lecture notes. This book was guided by three essential words: **practical, practical, practical!**

Teaching college is a filled with unique challenges, unique opportunities, and unique possibilities. My educational philosophy has always been that the best teachers are those who have as much to learn as they do to teach. I sincerely hope this guide will provide you with a lifetime of teaching success now and well into the future. It truly is a most exciting journey!

Cheers,
Anthony D. Fredericks, Ed.D.

PART ONE:

Starting Out

CHAPTER 1:

Help! I'm an Adjunct Professor!

The "Ancillary Army." "Turnpike Teachers." "Part-time Profs." These are some of the names and titles given to those individuals who are employed on a part-time basis to teach college courses. These folks may teach one or two courses at a single institution or in some cases, they may teach multiple courses at multiple institutions. Often, their "office" consists of an old cardboard box, the back seat of their car, or a recyclable grocery bag.

It is not unusual for these individuals to teach one course, jump in their car and brave traffic jams and road construction crews to speed to another course at another university, grab some indistinguishable fast food for lunch, and launch back onto the road for another course at another institution while maintaining some shards of sanity and, hopefully, teaching expertise and enthusiasm. In short, theirs is a world dictated by traffic lights, bad food, mad dashes down long hallways, delayed car repairs, and time management challenges that would make CEOs wince and army generals cry.

As an adjunct professor, you will, most likely, fall into one of three distinct groups (or, perhaps, even a combination of these groups).

1. **Teaching One Course a Semester.** If you are one of the lucky ones (e.g. you still have a "day job"), you may just teach a single evening course once a week. You will be someone who is not reliant on adjunct work for your livelihood or one who has some free time on your hands after retirement to teach a course each semester.

2. **Teaching Multiple Courses at the Same College.** If you are an adjunct professor who has the "luxury" of teaching one or more courses at the same institution, you may have a unique set of challenges. You may teach one course at 8:00 in the morning, teach another at 3:00 in the afternoon, and a third at 8:00 in the evening. That leaves lots of "free time" in between. However, without an office or work space, you may decide to leave campus, go home, and do the commute all over again. Or, quite possibly, you may have two or three courses back to back with no break or preparation time in-between. You may have to teach all evening courses, or weekend courses, or any courses scheduled for times that the full-time instructors shun.

3. **Teaching Multiple Courses at Multiple Colleges.** In southern California they're known as "Freeway Fliers." Along parts of the eastern seaboard they're called "Roads Scholars." You may be one of these adjunct instructors who cobble together a dizzying array of courses (anywhere from three to seven) each semester from an equally dizzying array of colleges in a broad geographical region.

For some adjuncts, the thought of teaching one or two courses on a part-time basis is appealing—a nice way to supplement their income. For others, the life of an adjunct professor is hell on wheels—literally and figuratively.

By definition, an adjunct professor is a part-time professor in a specific field or discipline. This individual is often hired on a contractual basis to teach one, two, or three courses a semester—a teaching load that is below the minimum necessary to earn full-time benefits such as health, dental care, retirement, and life insurance. The positions they hold are not permanent and may be cancelled due to low enrollments or changing course requirements, often at a moment's notice.

However, there are several benefits for individuals (such as yourself) wishing to work as adjunct professors. These include:

- Adjunct instruction allows you to share your expertise in a specific field.

- Adjunct instruction can supplement the paycheck of your regular job.

- The duties of an adjunct instructor do not include administrative assignments such as committee work or research responsibilities.

- At many institutions, the hours are flexible.

- You may decline a course at any time.

- For those with families and those who cannot work full-time, adjunct instruction can be a way of keeping current in a selected field.

- For retired individuals, adjunct instruction offers a way to provide students with real-world experiences and practical information.

RESEARCH POINT

In 2018, annual salaries for adjunct professors ranged from $12,338 to $70,573, with a median salary of $30,268.

Expectations and Concerns

Each year in the United States, as a new academic year begins; more than 16 million full- and part-time undergraduate college students fill untold numbers of classrooms, lecture halls, laboratories, seminar rooms and auditoriums. Waiting for them are more than 700,000 adjunct professors—some new and some experienced—ready to share their specific disciplines, philosophies, concerns, ideals and subjects with (hopefully) an eager and willing audience.

While your reasons for becoming an adjunct professor may be personal and unique, you need to know that you are among a select group of individuals. You are part of a tradition and a profession that has endured for thousands of years. From the ancient Greeks to the present day, teaching college students has engaged individuals in a process that furthers insight, inquiry and personal achievement.

Are you just about to begin your first teaching job as an adjunct professor? Have you just been asked to teach an evening course at the local college? Or, did you just find out that a department at your local college needed an instructor very quickly? No matter what group you fall into, you undoubtedly have many questions right now. Here are some of the major concerns of adjunct professors everywhere:

- **The first day.** How can I start a new course and get students excited about the topic?

- **Enthusiasm.** How can I maintain and promote student enthusiasm for learning throughout the semester?

- **Syllabus.** How can I design a course syllabus that covers all the relevant and necessary principals of my discipline?

- **Student needs.** How can I get to know my students as individuals?

- **Lectures.** How can I design dynamic and interesting lectures that will provide students with valuable information and keep them engaged?

- **Assignments.** What kinds of out-of-class assignments should students do that will extend and promote learning?

- **Discussions.** How can I lead classroom discussions that will promote learning and foster higher level thinking?

- **Assessment and evaluation.** How do I grade students fairly and equitably?
- **Academic integrity.** How do I promote or enforce the institution's policies on honesty, plagiarism, and cheating?

Does that sound like a lot? Not to worry! We'll be discussing each of those concerns in the pages of this book. I aim to provide you with practical, down-to-earth ideas and suggestions to help you become the best college instructor possible.

What This Book Can Do For You

Suffice it to say, teaching college is much more than standing in front of an auditorium full of undergraduate students and giving them a stimulating lecture. If you are wondering what you need to know in order to be a successful and effective college teacher, keep reading.

1. **Experience Pays.** The information in this book is not a collection of pedagogical theories or dull, dry research. What you will get is my own experiences as a college teacher for nearly forty years. You'll also get the experiences of scores of other college teachers from around the country who have been where you are now. I've interviewed them, visited them and borrowed their ideas to share with you. Their wisdom and suggestions are liberally sprinkled throughout this book. Most important, this book is a guide based on what actually works in college classrooms irrespective of discipline or institution.

   The emphasis in this book is on practicality. You want information and ideas that work. You want suggestions that can be used *right now*! You want support and encouragement from fellow adjunct professors who know what works and what doesn't. Every idea in this book has been "test-driven" by college instructors in every type of institution. There are no long boring theories here, simply what works based on the day-in and day-out experiences of seasoned professionals.

2. **Your Single Source of Information.** There are tons of journals, books, monographs, and websites you could consult. There are hundreds of outstanding college professors across the country (each honored with one or more teaching awards) whom you could contact. There are thousands of outstanding students in a variety of fields who would be willing to give you inside information about effective collegiate teaching. You could check them all yourself. To do so, however, would take more time than you have right now. I've consulted them and provided you with the most useful, most relevant and most necessary information. You can consider this book as your one-stop shopping guide to effective college teaching.

3. Your Personal Companion. Please use this book as your companion and as your guide. It's not important that you read it from cover to cover. Pick a chapter—any chapter—read it, and implement its practical ideas into your own college classes. Do the same for other chapters—in fact, I would suggest that you dip in and out of this book on a regular basis—read the chapters in any sequence that makes sense to you and that provides you with the immediate answers you need to answer your unique and personal questions. Keep this book on your desk or in your car and read a section every other day or so. In short, make this book your book, your companion. Use what you need when you need it.

4. Not a Panacea. Looking for guidance on becoming a successful and effective college teacher? I'll give you the basics—the strategies and methods that can create a course where students are learning with enthusiasm and you are teaching with passion and energy. But every course and every class is different, just like every student and every instructor is different. I don't pretend to know every student in your courses, the politics of your institution, or the dynamics of your specific field. But, what I can give you is a set of practices and procedures that will make your job less stressful and your undergraduate students more engaged in the learning

process. I can't offer you guarantees, but I can offer you practices that have worked in colleges, courses, and classes by undergraduate instructors just like you.

"OK, But I Still Have a Few Questions About Teaching College Students."

Right about now you have some concerns and worries. Yup, you and every other adjunct instructor has a ton of queries. As I've chatted with colleagues around the country, here are some of their most frequently asked questions:

1. What if my students don't like me? Guess what, not every student is going to like you. By the same token, you won't necessarily like every single student who takes up residence in your classroom. Look back on your own educational career. Did you like every single instructor you had in college? Most likely, no! The same will hold true in your own classroom. It's important to remember that good teaching is not a popularity contest, it is about changing lives for the better. If you go into this new position to be everyone's friend, then you're in it for the wrong reason. If you go into it to make a difference, then you've chosen the right reason. Face it, teaching has nothing to do with the number of "Likes" you have on your Facebook page; but it has everything to do with changing lives for the better.

2. What if I make a mistake? Terrific! That's what good teaching is all about. It's how you handle the mistakes that is more important than the mistakes themselves. You'll make lots of mistakes—hundreds of them, perhaps even thousands of them. Every teacher does. I've made a million or so. I recognized the fact that I'm imperfect and, in fact, I celebrated it. If I make a mistake in a class, I let students know, and then I set about fixing it. Perhaps I've shared some erroneous information or erred in computing a student's grade. I fully admit my error to students and show them I'm willing to correct the mistake and make things right.

3. I've been learning new things for a long time now and will continue to do so, as will you. Please don't try to be the "perfect professor" right out of the box. You'll frustrate yourself and pile more stress into your day than you need. Know that you might make a mistake or two on the first day, on your second day, on your one millionth day! That's OK, you're a human being and you're only being human by making mistakes, but you're being a teacher when you use those mistakes as learning opportunities—learning opportunities for you as well as for your students.

What if I don't know the answer? Great! You now have a most wonderful learning opportunity!! When students asked me a question where I wasn't sure of the correct answer or I simply didn't know, I usually responded with something like, "Hey, you know what, I'm just not sure of the answer to that question. Let's find out together." First, I admitted that I wasn't the font of all knowledge. I wanted to send a positive signal to students that teaching, for me, was also a learning process. I know a lot of stuff, but it's not possible for me to know everything about everything. The same goes for you. Admit to some of your shortcomings, celebrate them, and you'll be creating a very positive bond with your students. But, it's the second part of my response that I encourage you to adopt ("Let's find out together."). Here is where you send a most incredible message to students: Teaching and learning is a partnership; it's a joint effort by two parties to satisfy a curiosity or discover an unknown. By letting students know that I'm by their side in this intellectual quest—that I'm willing to share part of the load—I can help solidify a partnership that can reap untold benefits later in the semester. In many cases, I'll brainstorm with one or more students for ways in which we can work to find an acceptable answer—there's work to do for me and work my students need to do as well. We'll come together at a later date to discuss the results of our investigations until we arrive at a satisfactory response.

4. **What if a lesson "bombs"?** They will! Count on it! I've created lessons that bombed. I created some "bombed" lessons when I first taught and, guess what, I created some lessons that "bombed" just before I retired. That's OK. Not every lesson you write will be memorable, inspirational, or successful. Some just won't make it. But, that's all part of what makes teaching so exciting. If you set out to try and make every single lesson perfect, you will only add to your level of frustration. You need to face this reality: some lessons will fall flat on their face because you forgot a simple ingredient, a critical piece of technology (like, say, your thumb drive), a necessary fact, or slice of research. But, guess what, you will learn from that mistake. And, the next time you teach that lesson it will be much better and much more effective. Trying to write perfect lessons shouldn't be your goal; your goal should be to create learning opportunities to the best of your ability at this point in time. The longer you teach, the better your lessons will become. It's like playing the piano—the more you practice (over the years) the better you get. Unless you're a musical prodigy, you don't play Liszt's "Hungarian Rhapsody #2" the first time you sit down at a piano, it takes many years of constant and sustained practice to play this most-demanding piece. By the same token, it will take you lots of practice to perfect all the skills of an accomplished professor. Don't expect to do it all in your first college class.

5. **How do I know if I'm doing a good job?** For the thirty-plus years that I was a full-time college professor, I did something at the conclusion of every single class I taught. Before setting off down the hallway to the classroom, I placed a single three-by-five index card on my desk with the title of that class's lesson and the date clearly printed on the top. As soon as I returned from the class, I sat down at my desk and self-evaluated the lesson. I selected a number from one (low) to ten (high) and recorded it in the upper right hand corner of the card. Then I quickly wrote down some of the positives of the class, some possible areas for improve-

ment, and any ideas I might have to use the next time I taught that lesson again. In all, this took about three or four minutes.

For more than fifty semesters, I taught an undergraduate course called "Teaching Elementary Social Studies." Somewhere in the middle of the course, I addressed the topic of Multiple Intelligences (M.I.)—a two-week overview of one of the critical components of effective classroom instruction. My introductory lesson consisted of an overview of M.I., a video of several classroom teachers using M.I. in the classroom, and a hands-on activity in which students began generating their own M.I, activities.

One recent semester I returned to my office and gave myself a "3" on that particular lesson. I pulled the index card from the previous semester and noted that I had given myself a "3.5" for that same lesson. Clearly, there was something amiss, but I just couldn't figure out what it was. My lesson objectives were sound, my explanations were clear, students were provided with visual examples of M.I. in the classroom, and everyone participated in a scheduled "hands-on" activity. But, something was obviously not "clicking" with students.

So, I decided to go right to my students and find out. I found a trio of them in the hallway outside my office and invited them in for a cup of coffee and a discussion. I asked the three of them what they thought of the M.I. lesson. They all looked at each other and smiled. Finally, Jennifer spoke up and said, "Listen, Dr. Fredericks, that lesson was so out of date." I asked her to be more specific. It was then that the three of them told me, "Your video was so ancient. Nobody wears clothes like that anymore. The teachers were using chalk on a blackboard—nobody uses blackboards any longer. And there wasn't a single computer to be found anywhere in the classrooms. It was an ancient video." That's when it struck me: as soon as students saw the video and all its "ancient" references, they assumed that the topic I was sharing with them was also ancient; it wasn't current or up-to-date. The old guy was showing old stuff (A check of the copyright date on the video indicated that it had been produced four years before any of my students had been born—meaning the video was "older than dirt." Gulp!).

The following semester, when I was planning to teach that lesson again, I downloaded a video from YouTube (which had been filmed the year before) and used that as my introduction to M.I. When I returned to my office after that lesson I wrote an "8.5" on the index card. This time, students could "connect" to the teacher in the film and what she was sharing made a bigger impact. It was a most valuable lesson—for me as well as my students.

6. **What's your best advice?** I've got three tidbits. First, don't be so hard on yourself. Remember that every professor has a first class! This is yours! Celebrate it. Know that there will be some bumps in the road. You'll have a few hiccups, a few muddles, and a few gaffes. It's inevitable. We all did. Don't try to be perfect, you'll frustrate the hell out of yourself if you do.

Second, beg, borrow, and steal as many tips, ideas, and strategies as you can. Talk to colleagues, read other books (yes, you have permission to read books other than this one—my ego won't suffer), go to conferences, pour through professional magazines, and scour the internet. Build up file folders full of innovative, creative, and dynamic ideas to share with your students. Be a "packrat of ideas."

Third, feel free to take risks. We don't make any progress as a college professor, a hairdresser, an architect, a horticulturist, a doctor, an interior designer, or a computer technician without taking risks. Sure, you may trip or stumble. That's OK. You and I and a few billion other people around the world tripped and stumbled (and fell) when we first began to walk. But, guess what? There were there plenty of people around to pick us up and get us started again. And, guess what, that's how it is in teaching college, too. You'll have lots of people (and this book) around you to pick you up and get you started again. Your first steps may not be perfect, but with a little practice you'll be walking, then jogging, then running.

I sincerely hope you enjoy your journey through this book. It is a compilation of the best thinking, the latest research, and the finest advice from around the country. I'm here to help you choose the strategies and procedures that will make you an unforgettable college teacher—one who inspires students and has a long and productive career. I know your time is valuable, so let's get started.

CHAPTER 2:

What They Never Told You in the Interview

For a moment, think about all the courses you took in college—all the papers you had to write, all the lectures you had to sit through, all the seminars you had to attend, all the assignments you had to complete, and all the notes you had to take. You may, like me, have felt that college was a constant series of papers to write, exams to take, and requirements to satisfy. At times it seemed overwhelming; at times it was overpowering.

Wow, lots of stuff!

Well, now you're the one on the other side of the desk; now you're the one who will be handing out assignments to a classroom of bright-eyed freshmen, lecturing to large groups of students who are more interested in the latest tweet from their best friend, or grading a seemingly endless succession of papers hastily put together after all the partying on Homecoming weekend. Now, you're the one in charge of a small slice of your department's academic requirements, the one who hopes to inspire, motivate, encourage, stimulate, arouse, activate, and intellectually provoke a classroom (or two) of college students.

But, in your review of the job announcement, the application process, and the interview for the position, there may have been some information or data missing—some facts and realities that you weren't told or that were assumed you already knew. So, let's rectify that situation right now. Let's fill in some of those blanks with information you need to know.

1. **Your position is, most likely, temporary, tenuous, and fragile.** Here's how the dictionary defines "adjunct": something joined or added to another thing but not essentially a part of it. The brutal reality of adjunct professors is that they are not an essential part of an academic institution, they are something "added" to the institution, something not critical to the institution. In a nutshell, there is no job security. At most institutions, the position of adjunct professor is on a "semester by semester basis" and is highly dependent on student enrollment, instructor evaluations, and the teaching preferences of full-time faculty members.

2. **College students don't learn everything you teach them.** You'll put together a dynamic lesson, pull in some really interesting podcasts, schedule some fascinating guest speakers, and design the most creative PowerPoint presentation ever seen by human eyes—and your students won't learn! It's a sad reality, but the truth of the matter is that output is not always equal to input. There is no guarantee that the time and effort you put into a lesson will result in students ready to craft a Pulitzer Prize-winning novel or design a Nobel Prize-winning physics experiment. No matter how excellent you think your lessons are, the reality is that there will be some students that just won't get it. This is not the time to beat yourself up ("How can I get EVERY student in the class to learn this stuff?"), simply because you will fret over something that may be completely out of your control. Students may have family issues at home, or be afflicted with a certain disease or ailment, or

may be experiencing traumatic relationship issues, or they may simply be having "a bad day", just like you and I do at times.

The harsh reality is that you may not reach each and every student with each and every topic. That's as true for your students as it was for you. There have been some days in your educational career when you just weren't up to learning very much. Things may have been happening outside the classroom that affected what you were doing inside that same classroom. And, you couldn't (or wouldn't) learn a whole lot. Guess what, your students will go through the same process—perhaps many times. Just know that you have put out your best lesson and evidenced your best attitude and done your best job. It just may be that not everyone is on the same page as you this one day. And, you know what? That's OK.

3. **There are no benefits.** Life insurance, retirement contributions, and health care are not part of the contract with the institution. Costs for these benefits often come out of your own pocket. Your pay as an adjunct professor is, in most cases, a supplement to a "regular" income (or it may be your entire income), but it will not add one penny to your overall retirement portfolio. That's your responsibility, not the institution or institutions you work for.

4. **Your teaching schedule can be unpredictable.** Courses taught on a regular basis may "disappear," and new courses offered at the last minute may suddenly appear without advance notice. You may work all summer to prepare a course and get a phone call the day before the semester begins that that course has been canceled due to low enrollment. You may be scheduled to teach a course in one building and discover that the course has been shifted to the other side of town because someone else needed a particular room. You may prepare for a ten-student seminar and walk into the classroom to see more than fifty pairs of eyes staring back at you. You may think you're teaching an advanced course only to discover a classroom filled with freshmen enrolled in their first college course.

5. **The pay can be variable.** Your salary often depends on the whether you are an entry-level or experienced professional, your discipline or field of expertise, the institution's policy, your current degree, the geographical location of the institution, funding variables (state funds vs. institutional funds), gender, and tradition. The pay scale can change or be altered at any time depending on any number of economic factors. In short, there are no salary guarantees. According to data released in 2018, the median hourly rate (throughout the US) for adjunct professors was $37.06 per hour. That ranged from a high of $68.66/hour (late-career, research institution, Los Angeles area) to a low of $19.40/hour (entry level, community college, education courses).

6. **Who you are is more important than what you know.** Students will not judge you based on the quantity of "stuff" you have in your head. Nor will they judge you by how smart you are, what your GPA was as a college student, or by your IQ. All that means very little to students. Your evaluation, in the eyes of your students, will be based primarily on how you made them feel. Did you go out of your way to make them comfortable in the classroom? Did you acknowledge their presence on a regular basis? Did you give them valid opportunities to make choices and follow through on those choices? In all the years I taught college there was one kind of teacher that students universally despised: the "My way or the highway!" teacher. They are the one who supposedly had all the answers and controlled all the activities in a classroom. You've probably had those teachers in your educational career (and I know what you've said about them). Don't be one.

7. **You can't always get what you want.** Just like that old Rolling Stones song (1969), you may be asked to teach sections, courses, and classes that are in conflict with your personal schedule (e.g.: Saturday morning classes [ugh], evening courses, or late afternoon seminars). As the "new kid on the block" you may be given the courses and the schedule no one else wants.

8. **Students will blame you.**

    - They'll blame you if they fail a course or receive an unsatisfactory grade.

    - They'll blame you if there are too many assignments.

    - They'll blame you if there are not enough assignments ("How can you grade us when there's only a midterm and a final?").

    - They'll blame you if the room is too hot or too cold.

    - They'll blame you if the class is too early in the morning or too late at night.

    - You'll hear: "This is the first time I've ever taken a course and not gotten an A!"

    - You'll hear: "I have to get an A in your course or I'll lose my scholarship."

    - You'll hear: "You better give me a good grade or Coach will be very angry!"

    - You'll hear: "It was much better when _____ taught these courses. She was nice!"

    - You'll hear: "You've convinced me that I need to change my major."

9. **Good teaching does not come about overnight.** Kids learn to walk sometime around their first birthday (as did you and I). In many cases, a parent or guardian will place a child at the end of the living room couch or a nearby coffee table. The child will slap her or his hands on the furniture and take a sideways step (lots of giggling by the child is optional, as are lots of photos by the parents). Then there's another sideways step as the child begins to progress, very slowly and very methodically down the edge of the couch or table. Eventually the child will come to the end of the designated furniture, take one more step and—fall down. A parent will rush over, pick the child up, and place her or him back at the starting

point and the entire process will start over again. This may take some time (since several YouTube videos of little Johnny walking are being filmed by the parents), but each time the child comes to the end of the couch or table and falls down, there is someone there to lift her or him up, place her/him back at the beginning, and the process repeats itself. Eventually after some time (days, weeks), the child is able to walk on her or his own and a whole new learning curve begins.

You know what? Your first course as an adjunct professor is just like learning to walk. Your first steps will be tentative, your progress may be slower that you would have hoped, from time to time you may think you've reached the end of your rope, and from time to time you will take a step beyond your limits and (ta da) fall down. But, there will be a friend, colleague, or fellow instructor (and this book) there to pick you up, set you back on course, and encourage you to start the journey anew. And after some time (months, years) you will become an accomplished college professor just like you became an accomplished walker when you were considerably younger. Please remember this: Good college teaching (and good walking) take some practice and some persistence!

10. **Affect is more important than knowledge.** Here's an absolute fact of life about teaching college: The more I know about my students, the better teacher I will be. The fact that you can name all the democracies in sub-Saharan Africa or list all the elements in the Vanadium Group on the Periodic Table does not make you a good college instructor. It does, however, make you a good candidate for the TV game show *Jeopardy!* You will not distinguish yourself as a teacher by sheer brain-power; you will, however, dis-

---

RESEARCH POINT

In study after study, the single most important college teacher criteria expressed by undergraduate students nationwide was "instructors who show enthusiasm about their discipline and about teaching.".

tinguish yourself by what you do with your knowledge. The fact that you may have achieved a perfect 4.0 GPA throughout all your college courses does not ensure teaching success. There are considerably more important factors—detailed throughout the pages of this book—that will contribute mightily to your effectiveness as an educator. Memorizing a lot of "stuff" is not one of them.

11. **No one has all the answers.** Heck, I taught for nearly fifty years and I still asked for help on integrating more technology into my classes, more effective ways of assessing student progress, and innovative ideas for beginning any class session—ways to get students "mentally excited" about a forthcoming topic (to name a few). Asking for help, particularly during your first college course, can be one of the surest paths to teaching success. Please don't cocoon yourself from the larger teaching community. Please know that when you approach someone and ask for help, you are showing trust; and through trust, you are building community.

12. **There's also work outside of class hours.** Not only will you have teaching responsibilities, but you will also spend lots of time advising and counseling students. You will help them through their love lives, conflicts with their parents or roommates, career choices, money problems, part-time jobs, sinking GPAs, and a host of other personal issues. You'll also be asked to write dozens of letters of recommendation and meet with students outside of class to explain concepts or clarify important points. These are, as you might expect, non-compensated duties that every teacher from Kindergarten to graduate courses considers part of the job.

13. **Students will say things about you that you wouldn't want your mother to know.** They will talk about your attire, your mannerisms, your sense of humor (or lack thereof), your hair (or lack thereof), the kind of car you drive, your Facebook or LinkedIn profile, and a thousand other things that have nothing to do with your role as a college teacher. You will be rated and evaluated by

students in ways your department chair or the administration never intended. In fact, one of the most popular websites used by college students to rate, evaluate and share "inside information" about college professors is www.ratemyprofessors.com. This site allows students at almost every collegiate institution to provide comments about specific instructors and the courses they teach. Please note: the reviews are not always flattering!

14. **Expect the unexpected.** Students will ask, "I can't be in class on Thursday. Are you going to talk about anything important?"

AN EXPERT OPINION

According to Kim West, an associate professor of clinical education at the University of Southern California, and an employer of many adjunct professors, "There is a potential for a conflict of interest with adjunct professors, particularly if you are in the same program at three different institutions. There may be competition between the institutions, you may be a 'cheerleader' for one institution over the others, and you are a potential recruiter for every single institution."

A Persistent Myth

Many individuals teach college courses on a part-time basis in the hope that it will lead to a full-time or permanent position. Unfortunately, the reality is that that seldom occurs. The truth is that the odds are stacked against you if you are planning to use your part-time status as a stepping stone to a tenured faculty position. Here are the facts:

- It is considerably more cost-efficient for an institution to hire a part-timer to teach six courses an academic year at an average salary of $25,000 (with no benefits) than it is to hire a full-time tenure-track faculty member to teach those same six courses at an average salary of $80,000 (plus benefits). With a rise in operating costs, a slashing of budgets, and a need to keep tuition manageable, institutions look to reducing their largest expenditure: salaries.

- Adjunct professors provide a college or an academic department with "fluidity." That is, if students loose interest in a discipline or enrollment goes down, adjunct instructors can be let go. By the same token, if a new area of concentration or interest emerges, adjunct professors can be hired to fill the demand until the discipline "proves itself."

- Many universities and colleges require that their full-time professors hold terminal degrees (Ph.Ds or Ed.Ds) in their field. Without the terminal degree, full-time employment is not possible.

- Some fields (for example, the humanities, education, and history) continue to generate an overabundance of Ph.Ds. This over-supply means that these folks are often in a constant and continual scramble to snap up all the full-time positions available.

- One of the most discouraging facts of life is that search committees, who must go through scores of applications in order to fill a single full-time position, may question the qualifications of someone who's only taught on a part-time basis for several years.

I don't mean to discourage you if your ultimate goal is to obtain full-time employment as a result of dipping your pedagogical toes into the part-time waters. Every year people do it (two of the recent full-time hires in my department were folks who had done an outstanding job teaching part-time for a number of years). Be realistic, however; adjunct work is not an automatic ticket to a tenure-track position. Although national statistics are hard to come by, my conversations with people on several campuses seem to indicate that less than ten percent of adjunct professors will eventually move into full-time teaching positions.

That said, adjunct professors are frequently the lifeblood of a department or college. Not only do they bring in experiences from the "real world," so too, do they bring in their own unique brand of excitement and enthusiasm. In a nutshell, they do it because they love to teach and they love to share their expertise with a new generation of learners. The benefits are not necessarily in a paycheck, but rather in the mutual energy they share with students.

PART TWO:

Preparing to Teach

CHAPTER 3:

Best Practices: Seven Principles

The custodian in my building had a master key that she used to open all the offices and classrooms. Each morning, long before I arrived on campus, she came in to each faculty member's office and attended to her various chores. She entered each of the classrooms in our wing and got them ready for the 8:00 classes that would begin later in the morning. She could do all this with just one key. One key opened more than 40 different locks in a single building.

Wouldn't it be interesting if there was just one key that would open up the minds of all our college students? Guess what? It isn't going to happen. There are, however, several keys researchers have discovered that are critical to the success of college students as well as to the success you can enjoy in all your courses. Sometimes known as "Best Practices," these keys can help you teach more effectively and your students learn more positively. Let's take a look at them in a little more detail

The American Association for Higher Education (AAHE) Task Force on Best Practices in Higher Education began looking at all the research that focused the factors leading to undergraduate student success. They reviewed scores of longitudinal studies, examined reams of empirical research papers, and interviewed numerous individuals in institutions across the United States.

The results of this extensive review were published in the AAHE Bulletin. The report addressed seven conclusions or principles that have a significant impact on how well college students learn, irrespective of the course or discipline. These seven principles provide college professors, both experienced and novice, with important considerations in the development of any course. They are:

- Encouraging Student-Faculty Contact
- Encouraging Cooperation Among Students
- Encouraging Active Learning
- Giving Prompt Feedback
- Emphasizing Time on Task
- Communication High Expectations
- Respecting Diverse Talents and Ways of Learning

Let's take a look at these seven keys in a little more detail.

Student-Faculty Contact

One of the most interesting results to surface from this intensive multi-study research project was the fact that, "Frequent student-faculty contact in and out of classes is the most important factor in student motivation and involvement." That is to say, as faculty members, our job does not begin and end at the threshold to the classroom. It extends into our offices, the student union, administrative offices, sports fields, the gymnasium, dormitories, and even out into the larger community. In short, the more face-to-face time we have with students outside the confines of the college classroom, the more students will care about learning inside the classroom.

In fact, one research study found that relationships developed outside the classroom between faculty and students are the part of teaching that may have the greatest impact.

Here are some suggestions you can consider to effect and sustain student-faculty contacts:

- If you teach large classes, make arrangements to schedule some small seminar-type classes where students can interact in small groups. These need not be formal affairs, but can be done on an ad-hoc basis.

- In one introductory course I taught, I made a point during the first three weeks of the semester to have each individual student come to my office for a cup of coffee and some casual conversation. I used this time (fifteen to twenty minutes) to get to know them on a personal basis.

- If practical, set up a time and place in the college cafeteria, student union, or a vacant library room to meet with students to chat about the course or other items of interest.

- Set up a "brown bag" lunch with students once a month. Schedule a day and time when you can meet with students over some pizza or sandwiches for some informal conversation.

Cooperation Among Students

One of the results from the AAHE study was that, "Learning is enhanced when it is more like a team effort than a solo race. Good learning . . . is collaborative and social, not competitive and isolated. Sharing one's ideas and responding to other's actions sharpens thinking and deepens understanding." Most employers will state that one of the most valuable skills any prospective employee can bring to an organization is the ability to work with others and contribute to the welfare of a group.

Don't make the mistake of assuming that college students know how to work in groups. They may come from academic backgrounds in which individual achievement was more highly prized than cooperative ventures. It's critical that students be trained in the dynamics of group work if it is to having a significant impact on their learning.

The elements of cooperative work are woven throughout this book and are specifically addressed in Chapter 15 (page 203). However, here are some specific suggestions that will help students develop the skills they need for working together effectively:

- Invite students to discuss and record the factors and elements that contribute to effective group functioning. Consider editing and refining these suggestions and distributing them as a class handout.

- Emphasize the value of everyone contributing to a group discussion. There is no hierarchy in group work—everyone has an equal role.

- Groups should have a specific task. Make sure everyone within a group knows the final product or the ultimate goal of the group's work.

- Keep group sizes to a manageable level. Large groups seldom provide opportunities for everyone to contribute or develop positive social relationships. At least one research study examined the work produced by cooperative groups of various sizes. These included groups of two individuals, groups of three to four individuals, and groups of five to seven individuals. The report concluded that teams of three to four members were significantly more effective (in terms of what was learned) than groups of any other size.

- Groups should be heterogeneous in their composition. A variety of abilities, perspectives, viewpoints, gender, age, and other factors should be used to formulate groups.

- Consider using a combination of three different cooperative grouping patterns: Informal (ad hoc groups lasting a few minutes to a class period), Formal (groups organized to tackle a specific assignment,

- lasting a few days to several weeks), and base groups (these are long-term groups that stay together for the entire semester).

- Monitor group progress on a regular basis. Move around the room and listen in as students tackle a problem. Check to see that they are on track and on schedule.

Active Learning

The AAHE task force states, "Students do not learn much just by sitting in classes and listening to teachers, memorizing pre-packaged assignments, and spitting out answers. They must talk about what they are learning, write about it, relate it to experience, and apply it to their daily lives." In short, this means that students must not merely accumulate knowledge; they must have opportunities to process that knowledge. This is what is known as active learning.

Active learning is when students process (rather than just memorize) new information. Based on research in cognitive psychology, information is stored more deeply when it is manipulated through explaining, summarizing, or questioning. Discussion is the vehicle that helps students engage in active learning.

The principles of active learning are liberally sprinkled throughout this book. The emphasis is on providing opportunities for students to think about what they are learning by manipulating (or "playing around with") the data you share with them. Here are a few additional suggestions you can consider in designing courses in which active learning has a significant role:

- Provide regular opportunities for students to engage in formal discussion sessions.

- Frequently pose questions for which there are no right or wrong answers or no clear-cut responses. Inform students that you are not looking for a "right answer," but rather want them to intellectually wrestle with a concept or problem.

- Design your course so that students have opportunities for self-initiated learning tasks—work in which they can pursue the answers to their own questions.

- Invite students to share their learning experiences with each other. Consider small group, large group, or whole class experiences in which successes and challenges are shared.

- Offer students opportunities to apply their knowledge in practical situations. Simulations, problem-solving exercises, case studies, debates, panel discussions and the like are wonderful examples of active learning.

Prompt Feedback

The AAHE task force stated, "Students need appropriate feedback on performance to benefit from courses.... Students need frequent opportunities to perform and receive suggestions for improvement.... Students need chances to reflect on what they have learned, what they still need to know, and how to assess themselves."

> **RESEARCH POINT**
>
> One exhaustive review of over 8,000 studies concluded, "The most powerful single modification that enhances achievement is feedback."

Many new professors (and a couple of "old" ones, too) make the mistake of assuming that feedback is simply providing students with test scores in a timely fashion. True, returning tests within one week of administration is a significant factor in terms of student motivation, but it is not the only one. Feedback is a continual and continuous process of informing students about the quality of their learning. That may include test scores; but it is certainly much more than that.

Here are some suggestions you can easily incorporate into your course(s) to help students get the feedback they need:

- Consider all the forms of feedback at your disposal. These may include (but are not limited to) the following: test scores, personal conversations, interviews, verbal remarks in class, body language, whole class comments, written remarks on papers, etc.

- Feedback should come early and often. "Two quizzes and a final exam" are not sufficient to provide students with consistent and regular feedback.

- The feedback should be corrective in nature. The best feedback is an explanation as to what is accurate and what is inaccurate in terms of student responses.

- Feedback should be timely. The greater the delay between an assignment and receiving the results of that performance, the lower the achievement (for individuals and the whole class). My working policy was to return exams and papers within one week of submission. If I couldn't adhere to that "one week" policy, then I needed to examine the length or complexity of the assignments I made.

- Feedback should be specific. Telling a student that she did "poor work" is ineffective. Telling her that she didn't provide a rationale or substantial argument for the role of information technology in a global economy (in response to an exam question, for example) is more specific and more meaningful.

- Feedback should be constructive. Eliminate statements about a person's worth ("That was a pretty stupid response!") and use statements that emphasize improvement and learning ("How do the results of this research study compare with your position on the juvenile justice system?").

- Feedback should be individual, not group-oriented. The best feedback is when a student receives information relative to her or his performance in a course. On the other hand, when students get information about how they compare to others in a course, this tells them nothing about their learning.

- When practical, provide opportunities for students to self-evaluate. Students can maintain a journal, notebook, spreadsheet, or chart of the skills and abilities they acquire through a course. A growing body of research supports self-evaluation as a positive factor in student achievement.

Time on Task

The AAHE report suggested that college professors need to consider the effect of time on task on learning. The task force states, "Learning to use one's time well is critical for students.... Students need help in learning effective time management. Allocating realistic amounts of time means effective learning for students and effective teaching for faculty."

Time on task does not mean assigning students additional pages to read in the course textbook (or even adding more textbooks to the course). It means providing students with relevant learning experiences in concert with the time necessary to satisfactorily complete those assignments. In short, more assignments does not necessarily equal greater learning.

It is a "given" that many students arrive at college with little or no experience in time management. If we want those same students to become active learners in our courses, then we need to offer assistance in helping students manage their time more effectively. This is an institution-wide mandate, rather than simply the province of those who just teach freshmen-level courses.

Here are some time-on-task suggestions you can incorporate into your courses:

- Encourage students to maintain a formalized journal to record their thoughts, questions, and perceptions as they read various chapters in the textbook. These journals can become vehicles for class discussions.

- Provide students with a variety of out-of-class assignments. Go above and beyond the typical "read the chapter and answer the questions" assignments. Offer a host of projects in which students can apply their newfound knowledge in various venues (see Chapter 18, page 249).

- Provide students with choices ("Here are three different projects—written paper, PowerPoint presentation, speech—related to our discussion of sacred texts. Choose any one to complete.").

- You may wish to provide students with study questions to consider as they read outside material. Invite them to be prepared to discuss their responses in a follow-up class.

- The long-standing "rule of thumb" is that college students should prepare for two hours outside of class for every hour spent in class. If you subscribe to this maxim, plan your "outside" assignments accordingly.

- Most college campuses have learning resource centers that offer students tutoring assistance, study techniques, and instruction in time-management. Make sure your students are aware of the services available and mention those services frequently throughout a course.

High Expectations

Another significant factor that surfaced from the AAHE report relates to the academic expectations we have for our students. The task force stated that, "Expecting students to perform well becomes a self-fulfilling prophecy when teachers and institutions hold high expectations of them and make extra efforts." Simply put, students will achieve in accordance with how we expect them to achieve. Or, to use an old track and field metaphor, the higher we set the bar, the more students will work to get over that bar.

Here are some suggestions you can incorporate into your courses that will help you emphasize the high expectations you have for students:

- In preparing your course syllabus, try to keep the emphasis on learning rather than the simple memorization of information. The syllabus should reflect your concern about the value of process over product.

- From the first day of class, provide students with higher level thinking questions (see Chapter 13, page 169). Eliminate or significantly reduce the number of low-level questions and focus more on application, analysis, and synthesis questions. This holds true for all of your verbal interactions with students

- Share your goals for the course on the first day. Let them know what will be "covered," how it will be "covered," and, most important, what they will be able to do with that knowledge at the end of the course. It would be important to share these goals with students verbally, on the syllabus, and consistently throughout the semester.

- Interestingly, a significant body of research has demonstrated that many students are unaware of the fact that the effort they put into a learning task has a direct effect on their success relative to that task. It would be important, therefore, to emphasize (regularly) the effort that is necessary in order to master the concepts and principles of any course.

- After the first two weeks of a course, invite students to list their specific learning goals for the course. What do they want to learn? How will they go about accomplishing that learning? You may wish to do this as a whole-class activity or by inviting each individual student to list her or his personal goals.

- Plan to present your goals for a course sometime during the first week of class. Let students "in" on what they will be able to do by the end of the course as well as what you will do to help them reach those goals.

Diverse Talents and Ways of Learning

The seventh and final principle promulgated by the AAHE refers to the incredible diversity of students you may have in your classroom. The task force stated, "People bring different talents and styles of learning to college. Students need an opportunity to show their talents and learn in ways that work for them." It is quite easy to look out over a sea of faces at the beginning of a semester and see a mass of students without form, features, or personality. "Teach to the mass and let the chips fall where they may," I was told early in my professorial career. Unfortunately, we now know that to be a totally erroneous statement—one that inhibits learning more than enhances it.

It should go without saying, but you will have students in any course from a variety of educational institutions and with a variety of political inclinations, learning objectives, career goals, attitudes, interests, and a plethora of other factors that makes each one a singularly unique and distinctive student. There is certainly no such thing as an "average student;" in fact, one of the most exciting challenges of higher education is how to provide for the diversity of students in a fair and equitable manner.

> ### AN EXPERT OPINION
>
> Ed Ransford, a professor of sociology at the University of Southern California, says, "One of the most critical factors in any class is the creation of a safe, respectful environment. This is an environment where people hear each other, where everybody is respected, and where nobody is put down. It's an environment where differences are celebrated and enjoyed."

Considerable attention is spent on the diversity of students you will discover in your classes in several chapters of this book. Here are a few additional suggestions to consider:

- As you will learn later in the book, the most significant factor in getting a course off on the right foot is to learn the names (and pronunciation of those names) of all your students. Make this effort early and you'll be able to celebrate each person's individuality throughout the length of the course.

- As appropriate, learn about the cultures, religions, beliefs, and customs of individuals from countries other than the United States.

- Learn as much as you can about the various learning styles in your class. Some will be visual learners; others will be auditory learners. Some will be right-brained; others will be left-brained. Provide students with a brief self-evaluation form on which they can indicate their preferred learning styles. Consider these as you plan your presentations throughout the semester.

- Be aware that some students may have learning disabilities that may affect their in-class or out-of-class performance. Be prepared to provide alternate teaching or learning strategies.

- Check with your campus library or log on to selected websites and learn as much as you can about multiple intelligences. Become knowledgeable about the eight different types of intelligence and how you might be able to provide learning opportunities that respects each of these in your classroom.

Some Final Words

What becomes clear from all this research is that teaching is a complex interrelationship of various perspectives and practices. Learning, too, is a complicated arrangement of factors and events that vary from course to course and professor to professor. It is, in a way, an amazing juggling act, one that never stops and one you'll keep modifying and refining throughout your professional career.

One important point here: don't expect to master these seven constructs in your first year. No dean or department chair will ever evaluate you based on your total mastery of all seven principles. A good Cabernet takes a few years to achieve the peak of flavor. And like a good wine, you can too.

CHAPTER 4:

Designing a Course

My wife and I love to travel to Hawai`i. Each time we go, we spend considerable time in advance poring over maps, guidebooks, Internet sites, travel brochures, back issues of Hawaii Magazine, and other resources to determine the places we want to see and the adventures we want to experience. Each journey is different because we always try to enjoy new things; knowing that we can't include every aspect of the islands in a single trip.

Designing a college course is much the same thing. As a new professor, you may want to include everything about your discipline in your course, but realize that you have a limited amount of time or limited resources to do so. When we go to Hawai`i, we establish very specific "must-dos" prior to each individual trip. Designing a course also means designing specific (manageable) goals and outcomes that give you and your students both direction and accomplishment. The result can be a learning adventure full of great memories. Let's take a look.

There are two critical questions that confront every college teacher whether novice or experienced. Your response to these two queries will determine, in large measure, the success you enjoy as an adjunct professor and the academic success students will enjoy in your courses. They are crucial in the design of every effective course—from introductory freshmen courses to graduate seminars. They are:

QUESTION	TERM	DEFINITION
"What will I teach?"	Goals	These are the ideas, principles, concepts, or questions that you want to include in a course or that you want to teach. They are the end products of a course.
"What will students learn?"	Outcomes	Outcomes are what students will learn as a result of their exposure to those course goals. They are the skills that students develop throughout a course.

One of the classic errors many adjunct professors make is that they tend to concentrate on the first question almost to the exclusion of the second question. That is to say, they spend a lot of time planning what they will teach in their courses, but insufficient time on what they plan to have students learn in those courses. Many adjunct professors, particularly those fresh from graduate school, have all the latest theories, statistics, research, and content about a particular discipline. They often spend an inordinate amount of time trying to "fit" that content into the parameters of a fifteen-week semester. Little thought is given to the "learnings" they want students to have at the conclusion of that course.

> **AN EXPERT OPINION**
>
> Peter Filene, professor of history at the University of North Carolina at Chapel Hill, says that, "Professors have difficulty focusing on outcomes. They prefer to talk about what they themselves will do instead of what their students will do."

Reframing the Questions

One of the ways to begin designing your courses is to reframe the questions above. Instead of asking yourself, "What will I teach?" consider these two modifications:

- What do students need to know?
- What will they be able to do with that knowledge?

This reframing of the initial questions provides you with two critical focal points. It helps you zero in on the necessary content in concert with the utility of the content in students' lives. If your sole goal is to have students memorize the content (the traditional approach) then you are eliminating a critical component of the teaching/learning paradigm. That is, what do you want them to do with their newfound knowledge? In short, teaching is about changing—changing students' minds, changing their perceptions and outlooks, and changing their interpretations of the world. Giving them knowledge is one thing; giving them opportunities to use that knowledge is the *sine qua non* of a good college course.

Course Introduction

In Chapter 6 (page 65) we will discuss the components of a good course syllabus. Before you write that syllabus, however, you may wish to give some thought to constructing a course introduction (frequently the initial paragraph in many course syllabi). By focusing on the goals and outcomes of a course in your course introduction you will be able to address the two critical elements of any subject: what will you teach, what will they learn? Everything else in the course can stem from the answers to these two initial queries.

Following is a course introduction for a course I taught every semester—"Teaching Elementary Social Studies"—a course designed for pre-service teachers in their junior or senior year. Note how both the goals and outcomes of the course are embedded in the Introduction.

> This course is an introduction to the processes, practices, and procedures that encompass the elementary social studies curriculum. It is a course dealing with human interrelationships and interdependencies. The course is an examination of the issues, concerns, and connections that affect us every day and which are woven into the fabric of our culture and society. By the end of this course you will be able to affect a "process-driven" social studies curriculum which provides "hands-on, minds-on" experiences for youngsters to deal with those concepts. You will be able to make critical decisions that will help students explore the specifics of the six social studies disciplines. And, you will be able to demonstrate the methods and materials of effective instruction throughout the social studies program.

A colleague in the English Department shares this course introduction for a senior level course on Advanced Composition:

> Advanced Composition has one major goal: to help you to develop your repertoire of stylistic techniques. Learning to develop your "style," the third canon of rhetoric, means practicing writing at the micro-level: learning more about syntax—the way sentences function—and the ways that sentences are composed of carefully chosen words (in carefully chosen forms). We will also discuss the ways that all those carefully crafted sentences can be combined into paragraphs that are coherent, cohesive, and hence effective in given rhetorical situations. Writing is a craft; this course can make you a craftsperson.

The examples above encompass both goals and outcomes. They provide students with a blueprint for the semester, what they will learn and what they'll be able to do as a result of that learning. Just as important, they provide you with a forum through which you can answer the two critical questions of any course.

Let's say you're designing a course entitled "Survey of the Music Industry." Now, here's a course chock full of information and details! Potential topics include: career planning, creative careers, producing/directing, performing, teaching, songwriting, music publishing, copyright registration, sources of royalty income, performance rights, music licensing, union roles, music associations, arts administration, talent agencies, and artistic management. That's a lot of stuff for one course! How do you get it all in? My suggestion—don't try to.

In trying to "fit" all that information into a single course you will have a tendency to ignore or eliminate student outcomes for the sake of (or at the expense of) all your planned goals. Here's a sequence of activities that will help you respond to the two critical questions above (while also maintaining your sanity):

1. Make a list of all the goals, concepts, or principles that are part of the course. These can be obtained from your own experiences, a planned course textbook, suggestions from colleagues, or research. You can begin drafting your list of goals by providing answers to some of the following self-directed queries:

   - What is important for students to know?

   - What topics interest me the most?

   - What concepts should I emphasize?

   - What is the main idea of this course?

2. Identify the three most critical goals. These should be more general than specific. For example, "The mental processes and structures that compose the human cognitive system" rather than "The retrieval of memory."

3. Make a list of all the outcomes you want for your students. You can begin drafting your list of outcomes by providing answers to some of the following self-directed queries:

    - What do I want students to be able to do by the end of the course?

    - What new skills will students have after this course?

    - How will students' thinking be changed by this course?

    - What student perceptions or misperceptions do I want to challenge?

4. Select the two most critical outcomes. Be sure these are framed in terms of what students will be able to do with the information you provide them. For example, "Students will be able to use standard methods of solving ordinary differential equations and apply them to physics."

5. Design a one-paragraph introduction to the course which incorporates the three goals and two outcomes. You may wish to direct this introduction to students ("By the end of the course, you will be able to....") or you may wish to keep it impersonal ("This course is an introduction to the principles of ...."). Make this introduction the opening paragraph of your course syllabus (see Chapter 6, page 65).

You may argue that three goals and two outcomes are insufficient for your subject or course. I realize that most courses involve an overwhelming plethora of principles, concepts, factual information, and issues. But the key here, especially in initial course design, is simplicity. It's also to provide you with a manageable plan, one that helps you keep your focus without losing your way. Inevitably, you will deal with many issues and concerns throughout the semester, but the 3-2-1 plan will provide you with a reliable compass as you begin to design that course.

Know, too, that as you progress through your teaching career, you will refine, hone, and sharpen your course design. Suggestions from colleagues, ideas from periodicals and journals, research, conference proceedings, and other information sources will all become part of your courses. For now, you just need a solid platform on which to stand. Don't try to do everything the first time "out of the blocks." Keep the plan manageable, simple, and straight-forward. Remember that good courses and good instructors are always evolutionary. Start with a simple plan and then, as you add to your experience base, adjust and modify the course accordingly.

A Taxonomy of Significant Learning

L. Dee Fink, professor of geography at the University of Oklahoma, has examined the research on quality teaching and learning and has developed a taxonomy that leads to significant learning (and effective teaching) in any type of college course. According to Professor Fink, "For learning to occur, there has to be some kind of change in the learner. No change, no learning. And significant learning requires that there be some kind of lasting change that is important in terms of the learner's life."

Fink's taxonomy is significant in that it can help you design a course that addresses all the major factors that help students learn not just for the length of the semester, but long after the semester is over. Here are the six elements of this taxonomy:

- **Foundational Knowledge.** These are the major ideas and concepts of a subject: the facts, information, and ideas that are the underpinnings of a topic or course. These may include dates, terminology, basic research, significant events, definitions, people, or places.

- **Application.** This is the opportunity for students to engage in various types of thinking. The thinking may be critical, creative, or practical. It also includes the ability to manage complex projects or develop performance skills.

- **Integration.** The emphasis here is on students' ability to connect ideas, people and different realms of life (for example, between school life and occupational life). It also involves the ability to make connections between different disciplines (for example, between English and Physics or between Spanish Literature and the Colonial History of Latin America).

- **Human Dimension.** This category of the taxonomy involves learning more about oneself as well as about others. It is the personal and social implications of learning, including citizenship, leadership, teamwork, and character building.

- **Caring.** This element places a value on the affective value of a topic or subject. It's the degree to which students care about something and their willingness to make it part of their lives.

- **Learning How to Learn.** This final feature of the taxonomy focuses on helping students become better students throughout the course and afterwards. Learning how to learn is just as critical as learning *what* to learn. Continuing the learning process after the course is a significant factor in the success of the course.

Fink is quick to point out that this taxonomy is not hierarchical, but rather is interactive and relational. That is to say, it demonstrates the combination of components necessary for any course. This is a synergistic relationship—emphasis on any single component influences the development of other components. For example, if you include several opportunities for students to critically think and analyze a particular concept in your course, you will also be assisting them in caring about that concept. Why? Because now they have an active role in the learning process. They are beginning to *construct* knowledge.

I like the model above because it helped me to begin building a brand new course. I knew that I needed to incorporate all six elements of significant learning into the design of any course so that students could achieve the maximum learning benefits. By beginning with these six elements, I had a blueprint and a structural outline that shaped and guided overall course design.

Here's how I used this taxonomy to design an "Introduction to American Education" course:

> "By the end of this course, students will…."
>
> **Foundational Knowledge**
>
> » Understand the history of the American education system.
> » Identify significant individuals (Dewey, Piaget, Bruner) in American education.
>
> **Application**
>
> » Be able to identify and critique significant issues in American education.
> » Be able to analyze the work of a local school board.
>
> **Integration**
>
> » Identify the relationship between American education and European education.
> » Identify the role of education in the lives of people from varying socio-economic groups.
>
> **Human Dimension**
>
> » Identify the role of education in one's personal life—for better or worse.
> » Learn the responsibilities of educators outside the classroom.
>
> **Caring**
>
> » Understand and apply ethical behaviors in everyday teaching situations.
> » Develop a keen interest in the concept of "teacher as researcher."
>
> **Learning How to Learn**
>
> » Realize the importance of the teacher as a lifelong learner.
> » Develop a personal agenda for graduate work and long term professional training.

The items listed in each of the six categories became my working list of goals for the course. Obviously, your goals will look quite different from mine and will vary from course to course. What is significant here is that there is an emphasis on both *content* and *process*. That is, what students will learn is valued just as much as what you will teach.

In the "Old Days," college courses were put together topically. That is to say that professors typically compiled a list of topics, subjects, issues, and principles (in 1, 2, 3 or A, B, C order) and divided it over the length of the course. The basic intent was to cram as much information into a course as could be accomplished within the time limit of a fifteen-week semester. The thinking was that the more knowledge students were exposed to, the more they would learn.

We know from decades of research that that kind of thinking is both erroneous and fallacious. More content does not equal more learning. As we have seen earlier, learning is more complex than that. Learning involves the learner; it is not something done to the learner. This fact alone should be a significant element in the design of any college course. This requires a shift from the traditional brand of content-centered teaching (which focuses almost exclusively on "Foundational Knowledge") to a more learning-centered model in which students are intimately involved in the dynamics of learning.

> **RESEARCH POINT**
>
> A significant and overwhelming body of research has shown that students typically retain twenty percent or less of the content of their college courses. A few studies have found rare high values of fifty percent.

Four Factors That Make a Difference

How can you use "learner-centered learning" to design an effective and successful course? Here are some factors you may wish to keep in mind before you make a list of course topics:

1. Don't worry about trying to cover all the content in your discipline or subject area. You will only have your students for fifteen weeks;

thus, it would be impractical to expect that they should (or would) master all the essential information in that short time frame. Instead, identify a few key concepts for emphasis.

2. Keep in mind that the content (or "foundational knowledge") is only one element in the design of a course. There are other kinds of learning that need to be woven into the fabric of a course so that students understand its value in their lives and its relationship to the rest of the world. The content provides you with a launching pad from which students can begin to explore and analyze course elements in a variety of dimensions. Admittedly, achieving a balance between goals and outcomes is a tricky endeavor, but the rewards for both you and your students will be enormous.

3. Be cautious when using the textbook as an outline for your course design. The authors of the text do not know your students or your specific teaching situation. They are not aware of the dynamics of your institution or the experiences you bring to that institution. Therefore, you should use the textbook as a guide rather than as a "bible" in the design of a course. Feel free to eliminate sections, chapters, units, or resources if they are not appropriate. Additionally, consider rearranging the order of the chapters or topics to suit your specific emphases in a course (although you should minimize skipping around and always tell students your reasons for doing so). Always consider additional resources, research, and documents to augment your course design. Providing students with multiple perspectives will enhance their engagement in any subject.

4. In my interviews with successful college teachers across the country, no one said that they wanted students "to know all the facts" about a specific topic or course. They all indicated that they wanted students to use information in real-life situations, become lifelong learners, be able to think critically and creatively,

make connections between a topic in the class and events outside the classroom, understand interrelationships, and become active problem-solvers (among other topics). Almost to a person, these outstanding teachers said that a focus on outcomes was just as important (many argued that it was even more important) as goals. In designing your course, therefore, you may wish to think about the outcomes first prior to addressing the goals. Use the 3-2-1 model above, but consider addressing the "2" section first. Afterwards, you can identify the goals that will help you promote those outcomes.

Remember that a course—any course—needs to be flexible. A course will evolve over several semesters. It will also evolve during a single semester. You'll discover new resources, a potential guest speaker will unexpectedly arrive in town, a new webinar video will be released, students will take a discussion in a new and unplanned direction. It's important to remember that the design of a course needs to be flexible and malleable. Learning (and teaching) is never in a straight line. Be willing to modify, adjust, and make needed corrections just as you would want your students to do as they embark on the educational journey you've prepared for them.

CHAPTER 5:

Selecting and Using Textbooks

Several years ago, I wrote a college textbook on the teaching of language arts. In the Preface, I stated that if any topic, subject, or course is to be exciting and dynamic, then that attitude should be woven throughout every dimension of a college textbook. As both an author and college instructor, it was my fervent belief that the use of a textbook had the potential to "make or break" a course not just by its material or organization, but more importantly, by how it is used.

This chapter provides you with an overview of the attributes of quality college textbooks, how to integrate textbooks into the design and delivery of course concepts, and some of the tips and suggestions regarding textbooks used by some of the best college instructors. Consider these ideas as possibilities, not absolutes, for the design of your courses.

Textbooks: What's Inside?

Textbooks come in all shapes and sizes depending on the nature of the discipline, the materials to be covered, and the level of a particular course (lower division, upper division, graduate). By definition, a textbook is a collection of the knowledge, concepts, and principles of a selected topic or course. It is usually written by one or more college professors, researchers, or experts in a particular field or discipline. While there are disparate elements among textbooks and textbook publishers, here are typical features which, in varying degrees, are found in an "average" college textbook:

- Key Questions. Often at the beginning of a chapter to alert students to key concepts.

- Key Ideas. Highlighted sections throughout the chapter or at the end to summarize important points.

- Introductions. A brief overview of chapter content.

- Quotations. Statements from experts in the field that underscore a specific point of view.

- Student Activities. Projects or out-of-class investigations that reinforce chapter concepts.

- Commentaries. Specific points of views (either complementary or conflicting) about a specific issue.

- Vignettes. Brief stories or anecdotes that illustrate a specific point of view.

- Marginal Notes. Brief notes that highlight key ideas within a chapter.

- Chapter Summaries. A short and compact overview of key chapter concepts or ideas.

- Suggested Readings and Resources. Lists of print and Internet sources (often with annotations) for students to locate additional information on specific topics.

- Glossary. Definitions of key vocabulary.

- A Resource Handbook. This may be a supplementary publication that contains additional related readings, annotated bibliographies, out-of-class activities, charts and graphs, or practice materials for labs and/or seminars.

- Web Support. This may include self-assessments, exams, readings, web links, or a sample syllabus.

Textbooks provide you with several advantages for any college course:

- Textbooks are especially helpful for beginning college instructors. The material to be covered and the sequence of topics are spelled out in detail.

- A textbook provides you with a balanced, sequential presentation of information.

- A textbook should provide up-to-date information, research, and principles that is relevant or reflects current opinion and/or practice in a discipline.

- Textbooks provide a way for students to obtain a foundation of knowledge—particularly in subject areas where they have no previous experience.

- Textbooks provide a framework for the organization of research or current thinking about a course.

AN EXPERT OPINION

Professor Robert Rotenberg of DePaul University in Chicago says that professors need to distinguish between "an opportunity to teach the book, rather than looking for a book from which students can learn." In other words, a textbook is not an outline for teaching a course; instead, it is a resource that addresses students' needs relative to course content."

Selecting an Appropriate Textbook

College students have an expectation that there will outside readings for almost any course. That means that they will need to purchase one or more textbooks in order to obtain necessary background information, current research in the field, concepts, principles, opinions, and viewpoints. The careful and judicious selection of texts ensures that students will be able to come to class prepared and will be able to leave the course with appropriate levels of comprehension.

In most disciplines, there are many potential textbooks available. In disciplines that are relatively new (or for experimental courses) the range of available textbooks may be limited. How do you find out about the textbooks in your field? Here are some tips:

- As soon as you are assigned to teach a specific course, contact colleagues in your department. Ask them for the titles of textbooks they have used in the past or for the names of authors or researchers they admire or respect.

- Most textbook publishers have sales representatives, each of whom is assigned to a specific geographical region (a set of colleges). You can locate the name of these reps through each publisher's website. Ask them to provide you with complimentary desk copies of relevant textbooks for your review.

- Use publisher websites to order complimentary desk copies (i.e. free samples) of textbooks. You can often bypass the sales reps by ordering examination copies of selected textbooks directly on each publisher's website. This may be one of the first tasks you should accomplish as a new instructor.

- Whenever you attend a conference or convention in your discipline, take time to visit the display booths in the exhibit area. Here, you will discover the latest texts as well as the newest supplemental materials. Be sure to sign up for their mailing lists. Get the business cards of the sales reps, too. Often, publishers will grant you a conference discount if you would like to take a potential text home immediately.

- Also, while at conferences, peruse the listing of scheduled presentations, seminars, workshops, and discussions in the conference program. Plan to talk with some of the presenters about the texts they recommend or use in their courses.

- Ask to see the syllabi of colleagues in your department. Check out the texts they are using in their courses. You may wish to contact professors at other institutions (via the respective college websites) and ask them for complimentary copies of their syllabi or specific recommendations of potential textbooks for a specific course.

Textbook Evaluation Scale

Suffice it to say, textbooks come in all shapes and sizes. Some are like enormous unabridged encyclopedias, while other treat subjects superficially. Some are chronological in nature; others target specific concepts of principles. However, since textbook publishers tend to have fairly rigid guidelines on textbook authorship, there are many elements which tend to be repeated irrespective of discipline, topic or course.

The chart below has many of elements that are essential to a good college textbook. Since each course and each discipline is different, not every element will part of every textbook (a geometry textbook may not have recommended readings; a poetry text may not have any graphic elements). You can use this scale to evaluate various texts for a particular course. Rate each feature from five (high) to one (low). If an item is not applicable, circle NA. Upon completion, tally the ratings to determine the best all-around textbook for a course.

INFORMAL TEXTBOOK EVALUATION

Title of textbook_____

Author(s):_____

Date of publication:_____

Publisher:_____

Sequential table of contents	5 4 3 2 1 NA
Up to date (current)	5 4 3 2 1 NA
Glossary	5 4 3 2 1 NA
Bibliography	5 4 3 2 1 NA
Recommended readings	5 4 3 2 1 NA
Suggested websites	5 4 3 2 1 NA
Index	5 4 3 2 1 NA
Engaging writing style	5 4 3 2 1 NA
Thorough factual coverage	5 4 3 2 1 NA
Heading and subheadings	5 4 3 2 1 NA
Captions and labels for graphics	5 4 3 2 1 NA
Sidebars with relevant information	5 4 3 2 1 NA
Practice exercises/activities	5 4 3 2 1 NA
Chapter previews	5 4 3 2 1 NA
Chapter summaries	5 4 3 2 1 NA
Extension activities/homework	5 4 3 2 1 NA
Uncrowded page layout	5 4 3 2 1 NA
End of chapter questions	5 4 3 2 1 NA
Appropriate font, margins, line length	5 4 3 2 1 NA
Graphic elements (art, photos, charts)	5 4 3 2 1 NA
Technical support (website, exams, etc.)	5 4 3 2 1 NA

A textbook is only as good as the teacher who uses it. It's important to remember that a textbook is just one tool, perhaps a very important tool, in your teaching arsenal. Sometimes, teachers over-rely on textbooks and don't consider other aids or other materials for the classroom. Some teachers reject a textbook approach to learning because the textbook is outdated or insufficiently covers a topic or subject area.

As an adjunct instructor, you will need to make many decisions, one of those being how you wish to use the textbook. As good as they may appear on the surface, it's important to realize that there are some limitations to textbooks. The following paragraphs provide some of the most common weaknesses of textbooks along with ways of overcoming those difficulties.

Surveys of college students across the country reveal several issues with (read: complaints about) college texts. These negatives have remained constant over the years (you may have even voiced one or more of them in your undergraduate years). However common these negatives may be, they should also be considerations in your selection of appropriate textbooks.

- Textbooks are too expensive. Many students feel that textbooks are overpriced or are another way for the institution to pry more money from their wallets.

- Many textbooks are poorly written. Often textbooks are written by an expert in a specific field—someone who has a great deal of knowledge about a discipline, but may not be a professional author. As any good writing book will tell you, there is a tremendous difference between knowing a lot about something and being able to communicate that knowledge to someone else. Writing skills are often in short supply in textbooks.

- Textbooks are often "over the heads" of students. A great number of textbooks are sophisticated interpretations of relevant research. Those interpretations make sense to other practitioners, but may have little relevance for students just beginning their academic journey. In short, students often discover textbooks as incomprehensible, unfathomable, and/or unreadable.

- Textbooks are often all-encompassing. It is not unusual for students to reject textbooks simply because of what they are: compendiums of large masses of data for large masses of students. Students often find it difficult to understand the relevance of so much data to their personal lives.

One of the common complaints voiced by college students is "The [bleep] textbook cost a hundred twenty-five dollars, and we only read a few chapters. What a waste!" With the ever-escalating price of textbooks, it seems reasonable to students that they should get something for their financial investment in the academic materials of a course.

Effective Textbook Use

Professors typically designate one or more textbook chapters for each topic in a course. The sequence of chapter readings is outlined on the syllabus. Students are expected to read the assigned chapters (prior to class) and come to class prepared to discuss the content. While this is a traditional way of using a textbook, let's make textbook use more beneficial for your students by examining three critical components of reading texts:

- Before reading
- During reading
- After reading

This sequence is referred to as "Guided Reading" and it can enhance the utility of any textbook in any course. Let's take a look in a little more detail.

1. **Before Reading.** This stage is designed to link students' background knowledge and experiences to the text. Additionally, it is when a purpose for reading is established and specific direction is provided. In short, it's where connections are made in students' minds as well

as in course content. Here are some suggested strategies you can share with students before they read an assigned chapter:

- Encourage students to tap into any background knowledge they may have about the chapter topic.

- Ask students to talk about what they may already know about the topic of the chapter. Encourage them to place that information into various pre-reading categories.

- Encourage students to generate any questions they may have about the topic.

- Invite students to make predictions based on the chapter title or subtitles.

- Ask students to develop "links" between the assigned chapter and one previously read.

- Present and define potentially difficult vocabulary.

- Provide students with a study guide or outline of key concepts they should keep in mind while reading.

2. **During Reading.** This stage of textbook reading provides students with information necessary to the comprehension of important ideas and concepts. It is where students add to their respective "storehouses" of information while actively processing text. It implies that there is an interaction between the reader and the text. Here are some suggested strategies:

- Invite students to locate answers to previously generated pre-reading questions.

- Ask students to verify and/or reformulate predictions.

- Encourage students to integrate new data with prior knowledge.

- Ask students to generate questions (as they read) for classroom discussion.

- Invite students to write brief summaries of selected sections (or of an entire chapter).

- Invite students to respond to some of the following metacognitive questions: Why would this information be important for me to know? How does this information differ from other things I know? Why is this difficult for me to understand? Can I write a summary of this section? What do I know so far?

3. **After Reading.** Post-reading activities are critical to students' comprehension of textual material. Asking students to read a textbook chapter without any follow-up is both inappropriate as well as self-defeating. This is a wonderful opportunity for you to help students "build bridges" between what they knew (or didn't know) and what they need to know. This can be accomplished with some of the following practices:

   - Invite students to evaluate pre-reading predictions.

   - Engage students in a selection of problem-solving activities.

   - Provide opportunities for students to share perceptions and understandings in small groups.

   - Encourage students to pose unanswered questions.

   - Ask students to participate in debates, panel discussions, simulations, role-playing situations, journaling, interviews, and other extending activities.

   - Invite students to define selected vocabulary words or summarize significant concepts

One of the post-reading strategies I used in my college courses was a Chapter Log. Copies of this sheet were provided to students at the start of the semester. For each assigned chapter in the text, students were asked to partially complete one of the Logs. A critical thinking question was posed for students to record and respond to for each separate chapter. These

Logs served as valuable small group discussion vehicles (discussions lasted for approximately ten minutes). I listened carefully to the conversations and corrected misconceptions, provided additional explanations, or clarified important points in my follow-up lectures or presentations. Here's an example of a Chapter Log:

CHAPTER LOG

Chapter Number(s):_____ Pages:_____

Topic(s):_____

Group members: _____ _____

                   _____ _____

Critical Question for this chapter:_____

_____

My response(s) [to be completed before class]:

Group Consensus:

A significant quote from the reading is [to be completed before class]:

   Page:_____ Column:_____ Line:_____

Group Consensus:

Overall, I think today's experience
(chapter reading &/or group discussion) was:

❏ Very stimulating   ❏ Interesting   ❏ Fairly interesting

❏ Confusing   ❏ Boring   ❏ Other:_____

_____

The Textbook as a Tool

I like to think of textbooks as tools; they are only as good as the person using them. A scalpel in the hands of a competent surgeon can be used to excise a malignant tumor or correct a defective heart valve. In the hands of someone else, the result may be a permanent disfigurement or the shortening of a life. How you decide to use textbooks will be dependent on many factors.

I would like to add a personal note of caution here. That is, do not make the mistake of basing an entire course on a single textbook. The textbook needs to be used judiciously. A carpenter, for example, doesn't just use a hammer to build a magnificent oak chest. She may use a plane, chisel, circular saw, rotary sander, or any number of tools to create the masterpiece she wishes to build. A great college course, just like a great piece of furniture, needs many tools in its construction.

When thinking about how you want to use textbooks, consider the following:

- Use the textbook as a primary resource for students, but not the only resource.

- Use a textbook as a guide, not a mandate, for instruction.

- Be free to modify, change, eliminate, or add to the material in the textbook.

- Supplement the textbook with outside readings, research, and investigations.

- Feel free to eliminate chapters in order to provide more in-depth coverage of other topics.

- Feel free to "re-arrange" the order of the textbook chapters in accordance with the sequence of topics you wish to present to students.

Without a Text

Many adjunct professors eschew textbooks in favor of course packets. A course packet is a collection of relevant journal articles selected by the professor. The articles are duplicated and the reading assignments of the course are based on this compendium. Course packets are only as good as their currency. Don't use outdated research or "tired" articles. The best course packets are those that are refreshed on a regular basis (annually, for example). There are several advantages of these readings over textbooks.

Course packets:

- Provide students with the most up-to-date information and research on selected topics.

- Ensure that students receive a variety of opinions, viewpoints, or arguments about individual topics or the discipline as a whole.

- Encourage critical thinking through a focus on class evaluations, insights, and discussions.

- Provide multiple sources of information.

- Introduce students to the breadth of journals and research options in a selected field.

- Can be tailored for the specific level of students (lower division, upper division) or subject intensity (introductory level, advanced level)

- Can be used to sequence (from easy to difficult) the specific topics of a discipline

- Permits instructors to determine the topics they wish to "cover" rather than leaving that decision in the hands of a "pre-packaged" textbook

If you wish to provide your students with a collection of articles or a compendium of copyrighted material there are several clearinghouses who will obtain the necessary permissions, assemble the articles in any order you wish, duplicate sufficient copies for the students in a course, and make these documents available through your institution's bookstore. The costs for this service are part of the purchase price students pay at the bookstore. You can obtain the names (and services offered) of these businesses through your college library, department secretary, or appropriate dean.

Final Thought

Remember, no textbook is perfect and no textbook is complete. It is one resource at your disposal—a blueprint, a guidebook, and an outline. However, they do provide students with a ready "anchor point" for a course—a way to make sense of new or complex issues that can lead to higher levels of comprehension.

CHAPTER 6:

Designing a Course Syllabus

If you were planning to go on a safari in Africa, there would be quite a bit of work to do beforehand. You'd have to get a passport, make airline reservations, obtain appropriate clothing and other supplies, make hotel or lodging reservations, plan transportation, and a thousand other details. You might even sketch out a "to do" list in order to check off each of the various tasks as they are completed.

A syllabus is a "to do" list for both professors and their students. It is the instructional guide for a course—a way to map out what you want students to learn, how you will help them learn that material, and their responsibilities throughout the semester. Let's take a look at good syllabus planning and how you can effectively use syllabi in your courses.

Syllabi: What are they?

The dictionary defines "syllabus" as an outline for a course of study. It lists the topics covered, the requirements for a course, the expectations of students, and other types of basic information such as contact information for the instructor and grading procedures. But, a carefully designed syllabus is much more than that. Indeed, many institutions consider the syllabus to be a contract between the student and the professor; it lists the expectations of each in reaching a desired goal: the successful completion of a course.

In many respects, a syllabus is a blueprint, one subject to modification and revision from year to year and from course to course. The best way to look at a syllabus is as an evolutionary document, one that changes and adapts to the needs of students and the needs of a course or discipline. In short, a syllabus is a document that provides a sense of direction and the means to help students achieve appropriate levels of competence.

A good syllabus provides an outline for the accomplishment of specific tasks, while at the same time allowing for a measure of flexibility in terms of course concepts and instructor preferences. Syllabi exist for several reasons:

- To communicate to students what the course is about
- To clarify why the course is taught.
- To present the primary and secondary topics covered in the course
- To detail the logistics of the course.
- To provide a sequence or schedule of required tasks.
- To establish assessment and evaluation procedures.

Three of the biggest questions you will need to face as an adjunct professor is, "What material do I need to cover?", "How much of that material do I need to cover?", and "What is the sequence for delivery of that material?" As an adjunct professor, you may have an urge to cover everything "under the sun" (full-time professors fall into this same trap, too). You may feel that students need to be exposed to a wide range of information, concepts, and facts in order to fully understand the subject matter. In fact, there is convincing research that less material covered in-depth is more advantageous than more material covered superficially.

The two biggest demons you will need to wrestle in designing a course syllabus are time and material. How to balance the two will be a constant struggle both at the beginning of your teaching career and throughout all your years in academia. Here are a few suggestions to make that struggle more manageable:

1. **Decide on how you want to organize your course.** Select one of the following designs:

   - Deductive (general to specific). List all the topics as presented in a standard textbook for the subject (or use several textbooks and look for overlapping ideas). Assign each of the topics to a date on the semester calendar.

   - Inductive (specific to general). Make a large list of all the topics, ideas, concepts, facts, generalizations and principles that you, personally, would like to cover in the course. Assign each of the topics to a date on the semester calendar.

2. **Decide on a sequence for the course.** Select from one of the following possibilities:

   - From simple concepts to more complex concepts

   - Chronologically or historically

   - From knowledge to application

   - From theoretical to practical

   - Hierarchical

   - From general to specific

   - In order to make this step successful, you need to answer the following question: What do students need to know and when do they need to know it?

3. **Pare down.** Inevitably, you will have more topics than you will have available dates on the calendar. Now is when you need to make some difficult decisions, such as the following:

- Which topics are most important?

- Which topics need lots of time versus those that need little time?

- Which topics can you delete without affecting the overall content of the course (as described in the college catalog)?

- Which topics are favorites of yours and which ones are necessary, but not particularly engaging (for you)?

- Which topics will be confusing for students; which ones will be clear and apparent?

> **AN EXPERT OPINION**
>
> Peter Filene, professor of history at the University of North Carolina at Chapel Hill, cautions that, "the first time you teach a course is inevitably a dress rehearsal. You will identify the excesses, omissions, and confusions only as you perform it in dialogue with a live audience."

Now is when you need to decide on the various ancillary experiences (both in-class and out-of-class) you want your students to engage in. These would include (but are not limited to) reading assignments, written reports, exams, quizzes, seminars, forums, discussions, field trips, films, debates, simulations, interviews, observations, internships, and the like. Now, begin to "slot" those specific events into the developing syllabus.

What you will discover is that there are probably more things to do than there is time available to do them. Like a juggler in a circus, you have to strike a balance between the objects and the processes necessary to keep them moving effectively. Unfortunately, there is no magic formula; every subject, semester, class, and professor is different. Know that a syllabus (and the design of a course) is always evolutionary. What you create now might be vastly different from what you create ten semesters from now. That's O.K. In the end, a well-structured syllabus is founded on the answers to four basic questions:

- What are your goals for students in this course (cognition)?
- How will you involve students in those goals (methodologies)?
- How will students accomplish those goals (assignments)?
- How will you and your students know if they have realized those goals (assessment and evaluation)?

Design it Right - The Basic Elements

The following "ingredients" of a course syllabus are offered as an essential outline for any course or any subject. While the exact order of items is not critical, the inclusion of these basic parts will help ensure that your students are "up to speed' on the design and delivery of your course from the first day of class.

1. **Course Information.** The initial page or section of a course syllabus should include basic course information. The following is essential:

    - Course number
    - Course title
    - Credit hours
    - Semester or term (e.g. Spring 20XX)
    - Location of the classroom
    - Days and hours the class meets
    - Prerequisites/permission of instructor (as required)

2. **Instructor Information.** Be sure to provide basic information about yourself. Include most or all of the following:

    - Your name and title
    - Your office location (if available) or a meeting room

- Your office/meeting hours
- Your e-mail address (office and/or home)
- Your personal (or business) web page
- The course webpage (if any)
- Some instructors list their cell phone number on the syllabus in order to promote additional lines of communication after class hours. If you choose to do so, be sure to include the hours when students may call. For example, "No calls before 9:00 a.m. or after 8:00 p.m."

3. **Course Description.** This is a basic overview of the course and its objectives. Most instructors will include, at a minimum, the description of the course as included in the college catalog. Be aware, however, that the course may have changed or altered since the publication of the catalog, so it is essential that this description be up-to-date, accurate, and complete. Consider including the following information:

- The general content of the course
- Instructional methods (e.g. lecture, lab, seminar)
- Initial and final goals
- Need for the course
- Relationship of course to the major

4. **Course Objectives.** If the syllabus is the roadmap for the course, then the objectives are the destinations you want your students to reach at the end of the course. Objectives spell out what you intend students to know or be able to do when they successfully complete the semester (Please re-read Chapter 4, page 39).

One of the easiest ways to design the objectives for a course is to modify the catalog description. You may be able to locate appropriate objectives in the textbook(s) you plan to use for a course. Also, tap into the expertise of your colleagues and solicit their thoughts and ideas (particularly if they have taught the course previously). Take advantage of the resources available through your professional organizations and associations. Through the internet, you can access the syllabi (and course objectives) of others who teach comparable courses at other institutions.

Well-crafted objectives have two components: The audience (the students for whom the objective is intended) and the terminal behavior (the anticipated performance). Here's a sample set of objectives for a course on marine biology:

> Marine Biology is an introductory course designed to acquaint students with the diversity and ecology of marine organisms. The main objectives of this course are to understand:
>
> - How scientists investigate questions in marine science
> - Which organisms are found in the ocean
> - How marine organisms are adapted to the unique physical, chemical, and geological characteristics of various habitats in the ocean
> - Aspects of ecological theory as they apply to marine environments
> - How human activities are impacting the ocean"

Some courses, specifically those that are used to satisfy the standards of outside accrediting agencies (e.g. the state department of education, a national licensing board), are required to have syllabi that list specific objectives in line with state or national standards. These ensure students (and any outside reviewers) that course content is aligned with established and recognized standards.

5. **Required textbook(s).** List all the required and necessary texts that students will need for the length of the course. For each text, list the author, date of publication, edition, title, place of publication, publisher, ISBN, and price.

6. **Supplementary Readings.** For many courses, you will want your students to read materials in addition to the required textbook(s). It is important that you indicate whether these supplemental materials are required for the course, are strongly recommended, or optional. Inform students if these materials will be on reserve in the library or available for purchase in the campus bookstore.

7. **Additional Materials.** For some courses, specific materials and equipment will need to be purchased or obtained. Be sure to list those items in the syllabus. These may include the following:

    - *Art courses:* paint, brushes, special paper
    - *Science labs*: lab coats, microscope slides, tools
    - *Math courses:* laptops, graph paper
    - *Nursing courses:* medical equipment
    - *Psychology courses:* specialized tests
    - *Computer courses:* software

8. **Course Procedures.** This is typically a separate section of a course syllabus or can be designed as a series of subsections. In essence, this section outlines the rules or behaviors expected of students. It is vitally important that this section be included in any syllabus, but even more so for college freshmen and sophomores who need to be fully aware of your expectations. Be sure to include information on the following (this is a minimum list):

    - *Attendance:* Include a brief section about attendance. Is it required for each class meeting? Are points taken off for missed classes? Is the final grade reduced for poor attendance? Will attendance affect a borderline grade?

- *Lateness:* Include a statement about the need to be on time for each class session. Some instructors penalize students (e.g. lower their grades) for excessive tardiness.

On large campuses, it may not always be possible for students to get from one building to the next within the allotted time break between classes. The ever-present issue of securing a parking space for students coming from off campus apartments or part-time jobs may also affect their timely arrival in class. And, unfortunately, some of our colleagues may keep students longer than an allotted class time with "just one more thing before you leave."

9. **Class Participation.** If your course is primarily a lecture course, then this section may not be necessary. However, if you will be inviting students to actively engage in discourse with you or other classmates, then it would be important to include one or more statements about their need to be active participants. If class participation is a part of the final grade, you need to state that in this section, too.

10. **Missed Assignments/Exams.** Students realize that any missed assignments or exams will have an impact on their final grade. Be sure to include some information on how students can make up these course requirements (in the event of illness, participation in team sports, field trip with another class, family emergency, etc.)

11. **Safety Rules (if any).** If the course has any safety issues or is inherently dangerous (chemistry, engineering, biology, etc.) all safety rules must be listed in the syllabus. The syllabus must state the importance of these issues as well as any emergency procedures to follow. These may include evacuation procedures, location of a first aid kit, emergency phone number(s), location of infirmary, and contact information for campus security.

12. **Academic Dishonesty**. You should include a statement on academic dishonesty as part of the course syllabus. Because this is such a serious issue with many college students, I prefer to set aside a separate (and often highlighted) section concerning academic integrity.

> **RESEARCH POINT**
>
> In one national study comprising 6,165 respondents, one-third of the college students with As and B+s indicated that they had cheated. Two-thirds of 6,000 students at "highly selective" colleges indicated that they had also cheated.

Here is a statement regarding academic honesty. Consider this as an example of one you should include on your course syllabi, too:

> Academic dishonesty will not be tolerated at _____ College. Academic dishonesty refers to actions such as, but not limited to, cheating, plagiarism, fabricating research, falsifying academic documents, etc. and includes all situations where students make use of the work of others and claim such work as their own. Thus, it is expected that all assigned work for this course will be entirely original. In cases of academic dishonesty, the student involved may receive a grade of "0" for the course and the matter will be reported to the Department Chairperson and the Dean of Academic Affairs [or other appropriate administrators]."

Your own institution may have a specific policy statement about academic integrity. Find out what it is and make it a part of every course syllabus.

13. **Grading plan.** For most students, this may very well be the most important and most crucial element of your syllabus. It is therefore essential that students know from the first day of a course how they

will be evaluated and all the factors that lead to the ultimate evaluation: the final grade. Here are the elements you must consider and share with students:

- *Assignments:* How many assignments (written papers, lab report, original research, midterm and final exams, etc.) will comprise the course?

- *System:* What value (points, percentages, letter grades) will you give to each of the course assignments? Consider the following as one example of a point system:

ASSIGNMENT	VALUE
Lesson Plan	100 points
Internet Project	150 points
Research Paper	200 points
Quiz #1	100 points
Quiz #2	100 points
Final Exam	250 points
TOTAL	**900 Points**

Here's an example of a percentage system:

ASSIGNMENT	VALUE
Thematic Unit	25%
Outside Interview	10%
Self-Selected Project	20%
Multiple Intelligences Report	20%
Quiz	10%
Final Exam	15%
TOTAL	**100%**

- *"Extras":* If you will be using factors such as class participation, effort, attendance, or improvement to determine students' grades these need to be clearly stated on the syllabus, too.

- *College Policies:* Clarify the institution's policies regarding "Incompletes" (I), "Withdrawals" (W), or "Pass/Fail" (P/F) situations. Be sure to state the last day to withdraw from a course for the semester. In cases of incomplete grades, reiterate the college's policy on when the requirements must be completed (many institutions allow sixty days from the end of the semester to complete any outstanding assignments).

If you will be teaching any freshman or sophomore courses, it would advantageous to state the appeals process (your own, your department's, or the institution's) for students who feel they have been unfairly evaluated in a course. This is often presented in the college catalog or as a section in the student handbook. It never hurts to restate it here.

14. **Course Schedule.** This section outlines the basic plan for presenting the material of your course. You may wish to offer students a daily or weekly schedule of lectures, topics, textbook readings and the like. Consider this portion of your syllabus as the essential road map through the course—a way for students to discover new sights while following a prescribed route. At the very least, this schedule should include the following items:

- A daily or weekly schedule

- Topics/concepts/material for each of the designated dates

- Textbook reading(s) for each date

- Designated outside readings

- Dates of exams, quizzes, or other assessments

- Due dates for assignments, written reports, lab work

- Special events (guest speakers, videos, field trips)

Here's a partial course schedule for a course entitled "Topics in Children's Literature":

WEEK OF:	TOPIC	TEXTBOOK READING	OUTSIDE READING	OTHER
Aug. 29	Introductions; course syllabus; course expectations	Chap. 1		
Sept. 5	History of children's literature	Chap. 5		Guest Speaker—Ms. Samantha Pfeffer
Sept. 12	What is a good book?	Chaps. 2 – 3	"WOW, What a Great Story!" (article on reserve)	Quiz #1
Sept. 19	Engaging students in literature	Chap. 4		Author/Illustrator Unit due

You may be concerned that your class schedule is an inviolable outline. Not true! This schedule, just like any schedule, is always subject to change. Those changes may be due to your illness, unexpected weather problems, your attendance at a last-minute conference, power outages, special campus event, or a thousand other reasons. For that reason, it is always preferable to title this section as "Tentative Course Schedule." This will also avoid any legal difficulties later on if you need to depart from your pre-semester plan of action.

15. **Miscellaneous.** You may wish to include one or more of the following in your course syllabus. These are optional and not all are appropriate for every course or every instructor. Use the ones you

feel will provide students with essential information necessary to their academic success.

- *Suggestions for success:* You may wish to offer some pointers, tips, or ideas that will help students succeed in the course. These may include study aids, relevant outside materials, availability of tutors, or information from former students. One of the things I did each semester was ask one or two of the outstanding students in a course to write a generic letter to the students who will be taking the same course the following semester. I ask these students to share what they learned, how they grew as students, the challenges they faced in the course and how they dealt with them as well as any idiosyncrasies of the instructor (including his penchant for bad jokes and awful puns). Then, on the first day of the new semester, I read these letters to the new set of students as a way of introducing them to the course and inviting them to become active participants. These letters are a great way to kick off the new semester.

- *Privacy issues:* Depending on the nature of the course, you may need to include a statement on student privacy (e.g. names, e-mail addresses, and the like will not be shared).

- *Course or instructor evaluations:* For adjunct faculty, student evaluations of the course or instructor are conducted on a regular basis. You may wish to provide students with information on how this will be accomplished in your course.

- *Guest speakers, instructors, or observers:* If you are planning to have any guest speakers or other types of visitors in the class, you may wish to address this here. Protocol, rules of behavior, cultural taboos, and common courtesies should be shared with students.

- *Study sheets:* If you will be using study guides or discussion guides in your course, let students know when and where they will be available (on reserve, on your web page, distributed at the start of each class).

- *Permission forms:* Inform students of the need for special permission forms. In certain psychology courses, for example, students may be working with other individuals as part of a research project. Appropriate permission forms (e.g. human study) will need to be completed ahead of time.

- *Support services:* Consider the inclusion of a section detailing all the support services available to students. Start with the most obvious: the campus library. Let students know about the periodicals, journals, abstracts, collections, audiovisual resources, etc. that the library has. If your institution has a learning center or tutoring center, share that information with students, too. Inform students of any resources in the local community (museums, public libraries, galleries, social service agencies, laboratories, etc.) that can also serve as instructional resources. Reinforce the location, hours of operation, and availability of the campus computer center

- *Beliefs:* Some instructors create a special section in their course syllabi that lists some of their beliefs about the course itself as well as about students who take the course. These statements may outline her or his philosophy about teaching in general or about the course content specifically. They may include a brief overview of the instructor's personal philosophy about teaching (and learning). Or, they may include a sentence or two about the relationship of the course content to the "real world" outside the classroom.

The Bottom Line

I like to think of a syllabus as a roadmap—one that provides students with signposts, signals, detours, places to rest, sights to see, attractions, noteworthy venues, and a well-paved highway on which they will travel throughout the length of the semester. It is also a written document, an agreement between you and your students about what you will be doing and what they need to do to complete their "trip" successfully. Never keep students guessing about a course. If it's important for them to know, it's important to put it in writing.

That said, don't try to include everything about the course in this single document (the proverbial "kitchen sink" syndrome). Many well-written syllabi come in at four to five pages; other poorly designed ones frequently top twenty pages or more. The bottom line is: What do students need to know at the beginning of the course. Trying to include every single detail about the course in the syllabus may result on an overwritten document—one that students will be reluctant to read, particularly as they are trying to get to know you and the course you teach.

You may find it both appropriate and necessary to introduce other documents or information later in the course as students become more proficient with the course design, your expectations, and the tools they need to enjoy a measure of success. Again, ask yourself this question: What is the essential information students need to begin this course?

It's important to keep in mind that students will rely on you to provide them with a way to "enter" your course, your discipline, and your expertise. A well-written syllabus is the key they need to successfully gain this entry and to enjoy a measure of success throughout the semester. Please plan to review the sample syllabi in the Appendix for additional ideas and considerations.

/ **PART THREE:**

Teaching College Students Successfully

CHAPTER 7:

What College Students Want

When you go to see a new movie, you probably go with several expectations. You may want to be entertained. You might want to be intellectually stimulated. You want believable characters, an engaging plot, or a story line that is interesting or provocative. In short, you arrive at the movie theatre with a certain set of expectations. If the movie satisfies those expectations, then you might conclude that it was an enjoyable film. On the other hand, if the movie doesn't satisfy your preconceived notions of a good film, then you may feel that your money (and the evening) was wasted.

College students come to their classes with a preconceived set of expectations. They, too, want some "bang for their [tuition] buck." After all, they will be spending the next fifteen weeks or so of their lives with you and your course, and they want to know that it will be time well spent. Let's take a look at some of those student expectations and how they might shape the design and delivery of your courses.

Each year, I visited the classrooms of several colleagues at my institution. I selected different classes, various disciplines, and a variety of levels (freshmen, seniors). My goal was to solicit information relative to how students learn and how I could meet their learning needs in my own classes.

In each class, I distributed a blank index card to each student and asked her or him to respond anonymously to two or three specific questions. The questions were selected from the following list:

- At the beginning of a new course, what do you expect of a professor?

- What should professors do to help you learn?

- What is the most positive learning experience you've ever had (in school or out)?

- What factors inhibit your ability to learn a new subject or topic?

- If you could give one piece of advice to every college professor, what would it be?

While this little survey only takes about five to six minutes to administer, it has yielded some incredibly valuable information that has helped me in designing courses with student needs in mind. That's not to say that every one of my courses or every element of my classes is in response to student wants. Rather, it helps me in the planning of effective teaching methodologies that can ensure "well-developed characters, a good plot, and an engaging story line" throughout the length of the semester. The production of an effective college course is quite similar to the production (and directing) of a memorable movie.

Based on the information gathered over several semesters, here are the most frequent responses students share relative to the first question ("At the beginning of a new course, what do you expect of a professor?"):

- Everyone is treated fairly and respectfully.

- The instructor has clear expectations and is organized.

- The instructor is knowledgeable about her or his subject matter.
- The instructor is willing to help; she/he is approachable.
- The instructor is enthusiastic about teaching the subject.
- The instructor is human; she or he has good rapport with students.
- There is a connection between the material and "real life."
- The instructor creates a safe and comfortable learning environment.
- The instructor is flexible; she or he is willing to adjust or adapt as necessary.
- The instructor has a sense of humor.

> **WATCH OUT!**
>
> In a study of 700 undergraduate students, respondents were asked to list complaints about teaching behaviors they observed in all the college courses they took. Two of the most frequently mentioned complaints were: "being unhelpful and unapproachable" and "intellectual arrogance: talk-ing down to or showing a lack of respect for students."

It seems reasonable to assume that students come into our classes with a set of expectations. Whether or not those expectations match our goals for the course will have a significant impact on the success students will enjoy throughout the course. If we desire to help students learn our course content, then it is equally important that we pay attention and respond to their immediate and long-range needs. This is not coddling students, it's showing respect for their needs and responding to those needs. Let's examine some ways we can do that.

The Big Five

In numerous studies, several factors have been identified that have a significant and permanent impact on how well undergraduate students learn. This body of research has focused on identifying the needs or expectations students bring to the college class and the ways in which college professors can respond to those needs while teaching the necessary course content. I like to call these "The Big Five." Let's take a look at each one briefly:

1. **Real-Life Experiences.** It is probably safe to say that only an extremely small number of students in your freshman History of Western Philosophy course care much about "the development of epistemology, metaphysics, and ethics within several historically important systems of philosophy." The same holds true for all the non-majors in your Principles of Economics (Micro) course and their affection for "price and output determination as explained by the interaction of supply and demand."

   - Nevertheless, the impact of any lecture, presentation, or class discussion will often be determined by how well students "see" its relationship to their own lives. Students need to understand the connection(s) that exists between a specific topic and their lives and/or experiences outside the classroom. Without that connection, their level of comprehension diminishes significantly. Consider doing the following:

   - Ask questions that focus on connections between a topic and students' lives ("How might the disturbance at the game last Saturday be comparable to the current debate in the US Senate?")

   - Design and develop assignments that help students use course information in practical real-life situations in the outside world.

   - Provide relevant anecdotes, especially those from your own (or your colleagues') experiences in the field.

- Whenever practical, discuss the movies, books, podcasts, YouTube videos, or websites that students read or view. Draw parallels between those media and specific course concepts.

- Periodically construct and use classroom simulations to illustrate important ideas.

- Incorporate role-playing activities into your course as appropriate.

2. **Comprehensible Presentations.** As professors and practitioners, we are passionate about our subjects. We have spent considerable time (and tuition) learning as much as possible about our respective fields. The depth of our knowledge and the enthusiasm we have for that knowledge is extensive. We are steeped in the concepts, philosophies and terminology of our respective professions. But, students are not!

This does not mean that you should "talk down" to students; rather the implication is that you need to be both instructive as well as supportive. True, that's often a challenging task given some of the complex theories and concepts we need to present. Here are a few ideas:

- Today's students are visual learners. Whenever possible, supplement a presentation or lecture with some sort of visual aid. These may include (but, are not limited to) charts, graphs, maps, PowerPoint presentations, flowcharts, and webinars.

- Begin each class with one of the following: "What is one question you have about today's reading assignment?" "What is one question you have not found the answer to?" "What is one question that excites you right now?"

- Always provide opportunities for students to share and discuss course concepts in small group sessions. Learning occurs best when students have opportunities to talk about the implications of course content as well as their understanding of those concepts. Focused in-class assignments and projects are critical to their understanding.

- Always link new material to previously learned material. New information should always be tied to prior material learned in the course; information learned in previous (prerequisite) courses; and, especially, the "real-life" experiences of students outside the course.

- Students often stumble over new vocabulary. Plan to provide alternate definitions and explanations apart from those in the textbook. Invite students to participate in small group discussions about difficult terminology. Ask students to maintain vocabulary notebooks as they read which can be shared and discussed in class. One suggestion from Lana Becker and Kent Schneider at East Tennessee State University is "to create a 'living' glossary on [your] website where new terminology is added, explained, and illustrated throughout the course."

- Choose your course textbooks with care (see Chapter 5, page 51). Many texts are written by experts in their respective fields and are often authored to satisfy the demands of promotion and tenure. Terminology, concepts, and principles is frequently complex and difficult to comprehend. The "comprehensibility" of a course is often determined by the difficulty of the textbook. Choose wisely.

- When possible, provide students with opportunities to have some say in selecting what will be studied and how it will be approached. Offer students options on reading assignments, test design (essay, multiple choice), or written assignments.

- Make the course progressive. Begin the course with easy-to-comprehend concepts and principles. Offer multiple opportunities for students to succeed at this level with exams and out-of-class assignments. As their confidence grows, gradually increase the difficulty level of the information as the course progresses.

- Practice the following: "This seems to be a challenging or difficult piece of information. How can I help you understand it?" ==Don't assume that students will tell you when they don't understand something.== One of the best motivational devices at your disposal is to anticipate their intellectual discomfort and to be proactive in responding to it.

3. **A Supportive and Engaging Classroom Environment.** One of the most valuable ways we can promote a supportive classroom environment is through the feedback or responses we provide them both in and out of class. Feedback, to be effective, must be prompt, frequent, and efficient. Students want to see a direct connection between any effort or completed task (such as reading a textbook chapter or completing a midterm exam) and a response from you. Here are some suggestions for providing successful feedback:

   - Make feedback immediate. "I'm returning the test you took in the last class."

   - Always frame your feedback in positive language. "Wow, it looks like we're really on a roll today with quantum theory!"

   - Allow students to revise their incorrect responses. "I'm not sure that's a sufficient response. Is there another way we could explain this?"

   - Use verbal as well as written feedback. "You must be feeling pretty good about the progress you're making on this project."

   - Always make eye-to-eye contact in asking a question as well as when giving feedback. Let each student know that she or he has your complete and total attention. "Sandy, I see that you're a little unsure about some of the philosophical influences on the American system of education. What can I do to clarify?"

   - Allow students to control some feedback. "How do you feel about your effort on the titration experiment?"

- Make comments specific, and suggest corrections. "You provided a good overview of current thinking about the neural/hormonal regulation of sexual behavior, but you might want to address the topic from a historical perspective, too."

- Offer feedback in terms of a student's progress, not her or his comparison with others. "Look how you improved from seventy-eight percent on the first terminology quiz to ninety-one percent on the second one."

- Always comment on students' answers and always use part of a student's answer in your response. "Let me see if I can rephrase that. What you're saying is that the League of Nations was doomed from the very beginning, right?" (Note: This tip is so important that it should get five stars: ★★★★★)

In any verbal engagement with students, don't just accept a student's response to a question. Rather, prompt their thinking through one or more of the following:

- Always provide a reaction to a student's verbal contribution. "I like your interpretation of [the author's] main thesis."

- Always relate a student's comment back to the text. "Your summary of this article seems to concentrate on the author's last two points."

- Always use a student's words in framing a response. "You said that you thought that the author was 'less than honest, less than candid' in his summary. Please elaborate."

- Always turn a student's response into one or more higher level questions. "Given your position on this issue, how could we use that information to interpret [another author's] thesis?"

Another way instructors promote the concept of an engaging classroom is through the use of humor. Humor, when appropriately used, helps create a more relaxed, informal, and comfortable learning environment. It also has the advantage of revealing you as someone other than "just" an adjunct professor. In short, it humanizes both teaching and learning.

A recent study found that college students rated the use of humor as very effective to extremely effective in reducing their anxiety, increasing their ability to learn, and improving their chance of performing their best on problems and exams. Another study (which reviewed several decades of research on the uses of classroom humor) discovered a strong positive correlation among teacher uses of humor in the classroom, student evaluations of teaching, and student reports of learning.

This doesn't mean that you need to be a stand-up comedian in order to be an effective adjunct professor. It does mean that humor is a vehicle that can "lighten" a subject or specific topic while creating positive bonds of communication. Consider some of the following suggestions:

- Open each class with a humorous quote posted on the chalkboard. ("There comes a time in the affairs of men when we must grab the bull by the tail and face the situation." —W. C. Fields)

- Include a cartoon or two on your course syllabus, exams, or other written documents.

- Post a humorous cartoon or saying on your personal website or the course syllabus.

- If you're comfortable with it, use self-deprecating humor. At the start of a new course, I often make fun of my increasing loss of cranial hair by asking, "You know how people figure out that I've been teaching for more than four decades?" I wait a few moments, bend over, and point to the top of my head saying, "This is the result!"

- Often the best humor is spontaneous or situational humor, the kind that arises unexpectedly during a class discussion, an event outside the classroom window, a glitch with some form of technology, or a thousand other situations. Once, in the middle of an intense whole-class discussion of a significant educational theory, one of my students dropped her purse scattering the contents to the four corners of the classroom. Without thinking, she blurted out (quite loudly), "Oh, s**t!" She realized what she had said, put her hand over her mouth, and she (and everyone else in the class) waited for my response. I said, "That's OK; I probably would have said the same thing. It's just that the Dean docks my pay whenever I do." Everyone smiled, the situation was defused, and we moved on in our discussion.

4. Approachability and Respect. Repeatedly, in study after study, college students report that the "availability," "openness," and "mutual respect" of the instructor was a critical factor in how well they learned a subject and how well they retained that information long after the course was over. Students want to be treated fairly and respectfully. Their self-esteem and learning potential are significantly diminished whenever they are treated like "second-class citizens" without a voice or an identity.

> **AN EXPERT OPINION**
>
> Experienced professors know that college students learn best in humanistic (as opposed to dictatorial) classrooms. There is convincing evidence that "they want teachers who are real people, who recognize them as human beings—teachers who care about them."

Here are some suggestions that will help you address this principle:

- **Get to know each student by name.** This may be challenging, particularly if you teach large lecture courses, but the dividends are worth it. Conversations with students reveal that they feel more comfortable with and positive about a class when the professor takes time to learn (and use) students' names.

- Demonstrate that you care about students' enrollment, attendance, and participation in the class. This can be as simple as a friendly greeting to an entire class as you enter the classroom or asking to see random students after class to thank them for their contributions or progress on an assignment. Also, take roll in every class. This not only encourages attendance, but provides an opportunity to share (and learn) each student's name.

- Remove yourself from the "teacher role" every so often. Allow students to see you as something other than just a professor. I did this by sharing *relevant* anecdotes or stories about myself or my family periodically throughout the semester. I also share some of my foibles, mistakes, or learning challenges to let students know that I am certainly less than perfect.

- Always demonstrate respect for your students. Never put them down; never be disrespectful of their culture, religion, sexual orientation, beliefs, or opinions; and never make a joke at their expense. Use sarcasm sparingly, if at all.

- Open each class by posing a question for students. Invite each student to respond. You can begin the semester by asking general questions ("Who is your favorite actor?" "If you could only eat one dessert, what would it be?"). As the semester progresses, ask more specific questions ("What is the most important lesson you've ever learned?" "Where would you like to be in twenty-five years?"). You can also add some content specific question to your repertoire, too ("What is one unanswered question about organic chemistry that you have? "If you could tell the author of this poem one thing, what would it be?")

- Make it a point to frequently react to the ideas or comments of students. Acknowledge and validate each student's contributions to the class. This can be done through verbal responses ("Thanks for sharing that with us."), body language (smiling, nodding), or via an after-class e-mail ("I liked the question you raised today about the prospects for democracy in post-civil war Syria.")

5. Enthusiasm for Teaching; Enthusiasm for the Subject. A significant body of research has demonstrated that an instructor's enthusiasm is a crucial factor in college students' motivation and eventual success irrespective of the discipline or difficulty of material. According to Barbara Gross Davis of the University of California, Berkeley, "an instructor's enthusiasm comes from confidence, excitement about the content, and genuine pleasure in teaching."

Here are a few suggestions to keep in mind:

- Use a variety of teaching strategies and techniques (see Chapter 10, page 125). Vary your presentations each day, each week. Don't turn the semester into a non-stop series of lectures; not only will students be "turned off," so will you. For each class, consider an assembly of teaching options such as small group discussions, case studies, demonstrations, technological presentations, guest speakers, debates, role playing, brainstorming, and simulations. Not only will student interest be maintained with this variety, so will yours.

- Frequently tell students about some of the exciting reading you're doing, presentations you've seen, or influential articles/books. Occasionally inject some of your passion and enthusiasm into the course. Let students know what excites you about the discipline or field.

- Periodically share some of your teaching philosophy with students. Why did you become an adjunct professor? What have you learned as an instructor? What has been your most interesting teaching experience?

- The former mayor of New York Ed Koch used to stop people on the street and ask them, "How am I doing?" You can do the same thing with your students. Half-way through a presentation, ask them to fill in a simple two-minute evaluation form (What do you find interesting so far? What is less than interesting?). Periodically, invite students to engage in a short debriefing session about their level of enthusiasm for a topic relative to your level of enthusiasm. Invite a colleague to visit your class and assess your enthusiasm for a challenging or difficult topic.

- Whenever practical, use community resources. These may include local government officials, businesspeople, scientists, researchers, technicians, environmentalists, museum directors, and the like. "Outside" people provide you with opportunities to see your discipline through new eyes.

- Form a student panel and invite them to challenge your philosophy or viewpoints. Reverse roles and vigorously oppose your beliefs (students will defend your position).

- Provide opportunities for students to assume the role of a professional in your discipline (teacher, biologist, chemist, economist, mechanical engineer, respiratory therapist, paleontologist, psychologist, etc.).

- Take students with you when guest speakers, visiting performers, or other visitors come to campus. Plan time afterwards to discuss the work or information in terms of basic course concepts.

Here's a three-pronged approach that gives you the opportunity to exercise your enthusiasm within a class and throughout a course.

- Enthusiasm for the text ("Now, here's a really interesting statement for you!").

- Enthusiasm for student responses ("Congratulations. You really nailed it with that response!").

- Enthusiasm for what you are saying ("I think this is one of the most exciting ideas we've studied so far! Let me tell you why.").

Good courses (and the teachers who teach them) come from a recognition of, and a respect for, student wants. Being aware of the expectations of your students and integrating those expectations into the dynamics of a course can result in an educational experience that endures long after the semester is over.

CHAPTER 8:

How College Students Learn!

The human brain is a marvelous organ. This three-pound mass of gray matter is seventy-eight percent water, ten percent fat, and eight percent protein. The remainder is a combination of other substances. This organ keeps us alive and functioning. It also has the capacity to learn a wide variety of new information.

But, learning—particularly for college students—is not simply the memorization of new information in a particular discipline. It's much more than the attainment of high scores on midterm exams or the submission of lengthy papers with extensive bibliographies. Learning, as we will discover, is a multidimensional process—one that goes far beyond lectures, labs, assignments, or grades.

Psychology of Learning 101 (A Very Short Course)

In numerous studies over the last four decades, college students consistently define learning as "the accumulation of knowledge." Or, to put it another way, the more knowledge you accumulate, the smarter you get. Traditionally, college professors dispense vast amounts of information, students dutifully record that information in their notebooks, and the ability to retain (memorize) that information is assessed periodically throughout the semester via exams or written papers. Those that remember the most information get the highest grades; those that don't, get lower grades. As a result, students often envision learning as the simple transference of information from one head to another.

The sequence described above is referred to as a "transmission model" of learning (and teaching). In this model, the responsibility of instructors is to dole out a body of knowledge. The responsibility of students is to commit that knowledge to memory. The implication is that knowledge is transmitted by an expert and passively absorbed by a novice.

New research on how college students learn turns the traditional model (above) on its head. Educators now subscribe to the notion that learning involves an active and energetic relationship between the learner and the material. That is, the learner-material relationship is reciprocal and involves characteristics of the learner as well as the nature of the materials. This research, often referred to as a "transactional" or "constructivist" approach to learning, has particular applications for adjunct professors.

Here are two principles of transactional learning that will be particularly useful to you as you begin designing your college courses:

- Learning is a lived-through experience or event. The learner "evokes" the material, bringing a network of past experiences with the world and other information.

- Learning occurs best when there are opportunities for a reciprocal transaction between the learner and the material.

In brief, this suggests that learning is less about the products of a subject and more about the processes that engage students in using those products.

Changing Paradigms

There is an interesting shift taking place in undergraduate education. We are now seeing less of an emphasis on what to learn and more of an emphasis on how to learn. This paradigm shift places a greater emphasis on producing learning as opposed to providing instruction. The chart below illustrates this shift.

TRANSMISSION (TRADITIONAL)	TRANSACTIONAL/CONSTRUCTIVIST (CURRENT)
Information transferred from instructor to students.	Knowledge is constructed by an instructor and students.
Competitive	Cooperative
Instructor-directed	Student-centered
Focus on memorization	Focus on developing conceptual relationships
Evaluation is standardized	Student self-assessment
Instructor talk predominates	Inter- and intra-class discussions
Focus on the products of thinking	Focus on the processes of thinking
Students answer questions with predetermined answers	Students generate (and seek answers to) queries
Goal: Course completion	Goal: Lifelong learning
Authoritative	Power is shared; students are empowered
Prior knowledge is disregarded	Prior knowledge is respected and built upon

Laws of Learning

From my conversations with colleagues around the country about how students learn and how professors teach, I have discovered that there are certain laws that govern the learning process. These laws apply to any student in any course or at any level (freshman, senior). Just as important, they are also supportive of what we know about how learning takes place and how we can facilitate that learning.

- **Law of Readiness.** Students learn more easily when they have a desire to learn. Conversely, students learn with difficulty if they are not interested in the topic.

- **Law of Effect.** Learning will always be much more effective when a feeling of satisfaction, pleasantness, or reward is part of the process.

- **Law of Relaxation.** Students learn best and remember longest when they are relaxed. Reducing stress increases learning and retention.

- **Law of Association.** Learning makes sense (comprehension) when the mind compares a new idea with something already known.

- **Law of Involvement.** Students learn best when they take an active part in what is to be learned.

- **Law of Relevance.** Effective learning is relevant to the student's life.

- **Law of Intensity.** A vivid, exciting, enthusiastic, enjoyable learning experience is more likely to be remembered than a boring, unpleasant one.

- **Law of Challenge.** Students learn best when they are challenged with novelty, a variety of materials, and a range of instructional strategies.

- **Law of Feedback.** Effective learning takes place when students receive immediate and specific feedback on their performance.

- **Law of Expectations.** Learners' reaction to instruction is shaped by their expectations related to the material (How successful will I be?).

- **Law of Emotions.** The emotional state (and involvement) of students will shape how well and how much they learn.

Constructivism

One of the most exciting developments in undergraduate education is a shift away from a delivery system of teaching to a constructivist model of education. The traditional form of teaching relies on a professor giving or delivering instruction to students (sometimes referred to as an "information dump"). You may recognize this as an instructor lecturing students and students dutifully recording the information in their notebooks. In short, an expert tells novices what they need to know.

Psychologists have helped us look at the teaching-learning partnership in a new way. Through intensive research, we have learned that learning is not simply the accumulation of knowledge (which is often passive), but rather how we make sense of knowledge.

Constructivism recognizes that knowledge is created in the mind of the learner. Professors help students relate new content to the knowledge they already know. In addition, students have opportunities to process and apply that knowledge in meaningful situations. We could say that constructivism is not the passive transfer of knowledge from a professor to a student. Rather, it is how knowledge is constructed in the mind of each student. This is active learning and also active teaching.

One of the oldest ideas in postsecondary education is that students must be presented with a large body of information (typically shared via a lecture). This body of information is then stored in students' brains and is available for regurgitation on papers, quizzes, and exams. Presumably, the more information one can store in the brain, the more they know about the subject and the higher the grade they will receive (grades = memory power).

RESEARCH POINT

Research from a number of cognitive scientists has demonstrated that when students think about material in more meaningful ways (as opposed to simply memorizing it), their underlying brain structures are changed in such a way that more lasting learning is promoted.

People learn because they construct knowledge. That is to say, they use what they already know as a foundation for a new topic, then try to relate the new information to that old information. In other words, we are all trying to make "mental connections" whenever we encounter new information. To make sense, new information must be related (or connected) to other information. When a carpenter remodels your kitchen, she is using new materials in combination with previous materials to form something new and more beautiful. This is constructivism at its best.

Here are some suggested practices:

- Assess what your students know and allow them to vocalize their past experiences, readings, or backgrounds of experience. Knowing what your students know and using that knowledge to construct a lesson is a powerful teaching tool.

- Provide students with opportunities to challenge their own preconceived notions or concepts. This can be accomplished through a systematic ordering of questions such as these:

  - Is this idea similar to anything you may have read before?
  - What were you thinking when you read this part of the chapter?
  - What have we learned so far?
  - Did you change your mind about anything after our discussion?
  - Do you have any personal questions about this material that have not been answered so far?
  - What did you do when you didn't understand something in the text?
  - What makes you feel your interpretation is most appropriate?
  - What new information are you learning?
  - How did you arrive at your interpretation?

- Challenge their misinterpretations, preconceptions, misperceptions through dynamic problem-solving. Provide supportive opportunities for students to wrestle with real-life challenges in your respective field. This should be done in a "safe" environment—one which encourages students to try something, fail, receive encouraging feedback, and then be encouraged to try again.

- Always focus on the utility of the information presented. Indeed, the universal question in the mind of every learner is, "Why do I have to know this stuff?" By providing opportunities for students to use information in practical situations, they will not only learn the essential facts, but understand the reasons why they need that data. Be sure students have opportunities to respond to the following questions:

  - How is the information used by practitioners?
  - How can it be used to solve problems both in and out of class?
  - What are some of the clinical implications of the data or research?
  - How have others struggled or wrestled with this information?
  - And, most important, what has this information got to do with real life?

Learning is Questioning

Often students come to college with limited backgrounds, limited life experiences, and limited exposure to a field of study. Their learning has been narrowly defined. However, that learning can be expanded and enhanced considerably through questioning. Questions help learners (specifically college learners) begin to make sense of a topic. Questions assist learners in categorizing and "filing" information in their memory banks for later retrieval. Most important, questions are essential in helping students construct knowledge, simply because they help students think about their knowledge, its importance, and its relevance to what they already know.

Here are some suggested practices:

- Use penetrating, critical, and higher-level questions to help students look deeper into a topic or subject. Use questions to challenge students' thinking, but also use them to challenge conventional thinking (by the general public), as well. A judicious use of "higher level" questions can help students see some of the inconsistencies in their own thinking in addition to the strengths (or fallacies) of principles, issues, and concerns in your field. Here are some examples:

- **Comparing.** How are these things alike?
- **Classification.** Into what groups could you organize these things?
- **Induction.** Based on this information, what is the likely conclusion?
- **Deduction.** What predictions can you make or what conclusions can you draw?
- **Error Analysis.** How is this information misleading?
- **Constructing Support.** What is an argument that will support this claim?
- **Abstraction.** What is the general pattern underlying this information?
- **Analyzing Perspectives.** What is the reasoning behind this perspective?

• Provide multiple opportunities for students to generate their own self-initiated questions. Learning occurs when we obtain answers to questions that mean the most to us. Those are typically questions that we ask and that we want the answers to. When students begin asking questions about what they are learning, they are beginning to assume one of the major roles of an accomplished, active learner. With self-generated questions, learners are motivated to learn because they have a personal stake in the information, research or concepts. In short, they become "constructors" of knowledge. Consider the following possibilities:

- Write one question about the title of the next chapter.
- Turn to a partner. What are two questions you have about today's reading?

- So far we have talked about X; what about Y?
- (At the end of class) What is one question that is unanswered for you?

> **AN EXPERT OPINION**
>
> Kay McAdams, an associate professor of history, says, "Content is merely the vehicle for learning. The real challenge is to get students to question the content—to interpret it from a variety of viewpoints. That's when learning occurs."

Learning is a Psychological Endeavor

For years, psychologists have told us that knowledge is socially constructed and that a student's perception of self is critical to the construction of that knowledge. To look at it another way, undergraduate students become more knowledgeable (about a subject or discipline) commensurate with an emphasis placed on their identity (self-concept) and interactions with others.

Equally important is the fact that postsecondary students learn something best when they care about the material on a personal or emotional level. As faculty members we often say that we want our students to "be excited," "be curious," "be interested," "be stimulated," etc. We want our students to put a value on what they are learning. Students, too, want to know about the value of their educational experiences. Again, it comes back to a previous question: "Why do I have to know this stuff?"

The key is in how students are motivated to learn. Simply stated, motivation is of two types. Extrinsic motivation is when one person has control over another person or an individual relies on others to establish personal goals and the reward system for meeting those goals. Intrinsic motivation, in contrast, is when drive and ambition are determined internally; that is, an individual sets her or his own goals and feels empowered to pursue them. Extrinsic individuals feel they are strongly influenced by others (parents, teachers, peers). Intrinsic individuals feel they are primarily responsible for the events that happen to them. As you might expect, both logic and research support the notion that intrinsically motivated students do better academically than extrinsically motivated students. Specifically, externally motivated students:

- Are engaged in a competitive atmosphere that becomes self-defeating in the long run.

- Work only for rewards. The queries "How long should this paper be?" and "What grade did I get?" are typical indicators of extrinsic students. Thus, motivation to learn is subverted at the expense of reward accumulation (grades), the relationship between effort and achievement is not apparent, and process is not valued.

- Avoid creative and problem-solving activities in favor of low-level thinking (memorizing).

- Have goals (if any) that are short-term and immediate. Long-range projects and thinking are avoided.

- Do not take personal responsibility for their learning, but rather see the things that happen to them as a matter of luck or chance.

- Become part of a self-perpetuating cycle in which a lack of academic success substantiates a belief that one may never be successful.

Because there is a strong relationship between motivation and learning, we need to be mindful of the behaviors we exercise in the college classroom that can lead to heightened levels of intrinsic motivation and, in turn, heightened levels of achievement. Here are some suggested practices:

- Remember that learning happens best in a social context. The use of cooperative learning opportunities (see Chapter 15, page 203) allows students to process material and entertain a variety of viewpoints. Participation is valued and celebrated in group work. Students see a host of perspectives on a topic, rather than a single teacher-oriented view.

- Offer regular and consistent encouragement that recognizes a student's effort ("You worked really hard on this project."), promotes self-evaluation ("How do you feel about your work so far?"), and emphasizes effort and progress of a task ("You've certainly made quite a bit of improvement on this project, don't you think?"). Encouragement places a value on the development of intrinsic students—those who begin to assume responsibility for their own learning.

- Establish an "invitational classroom"—one in which students are afforded some decision-making power in terms of emphasis or direction. For example, provide opportunities for students to establish their own goals for a course. What would they like to learn? How can this course be made relevant to their personal life? What would they like to get out of it? Invite students to suggest alternate or additional readings (from their own experiences) for a specific topic. Provide them with two to three different viewpoints on a specific topic and ask them to select the one they are most interested in pursuing for an assigned paper.

- I always extended a challenge to students in every course I taught. At any time during a class or at any point in the semester, they are invited to raise their hand and ask, "Why do we need to know this?" That's often a signal to me that I've gotten too wrapped up in what is important to me, rather than what is necessary for students. It's the time when I need to stop and share with my students why the material is important to their lives or careers and how it relates to the overall course in general.

Caution!

A constructivist philosophy of teaching and learning can reinvigorate any college subject and promote learning as an active process. But if you are more familiar with traditional forms of teaching where the teacher delivers all the instruction, you may find constructivism challenging.

There's a saying that has been around for a long time: we tend to teach as we were taught. If we have been taught with more traditional forms of instruction (such as lecture) we have a tendency to teach in roughly the same way. Yes, we are products of our experiences. As a result, moving your philosophy to a more constructivist view may be a challenge. I suggest that you talk with colleagues, read current educational periodicals and observe constructivist teaching (and learning) in action. Observe how students behave in a constructivist classroom; especially how they are actively engaged in the learning process. You may discover, as I did, that this shift in philosophy can result in some exciting and dynamic lessons no matter what course or discipline you teach.

CHAPTER 9:

The First Day; First Impressions!

Remember the first time you ever drove a car? Do you recall the anticipation, the fear, the anxiety, the trepidation? Do you remember all the various thoughts that were bouncing around in your head? What if it stalls out in the middle of the driveway? What if I crash into something? What if I run over Mrs. Mulrooney's flowers? That was certainly a scary time, right?

Well, your first day of teaching college is just like the first time you ever drove a car. You may have seen expert professors create magic in a classroom. On the other hand, you've probably experienced instructors who, to put it gently, couldn't teach their way out of a paper bag. Now it's you in the front of the college classroom, and you're scared! Guess what, you are not alone. Of all the questions that adjunct professors ask, "What do I do on the first day [or week] of my course?" is one of the most common.

Think back to your days as a college student. How did your instructors approach the first day of a new course? Did they fill up that initial class with the demands, requirements, and assignments of the course? Did they tell you about the difficulties associated with the course or subject matter?

Did they spend an inordinate amount of time on a confusing and abstract syllabus? Did you leave frustrated or with a heightened sense of anxiety about your ability to complete the course(s) successfully?

Every college student, no matter whether they are at an Ivy League institution, a liberal arts institution, a state college, a private institution, or a junior college, approaches each new course with some degree of trepidation and anxiety. If it is true that "first impressions are lasting impressions," then it is equally true that we need to help our students get off on the right foot at the start of each new course or each new semester. Indeed, the success students enjoy in your courses will often be determined by the impressions they take away from that all-important first class session.

You can alleviate many of their fears (as well as most of yours) by focusing on two basic concepts. While these are areas you need to focus on during the first day of class, they are also important areas of concentration throughout the entire semester, too:

- Building a Community (student to student interaction)

- Building Rapport (professor to student interaction)

> **RESEARCH POINT**
>
> Several studies have demonstrated that one of the most significant factors in whether undergraduate students stay at an institution is whether a sense of community is established in their courses.

Building a Community

One of the most frequently used opening activities of the semester, particularly for novice professors, is to spend the first class period going over the course syllabus. All of the requirements for the course are dutifully laid out, the grading of assignments and assessment of students is spelled out in minute detail, and the procedures and practices of the course are systematically provided. Afterwards, the question is posed, "Are there any questions?" Hearing none, the instructor dismisses the class with a final comment, "See you next time."

The problem with this typical semester opening is that an inappropriate message is being sent to students. That message is, "The material is more important than you." Students often walk away from these first sessions bewildered, dazed, confused, and often upset. They are certainly intimidated. Their first impression is that what they do is much more important than who they are.

On the other hand, professors who take time to begin establishing a "community of learners" on that all-important first day will send a powerful message to students. That is, the value of people is to be celebrated as much as the value of the material. Here are some opening day activities, ideas, "icebreakers," suggestions, and processes that will get your semester off to a positive start and establish your own "community of learners."

- At the end of each semester, I collected comments from the course evaluations students completed at the end of the previous semester. At the beginning of a subsequent semester, I took time to share some of these (both positive and negative) and invited student reactions, comments, and discussion. This sent two powerful messages: other students successfully completed the course, and there is an important "thread," or bond that exists between the two groups of students.

- Students begin building a classroom community most effectively through the use of each other's names. Invite students to pair up with someone they don't know. Ask the students to interview each other about the origin, cultural background, reasons, family traditions, nickname, and significance of their first name. After the interviews, invite each member of a pair to introduce her/his partner to the entire class, with reference to the background information about that name. Record each student's name on the whiteboard with a short note about its background. Plan time, as appropriate, to discuss the variety of names in the class and why each is special.

- Gather students together in a large circle of desks. Tell students, "As a class we share certain similarities that may be cultural, philosophical, historical, or personal. We also have some differences as well. The following activity is designed to identify our similarities [You are an active participant, too.] as well as areas in which we might differ. Please keep in mind there are no right or wrong responses and that you will not be forced to respond to any statement with which you may be uncomfortable. OK, please raise your hand or stand up if the following applies to you:" (This is a suggested list of items. Feel free to modify, adjust, or supplement these items with ones of your own creation.)

- I live in another state.
- I ate a pizza in the last week.
- I drive a red car.
- I am blue-eyed.
- I speak a European language.
- I am left-handed.
- I have birthday in February.
- I watch a reality show regularly.
- I am married.
- I am older than twenty-five.
- I used a skateboard in the last week.
- I am a middle child.
- I have more than three roommates.
- I am a natural blond.
- I was born outside the US.
- I have a three-syllable first name.

- I have more than two grandparents still living.
- I hate math.
- I traveled to Asia.
- I am a athlete.
- I haven't selected a major yet.
- I am an environmentalist.
- I have broken a bone.
- I have a red-headed relative.
- I am an only child.
- I know or am related to someone famous.
- I would rather be in Bermuda right now.

Plan time afterwards to discuss shared characteristics as well as those characteristics with no representatives (students).

- As a variation of the activity above, pose a number of general questions to students. Invite students to raise their hands in response to queries such as the following (inform students that they should note other students who also raise their hands to selected questions):

How many of you…

- Have more than three siblings?
- Have traveled to a foreign country?
- Have done something dangerous?
- Come from a rural background?
- Own a pet other than a dog or cat?
- Have recently seen a lousy movie?

- Are nervous about this course?
- Have ever been hospitalized?
- Have a very strange family member?
- Can juggle?
- Have ever published something?
- Play a musical instrument
- Have ever swallowed a live animal?
- Can speak another language fluently?
- Listen to hip-hop?
- Are on a sports team?

Design and develop your own list of questions in addition to (or in place of) the ones above. After students have had an opportunity to respond to several questions ask them to form mini-groups of two or three individuals, all of whom responded positively to the same question (they all have at least one thing in common). Invite them to interview each other for five minutes to discover at least three other things that they have in common (irrespective of the questions above). Provide an opportunity for the groups to share their commonalities with the whole class.

- Divide the class into several groups. Provide each group with paper and writing instruments. Invite each group to find five things they all share in common. The commonalities can be cultural, physical, personality, outside interests, family-oriented, etc. They may use words, symbols, phrases, or pictures to describe their similarities. After five or ten minutes, invite each member of a group to introduce herself or himself to the entire class and share one of the items in common with the other members of her or his group.

- Divide the class into several random groups. Provide each group with a sheet of newsprint and several markers. Tell each of the groups that they (collectively) represent an incredible array of talents and experiences. Invite each group to compose a group resume. The resume should include any information that promotes the group as a whole. Each group may chose to include any of the following: educational background, knowledge about the discipline, hobbies, major accomplishments, travel, job experiences, etc. After sufficient time, invite each group to share their resume with the whole class.

- Schedule a class meeting or roundtable early in the course. This can be a circle of chairs or tables. Take time to talk about some of your expectations as well as some of the exciting learning opportunities you've planned. Invite students to share some of their fears or anxieties, too.

RESEARCH POINT

One impressive research study out of Harvard University concluded that for college students, "the emotional climate of the classroom is directly related to the attainment of academic excellence, however defined. Students feelings about what they will experience in class ... cannot be divorced from what and how well they will learn."

Building Rapport

A plethora of research, and my own interviews with college students in a variety of institutions, has revealed that one of the most significant factors that ensures the success students experience in a course is the rapport established between the professor and themselves. On the other hand, professors who are arrogant, "stand-offish," elitist, or distant are those who create uncomfortable classroom environments: environments that impede the learning process and inhibit students' engagement in the subject.

In my annual informal assessments of students, the following comments are those that are frequently proffered in response to the question,

"What characteristics of an instructor help you learn best?" Here are the top eight responses (those ranked highest over the last five years):

- Respectful of students
- Approachable
- Caring
- Willing to help
- Open-minded
- Supportive
- Fair
- Considerate

It's interesting to note that none of the top eight responses have anything to do with knowledge of subject matter, number of books or articles published, tenure, rank, graduate institution attended, gender, or age. They all center around the interpersonal relationships between students and professors. In short, the rapport we establish with our students has more to do with their academic success than does the number of degrees we hold, the number of years we've been teaching, or our stature in the academic community.

Here are some first-day suggestions and activities that will help you establish a level of rapport with your students. As with the previous list, feel free to select those ideas with which you are most comfortable. By the same token, consider the inclusion (and extension) of these suggestions throughout the length of the semester.

- Make sure your students see you as a human being first, rather than an authority figure in the classroom. Take time early during the first day to introduce yourself. Tell students something about yourself, particularly about your life outside the classroom. This can include:

- Your youth and educational experiences
- Hobbies and interests
- Your family
- Places traveled
- Books read

It's important for students to know that you have experiences and interests that are not unlike those of other adults. In fact, I've often found it helpful to share a funny incident from my past, an embarrassing moment I had in school, or some self-deprecating humor. These humanizing touches cue students that their professor does human things and is not always perfect.

- Take time during the first class to disclose some information about yourself that may not be evident to students. You might want to describe some of your experiences as a college student, particularly those related to the discipline you are now teaching. Tell students about your early years: where you grew up, schools attended, hobbies, interests, and places traveled. I often tell my students about growing up in southern California in the '50s and '60s and how I used to be a body surfer, a skateboarder, and how I could play a pretty mean game of beach volleyball. This opens the door to all sorts of conversations (and revelations) critical to building good relationships.

- Invite a student from the previous semester to write an open letter to the students in the current offering of the course. The student may wish to comment on course requirements, personality of the professor (you), ways of being successful, study hints, how to handle the textbook, or other appropriate items. I always invite the student writer to comment on some of my idiosyncrasies or mannerisms (Note: Students have noted that I have a particular fondness for the word "plethora."). I read this letter at the first meeting of the course and invite student comments.

- Divide the class into several groups. Invite each group to decide on a series of three questions they would like to ask you (questions unrelated to course content or procedures). The questions may relate to your family life, background, education, political preferences, favorite restaurants, travel, or reading material. Invite students to record the questions on individual index cards. Collect the cards (this allows you to pre-screen the questions) and respond accordingly.

- Take time to share anecdotes about your discipline or area of study.
  - Why did you choose this field?
  - What have been some of your most memorable learning experiences in this field?
  - Did you choose the field or was it chosen for you? Who are some of the memorable people you've met in this discipline?
  - What gets you excited about teaching this discipline? What has been the greatest lesson you've learned in this field?
  - If you had to do it all over again, would you still make the same choices in this field?

- Divide the class into several groups. Instruct the groups that they will be making predictions on how you will respond to certain questions you have prepared for them. Here are a few possibilities:
  - Where did you grow up?
  - What are some of your hobbies or free-time activities?
  - What kind of music do you like to listen to?
  - What kind of childhood did you have?
  - What do you do during the summer?
  - What got you interested in this subject?

Provide time for each group to make (and record) their predictions on how you will respond to those queries. Tell them not to be afraid of bold guesses. When each group is finished, invite them to share their predictions with the whole class. Be sure to allow time to share the appropriate information about yourself and to "correct" any misconceptions.

- Prepare a set of index cards with a series of pre-arranged questions for students to ask you (twenty to thirty questions would be appropriate). Distribute the cards to the class and invite students to each select one of the cards with a question they would like to ask. After students have selected appropriate cards, invite them to query you (since you generated the questions you will, of course, already know the answers). Provide students with the option of declining to ask a question. Here are some possible queries to record on the cards:

  - Why did you become an adjunct professor?
  - What do you like so much about this particular discipline?
  - Who has been the greatest influence in your life?
  - If you could be anywhere else right now, where would you like to be?
  - Were you a good student in school?
  - Where do you like to travel?
  - What was one of your most embarrassing situations?
  - What kinds of books do you like to read?
  - Did you party a lot when you were in college?
  - What really irritates you in life?

- When did you know you wanted to be a college teacher?
- Would you like to tell us something about your family?
- What is the greatest honor you've ever received?
- If you could have a conversation with any historical person, who would it be (and why)?
- What would you like to change about your past?
- What's the best advice you've ever received?
- What do you like to do in your spare time?
- What is your philosophy about teaching?
- Are you a hard teacher?

• As a variation on the idea above, distribute a few blank index cards along with the cards with pre-composed questions. Invite students who receive the blank cards to create their own question for you—one not part of the pre-arranged set of queries. After students have heard an array of the pre-arranged questions, they will be more inclined to create their own original questions to ask you.

• Take attendance the first day. Spend time learning the correct pronunciation of each student's name. Make a positive comment or ask a brief question as you go through your class list. Consider the following:

- "Thanks for coming."
- "I'm looking forward to working with you"
- "How does the field hockey team look this year?"
- "I like that outfit."
- "It's good to see there's another Anthony in the class."
- "How are you doing?"

- "What's one adjective you would use to describe yourself?"
- "I'm curious, why are you taking this course?"
- "Seen any good movies lately?"

The comments you make or the questions you ask aren't important. What is important is that you are making an effort to reach out to students to welcome them and learn something about them as individuals.

- Start off the first class by posting a philosophical statement on the chalkboard or whiteboard. This should be a statement that is reflective of your own personal philosophy. Here are some I have used:
  - "Imagination is more important than knowledge." —Albert Einstein
  - "There is nothing more dangerous than a closed mind."
  - "Education is a process, never a product."
  - "I touch the future, I teach." —Christa McAuliffe
  - "Education is not the filling of a pail, but the lighting of a fire." —William Butler Yeats
  - "Humans and amoebas are both imperfect. But humans have the capacity to change."

Talk with students as to why that particular philosophical statement is reflective of your outlook on life or your outlook on teaching college.

- How did you arrive at that philosophy?
- How do you practice that philosophy?
- Has that philosophy ever let you down?

- What do you do to share that philosophy with others?

Then, invite students, either individually or in groups, to design their own philosophical statements.

- Just prior to the first meeting of the course, send a group e-mail to all the students and provide them with a brief introduction to the course and to yourself. Use this opportunity to welcome them to the course, provide some background information about you, some of the exciting things you have in store for them, and an invitation to respond to the e-mail with any "pre-first day" questions or concerns.

- Give each student two blank index cards (each a different color). Invite them to each write a question on one card they would like to ask you (about you personally). On the other card, invite them to write a question about the course in general. Pass the cards around the class. As each card is passed to the next person, she or he should read it and place a check mark on the card if it contains a question of concern for the reader as well. When all the cards have circulated, collect them and respond to the ones that received the most votes. If time permits, you may wish to have some students share their questions, even if they did not receive the most votes.

Other First Day Suggestions

If it is true that first impressions are lasting impressions, then what we do during that all-important first day of class helps set the tone (and the expectations) for the semester to follow. Here are a few more "first day" tips I've gathered from colleagues around the country:

- This is not the time to pontificate. It's an opportunity to establish a bond between you and your students.

- Take time to get to know your students; provide your students with time to get to know you.

- Provide study tips or note taking tips that lead to success in the course.

- The best learning takes place in a cooperative atmosphere—one in which everyone has an equal voice. Be sure to make that clear on the first day.

- Share your attendance policy in a positive manner.

- Here's a statement I included in my syllabi: "Valuable information and ideas are presented and shared during each class session. It is to your benefit as well as the benefit of your classmates to be present for each and every class session. Your attendance, participation, and input are enthusiastically solicited and will help ensure mastery of all concepts."

- Students always want to know how grades will be determined. Make sure those procedures are clearly spelled out on the first day.

- Distribute index cards to students on the first day. Solicit some (or all) of the following data: Name, contact information (e-mail, cell phone number, hours they can be reached), major, current part-time jobs, other courses taken in the discipline, other courses this semester, reasons for taking this course, personal information (about how they learn best), and a philosophical statement.

The most frequently suggested tip shared by outstanding college teachers nationwide was that the time you take on the first day (or in the first week) to establish positive relationships between students and between yourself and your students will pay enormous dividends throughout the course. This is not wasted time!

CHAPTER 10:

Conducting a Class

Somewhere along your educational journey, you probably remember a class that was so intellectually stimulating and so engaging that it has remained in your memory bank for years afterwards. It doesn't make any difference what the discipline was or the topic; it's just that that particular class was one that left a lasting impression on you and may even have contributed to your desire to become an adjunct professor.

What do some professors do to make their classes dynamic and productive learning environments? What do other professors do that turn their course into "intellectual wastelands" where students feel as though their time, money, and effort are all swirling down a drain? Perhaps the best question to ask is, "How can I make sure that each of my classes is a successful learning experience for my students?" In this chapter we'll take a look at the answers to that query.

Lesson Design

Effective public speakers always follow three essential rules of a good presentation:

1. Tell the audience what you're going to tell them (Stage 1).

2. Tell them (Stage 2).

3. Tell them what you've told them (Stage 3).

Those three stages also hold true for the design of effective college classes. In its most simplistic form, a good college class is separated into three critical components: the beginning, the middle, and the end. While that division may seem simple, it is a coordinated series of learning opportunities that offers students valuable information and ways of dealing with that information in productive intellectual activities. The focus is not on the information itself, but rather how that data can be processed by students and ultimately made important for them.

Lets take a look at each of those three stages in a little more detail.

Stage 1: Opening a Lesson

Good college teachers are aware that it is often the first five minutes of a class that sets the tone for the rest of a lesson. These critical minutes not only provide an intellectual introduction for students, but also gives you an opportunity to begin building bridges of comprehension between what they know and what you would like them to know.

There are four elements that you must address during this critical time. They include: grabbing their attention, tapping into their background knowledge, providing an advance organizer, and developing a connection with students' lives. Let's take a look at each.

1. **Grabbing Their Attention.** When I was just beginning my tenure as a college instructor, one of my colleagues used to tell me, "It's critical that you grab students' attention in the first thirty seconds of class. Remember that their minds may be somewhere out on the

planet Neptune; you've got to bring them down to Earth." It was (and still is) a telling analogy, and the truth is that it is a positive stimulus to learning—it sets the tone for the day and signals students that there is something valuable ahead. Here are some tips:

- Start with a provocative question ("You're a presidential candidate and have just been asked about your policy on immigration. How do you respond?").

- Start with a current event that relates to your topic ("There was an article in this morning's newspaper about stem cell research. I'll read it to you and you can tell me what you think based on what we discussed on Tuesday.").

- Start with a problem that challenges their common assumptions or beliefs ("If you had a choice between raising taxes or eliminating social services, which would you choose?").

- Start with a "close to home" issue ("OK, it seems like the trustees want to raise tuition again. How does this relate to our current discussion of 'competition and efficiency?'").

- Start with a challenge to their mental models ("You know what I think? I think we should eliminate the welfare system. If people can't get a job, tough! Why should I have to support them with my taxes? They're bleeding us dry.").

Educators refer to this step as an "anticipatory set." It's when students are "set up" with a question, challenge, or problem that helps build an anticipation or expectation for the learning to follow. It stimulates the mind to begin processing information, not with meaningless facts or figures, but rather with an intellectual challenge that initiates the discovery process.

2. **Tapping into Background Knowledge.** Students bring a certain amount of background knowledge, prior experiences, perceptions, and misperceptions to any lesson. It's vitally important that

you discover what they know (or think they know) before beginning any lesson. That background knowledge will "color" their interpretations and comprehension of the material as much as it will affect their retention of that information.

Don't make the mistake of assuming what students know. Take the time to assess their background knowledge and you'll be rewarded with more successful lessons. Bottom line: Always know what your students know!

Here are a few strategies:

- *Self-Questioning:* Invite students to generate two to three questions about a forthcoming topic at the beginning of each class ("After reading the chapter in your textbook about population density patterns in Canadian provinces, what are two questions you have?"). These initial questions provide you with insights about students' thinking and how it may affect their interpretation of the material. I have also found that when students are provided opportunities to generate their own questions about a topic, then they will be motivated to seek answers to those questions.

- *Predictions:* Predictions are educated guesses about what may or may not happen. Predictions are valuable in terms of providing students with some self-initiated directions for a lesson. Predictions also give you insights about what students believe to be important or necessary ("Now that Horner has discovered the *Maiasaura* eggs, what do you think he will do next?").

- *Brainstorming:* Encourage students to brainstorm for everything they may know about a forthcoming topic. Remember that the emphasis in brainstorming is on gathering a quantity of ideas, irrespective of their quality. Brainstorming allows students to share much of their prior knowledge in a supportive arena.

3. **Providing an Advance Organizer.** Let's say you were planning a driving trip to Carbondale, Colorado. What would be one of the first things you would do? For many of us, the first thing would be to get a map, find out where Carbondale was on that map, and look at the highways, routes, and roads we would need to travel to get from here to there. In short, before we began, we would need to know how to get there. An advance organizer is students' roadmap for a lesson.

An advance organizer provides students with an intellectual scaffold that helps them understand and retain material. It alerts students as to what is important in a lesson (from the start) and offer "anchor points" upon which students can begin collecting the necessary material in advance.

> **RESEARCH NOTE**
>
> Advance organizers have been studied in considerable depth in the educational literature. A synthesis of that research shows that students who were provided with advance organizers at the beginning of a lesson showed average gains (on standardized tests) of from fourteen percent to twenty-nine percent as opposed to students who did not experience advance organizers.

Basically, there are four different types of advance organizers. They include:

1. *Expository:* Simply stated, this type of advance organizer describes the new content to which students will be exposed. It's a brief overview of the content by the instructor (time needed: three to four minutes).

2. *Narrative:* This is when the instructor presents information to students in a story format. It may include anecdotal information or fictionalized events (time needed: three to four minutes).

3. *Skimming*: Students are afforded the opportunity to quickly skim reading material in advance of reading it or in advance of discussing it in class (time needed: five to six minutes).

4. *Graphic organizers:* Graphic organizers are charts, graphs, or outlines of the essential information in a lesson. They serve to provide students with a pictorial representation of the major points in a lesson and how those points are related to each other (time needed: five to six minutes).

The key to the success of advance organizers is that they alert students to, and they focus on, what is important in a lesson. As a result, students have a "mind set" at the beginning of a lesson—a framework that they can begin to fill in as you share the necessary information.

4. **Developing a Connection with Students' Lives.** Recently, I observed an upper-division course on communication theory. I watched as the instructor opened a class with a discussion of a current episode of the TV program *Gray's Anatomy* (which, through earlier assessments, he knew students watched regularly). He briefly discussed the specific episode with students and then wrote "Social Penetration Theory (Altman & Taylor)" on the whiteboard. He turned back to the class and said, "Did you know that that episode was all about 'Social Penetration Theory,' our topic for today? Let's take a look," and the lesson began.

That instructor was able to effectively draw a relationship between students' lives (a TV show) and a classroom topic. It shouldn't be too surprising that he quickly had their attention and that he was able to begin drawing parallels between a theoretical construct and something that students could relate to.

This critical element of every lesson doesn't need a lot of time—one to two minutes at most—but, it is essential to the success of that lesson. Take the time to make the connection and you will always find it to be time well spent.

Stage 2: Teaching the Lesson

This is the heart of any lesson—that portion where you teach and where students learn. This is also where students obtain valuable information, manipulate data, and engage in active discovery through total involvement.

Not only is it important to give some thought as to what you are going to teach, it is equally significant that the methods of presentation be considered as well. I'm sure that you have been in a course composed of nothing more than dry, stale lectures. You undoubtedly found the course boring and wearying. The same fate awaits your students if you provide them with an overabundance of one type of teaching methodology to the exclusion of others.

Here, in the body of a lesson, you want to focus on three critical elements. These include:

- **Knowledge.** How will you present the basic information to your students?

- **Synthesis.** How will you provide opportunities for students to actually do something with the information they receive?

- **Performance.** How will you provide opportunities for students to use their knowledge in productive, hands-on learning tasks?

Let's take a look at each of these critical elements in a little more detail.

1. **Knowledge.** How do you present basic information to your students? It makes no difference whether you are teaching college freshmen in an introductory English course or instructing college seniors in an advanced level Anthropology seminar, you must teach them some basic information. Here are the ways you can do that:

- *Lecture:* Lecture is an arrangement in which information is shared directly with students with roots going back to the ancient Greeks. We discuss this "popular" form of knowledge sharing in the next chapter (page 139).

- *Reading Information:* With this method, you assign material from the textbook for students to read independently. You may also choose to have your students read other supplemental materials in addition to the textbook.

- *Audio-Visual Presentation:* In this format, you rely exclusively on the use of YouTube videos, PowerPoint presentations, photographs, webinars, podcasts, interactive websites, or other technology.

- *Demonstration:* In this format, students witness a real or simulated activity in which you use materials from the real world. These materials may include artifacts and objects used by individuals in a specific line of work. For example, microscopes (biologist), barometer (meteorologist), transit (surveyor), or word processing program (writer).

- *Observation:* This format allows students to watch an event or occurrence take place first hand.

- *Field Trips:* In this case, you are able to take your students out of the classroom and into a new learning environment.

- *Interviewing:* This format may include the personal interview in which one person talks with another person. It may also involve the group interview in which several people talk with a single individual.

2. **Synthesis.** One of the objectives of any lesson is to provide opportunities for students to pull together various bits of information to form a new whole or basic understanding of a topic. This process underscores the need for students to actually do something with the information they receive.

Here are some synthesis strategies:

- *Small Group Discussions:* Here, the class is divided into small groups of two to four students. Each group is assigned a specific task to accomplish. The group works together and members are responsible for each other. Some professors think that small group discussions are non-productive because no actual teaching takes place. Empirical research studies have shown that they are highly productive. They allow for the absorption of valuable material, a reflection on different points of view, and an informal means of assessing students' comprehension of material.

- *Experimenting:* Students participate in a planned experiment in which materials are manipulated in order to discover some scientific principle or truth.

- *Graphic Organizers:* Graphic organizers assist students in categorizing information. Most important, they help students understand the connections between their background knowledge and the knowledge they are learning in class.

- *Problem-Solving* Activities: In this situation, the class, small groups, or individuals are given a problem or series of problems and are directed to find an appropriate solution. It is important to include problems for which you do not have a preordained answer.

- *Buzz Sessions*: In this instance, temporary groups are formed for the purpose of discussing a specific topic. The emphasis is on either the background knowledge students bring to a learning task or a summary discussion of important points in a lesson.

> One widely used graphic organizer is **semantic webbing**. Semantic webbing is a visual display of students' words, ideas, and images in concert with textual words, ideas, and images. A semantic web helps students comprehend text by activating their background knowledge, organizing new concepts, and discovering the relationships between the two. A semantic web includes the following steps:
>
> 1. A word or phrase central to some material to be read is selected and written on the whiteboard.
>
> 2. Students are encouraged to think of as many words as they can that relate to the central word. These can be recorded on separate sheets or on the whiteboard.
>
> 3. Students are asked to identify categories that encompass one or more of the recorded words.
>
> 4. Category titles are written on the board. Students then share words from their individual lists or the master list appropriate for each category. Words are written under each category title.
>
> 5. Students should be encouraged to discuss and defend their word placements. Predictions about lesson content can also be made.
>
> 6. After the material has been read, new words or categories can be added to the web. Other words or categories can be modified or changed depending upon the information gleaned from the lesson

3. **Performance.** Having a bunch of knowledge is one thing. Being able to pull together bits and pieces of knowledge is another thing. But, the crux of a good lesson is the opportunities for students to use their knowledge in productive, hands-on learning tasks.

- *Independent Practice:* This method is one in which each student has an opportunity to use previously learned material on a specific academic task. For example, after learning about surrealism in an art theory class, students could create a PowerPoint presentation of a representative sampling of surrealistic paintings. In an Intermediate German class, students could assemble a German/English dictionary specifically for German college students visiting the US.

- *Debriefing:* Usually conducted at the conclusion of a lesson, debriefing allows students to condense and coalesce their knowledge and information as a group or whole class. It is an active thinking process.

- *Role Playing:* In this event, a student or students take on the role of a specific individual (a historical person, for example) and acts out the actions of that person as though they were actually the person. The intent is to develop a feeling for and an appreciation of the thoughts and actions of an individual.

- *Simulations:* Simulations are activities in which students are given real-life problem situations and asked to work through those situations as though they were actually a part of them. If you have ever played the game Monopoly, then you have been part of a simulation.

- *Reflective Inquiry:* This method is student-initiated and student-controlled. Individual students are encouraged to select a topic that they wish to investigate further. In so doing, they pose a series of questions that they wish to answer on their own. The questions are typically higher order ones (see Chapter 13, page 169) and emphasize a variety of divergent thinking skills.

If you'd like to make every lesson successful, you must do one thing: include a variety of teaching and learning methods in every lesson. If variety is the spice of life, then fill your lessons with lots of spice as you incorporate multiple teaching strategies.

Here's a good rule of thumb: For every lesson, try to include at least one knowledge method, one synthesis method, and one *performance* method. That way, your students are getting the necessary information; they're pulling that information together into a comprehensible whole; and they're afforded opportunities to use that information in a creative and engaging way.

Stage 3: Concluding a Lesson

It is essential that some sort of closure be incorporated into the lesson. This may mean a few minutes at the end of the lesson in which you or your students summarize some of the significant points, an activity in which students share perceptions with each other, or a time in which students recall their positive or negative perceptions of a lesson.

Here are some closure suggestions:

- **Teacher Summary.** Be sure to summarize the important points or critical elements of a lesson for students. Discuss what was taught and what was learned. This may be the most valuable three to five minutes of any lesson.

- **Student Summary.** Provide opportunities for students to summarize a lesson as well. Inviting them to put a lesson into their own words can be helpful to you in determining how well they learned the material.

- **Pose a Question.** Use a question that was asked at the beginning of the class as a concluding question, too. If you began with a provocative question to gain students' attention, you may choose to close with that same question.

- **Provide Feedback.** Remind students of what they learned and how well they were able to process the information ("We covered a lot of ground today on the differences between good reasoning and poor reasoning. It was some tough territory, but you did well.").

- **Provide an Anticipatory Set for a Follow-Up Lesson.** "From our discussion of the economics of the Aztec empire, I think you're ready to begin looking at the long-term social implications – which we will do tomorrow."

- **Use a cliffhanger.** Whenever possible, use a cliffhanger at the end of a lesson. This can be an unanswered question on the board, an unfinished project or an enticing bit of information ("Our discussion of sight and vision in invertebrates covered a lot of ground. But, wait until tomorrow. I'm going to bring in a creature with eight eyes. You won't want to miss it!").

A Sample Lesson (Briefly)

Here's a very brief summary of a lesson an adjunct professor of biology taught one day (she invited me to observe.). The lesson was part of a course on marine biology and focused on specific groups of marine invertebrates (*Porifera, Cnidaria, Ctenophora, Annelida,* and *Mollusca*).

1. **Stage 1: Opening a Lesson**

    - *Grabbing Their Attention:* "Remember what we discussed yesterday? Are you ready for some critters that are even more amazing?"

    - *Tapping into Background Knowledge:* "How many of you have been to the shore? How many of you have ever seen jellyfish in the water or on the beach? What did you notice about them?"

    - *Providing an Advance Organizer:* At the start of class, the instructor provided students with a study guide which listed the various groups of creatures along with representative examples. The guide also included a reading list and definitions.

    - *Developing a Connection with Student Lives:* "Why should we care about Ctenophores (comb jellies)?" She then explains that these creatures multiply very quickly and that they have taken over an entire ecological niche—the Black Sea. Discussion then centered on the implications if they were introduced into the Great Lakes or other freshwater ecosystems.

2. **Stage 2: Teaching the Lesson**

    - *Knowledge:* Using the study guide, the instructor reinforced the printed information with illustrations, a PowerPoint presentation, and other media. New vocabulary was written on the whiteboard and explained.

- *Synthesis:* The instructor frequently brought in the knowledge students have learned in other classes to help build "connections." She then provided students with extended opportunities to view hydras and water fleas via classroom microscopes.

- *Performance:* The instructor engaged students in a brief role-playing scene in which they pretended they were feather-duster worms. She invited them to act out the movements of these invertebrates as they slowly emerge from their shells to seek food.

3. **Stage 3: Concluding a Lesson**

    - *Teacher Summary:* The instructor provided the class with a brief overview of the important concepts they studied in the class.

    - *Student Summary:* The instructor invited selected students to provide personal insights as to why the information is important not only in terms of marine biology, but also in terms of their own lives.

In a conversation with her afterwards, the instructor said, "I can help students succeed in two ways. One, since many students have a fear of science, I can't just throw things at them. They would all shut down. I need to take small steps and then add things as we go. Second, I have to have enthusiasm for what I teach. I put in things that I find exciting. I want students to say, 'I got excited because you were excited!' This means that I have to give them good information, but also opportunities to do something exciting with that information. It's students' interaction with me and with the material that's important!"

CHAPTER 11:

Effective Lectures = Effective Learning

Ever since the time of the ancient Greeks, lectures have been a ubiquitous element of almost every collegiate experience. It is the most widely used way of transferring knowledge from one individual to another and, for better or worse, one of the memories students cite most about their college days. They will remember excellent lecturers as much as they will forget those who "put them to sleep" or droned on and on and—

There has been a lot written about lectures and lecturers. Some say that it is overused, misused, or abused. Others are just as adamant that it is the only way to get lots of valuable information in the heads of students. Still others will advocate for a reform in the traditional methods of lecturing—a reform that can make this delivery of information meaningful, productive, and intensely valuable. Let's take a look at the processes and procedures that will make your lectures dynamic and engaging.

The Nature of Lectures

By definition, a lecture is an oral presentation of material. It is a verbal delivery of material from an expert (you, the adjunct professor) to the ears (and, hopefully, minds) of students. The basic premise of a lecture is that students have a "knowledge gap" which needs to be filled through the delivery of specific information. Specifically, a lecture is the oral delivery of a body of knowledge from an expert to a novice. Its traditional form in college classes is the verbal transfer of information from a professor to a group of students.

College professors use lectures for several different reasons. While not all of these reasons are pedagogically sound or research-based, several have become part of the *modus operandi* of college professors since the beginning of time (or close to it). That these reasons are part of the tradition of the college experience for students does not, in any way, validate their use. They have simply been used so often that the reasons for their use may be nothing more than "that's the way it's always been done."

- A professor has a large (often overwhelming) body of knowledge to deliver in a fifteen-week semester.

- The discipline is so complex and the research so extensive that lecturing is the only way of presenting all that material.

- "How else can I teach 250 students crammed into an airless lecture hall?"

- There is more information than there is time.

- The textbook is so complex that lecturing is necessary to explain obtuse points and convoluted theories.

- "That's the way I was taught, so that's the way I will teach."

- The professor wants to impress students with her or his vast amount of knowledge.

RESEARCH POINT

There is an enormous body of research on lectures and their value in the college classroom. Space limitations prevent me from presenting all that data in this chapter. However, here is some interesting research for your review. Please consider this information carefully as you plan your courses—particularly as you plan the methods and procedures of sharing information about your discipline with students.

» A study of more than eighty undergraduate institutions showed that lecture was the instructional method of choice in eighty to ninety percent of all courses.

» Another study showed that up to fifteen percent of students' time in lectures was spent fantasizing.

» Several studies have indicated that when students are tested immediately after a lecture, they are only able to recall about forty percent of the material. Most of the recalled information was delivered in the first ten minutes of the lecture.

» Students' attention drifts after only ten to fifteen minutes of lecture.

» The human brain has "memory limits"; it can only hold or remember a selected amount of data at any one time. For college students that limit is seven "chunks" of information.

Educational researchers tell us that genuine academic attention can be sustained at a high and constant level for only a short time. For kindergarten and first grade students, that time limit is five to seven minutes. For college students, the time limit is ten to fourteen minutes.

In the college classroom, constant attention may be counterproductive. Much of what students learn cannot be processed consciously because it happens too fast. Students need time to process it. And to create new meaning, they need internal time. Meaning is always generated from within, not externally dictated. Also, after each new learning experience, students need time for the learning to "imprint."

> **RESEARCH POINT**
>
> One of the most important pieces of pedagogical research I ever read, and one that guided much of what I did in a classroom, is: "Eighty percent of what students hear is typically forgotten within forty-eight hours." That is to say that if I lecture students for an hour on Tuesday, they will only be able to remember about twelve minutes of that lecture by Thursday's class.

A Plan of Action

Good lectures don't just happen, they are the result of careful and systematic planning. The worst you can do to your students is to walk in "cold" to a lecture hall with a sheaf of yellowed notes in your hand, park yourself behind a podium or lectern, and talk at them for sixty minutes or more. In simple language, you've wasted their time and yours.

In designing an effective lecture, there are four elements that you must consider. It doesn't make any difference whether you are planning to talk about the intellectual evolution of European civilization from the decline of the Roman Empire to the late 14th century, how ecosystem stability leads to maintenance of biodiversity, or even why Pluto is no longer a planet—the key to a successful lecture revolves around four critical elements:

- Preparing your notes
- Beginning the lecture
- Continuing the lecture
- Concluding the lecture

Let's take a look at each of these elements in a little more detail.

Preparing Your Notes

I'm going to begin this section with a loud and vociferous "Don't." That is, don't write out your lecture notes verbatim! What often happens is that you become a "prisoner" to your own notes, disregarding the attention, interests, and motivational aspects of the students you are addressing. Equally important is the fact that, as learners, students process information quite differently in a verbal format than they do in a written format. Explicitly written notes satisfy your desire for detail and explanation, but often do not satisfy students' needs for participation and comprehension.

> **RESEARCH POINT**
>
> In one study, researchers examined the lecture notes of professors at more than seventy-five colleges. The conclusion was that extensive lecture notes promote passivity on the part of students. When professors read from detailed notes, they lose an important component of any learning situation—eye contact. More eye contact promotes more active involvement on the part of students.

Here are three "time-tested" tips that will assist you in preparing and organizing your notes for a forthcoming lecture:

1. **Graphic Organizers.** A graphic organizer (discussed earlier) is a visual arrangement of information, ideas, and concepts. Typical graphic organizers include semantic webs, tree diagrams, flow charts, and story maps. A graphic organizer allows you to focus on the relationships and connections that exist between ideas and information. The emphasis is not on the details, but rather on the concepts developed from those details. In a nutshell, a graphic organizer is a visual arrangement of words, concepts, or factual information grouped together into various categories.

2. **Color Coding.** I like to write my lecture notes with colored markers. Then, as I progress through a lecture I can quickly glance at my notes and determine what type of information I am to present next. This frees me from an over-reliance on those notes and allows me to maintain eye contact with the audience. Color coding is also a self-checking process that ensures that I am including essential elements of a lecture (see below) in every presentation. Here is my coding system; feel free to develop one appropriate for you:

- *Red:* An anecdote, story, or reading from a book
- *Green:* An open-ended or higher level cognitive question
- *Orange:* A little bit of humor
- *Black:* A "connection" with students' personal lives (movie, recent sports contest, campus event, future profession)
- *Purple:* A problem-solving situation, small group discussion, or synthesizing activity.
- *Pink:* A visual (You Tube, PowerPoint, webinar, etc.)
- *Blue:* Specific details or information

3. **Blocking.** You may find it helpful to design a lecture in blocks. I prefer time blocks – that is, I arrange my information and all ancillary activities (see above) into individual blocks of eleven to thirteen minutes each. Here are some other "blocking" strategies you may wish to consider:

- *Topic Blocks:* Select the three most important topics.
- *Chronological Blocks:* Arrange the information in chronological order. For example, three blocks each focusing on a single decade of time.
- *Controversial Blocks:* Arrange the information in a series of blocks that moves from "pro" to "con" to "resolution."
- *Progressive Blocks:* Set up your blocks so that students are introduced to the "theory," "research," "facts," "practice," and "applications" of a topic.
- *Hierarchical Blocks:* Organize the information into a progression of blocks that move from easy-to-understand to more challenging information.

- *Question Blocks:* This form is guided by a challenging question posed in each block. The questions may be generated by you or ultimately by your students ("Based on what we have discussed today, what questions do you need answered in Wednesday's class?")

Beginning the Lecture

The introduction to a lecture may be the most important part of any presentation. It alerts students to the information to follow, taps into their background knowledge, helps them make "connections" to the new material, and provides a motivational factor that stimulates engagement in the entire lecture. My own experience has been that the time spent on developing the introductory elements of a lecture will result in more effective lectures irrespective of the material or concepts covered.

Here are some valuable tips and ideas for your consideration:

- Begin a lecture with a story, vignette, or anecdote. This personalizes the information and places it in a context that is memorable for students.

- Start with a provocative question or interesting fact. This helps students quickly focus on the specific material to be presented and arouses their interest. For example, a mathematician might ask, "Did you know that some cultures never used the number zero?" A human anatomy instructor might ask, "Does anyone know what the largest organ of the human body is?" An oceanographer might say, "A tsunami can travel through the ocean at speeds greater than a jet airplane."

- Begin with a current event that directly relates to the material. For example, an article on declining attendance at professional baseball games would be appropriate to share in a sport management class. An article on an increase in white-collar crime would be appropriate in a business ethics class.

- Consider the use of an interesting visual to begin a lecture. This may include a cartoon, a quote, a photograph from a magazine or newspaper, or a short section of a video.

- Project the one to three objectives for the lecture for everyone to see (via PowerPoint). This provides students with your "plan of action." Refer back to these objectives periodically throughout the lecture.

- Sometime during the first five minutes of a lecture, discuss how the subject matter relates to students' lives. Draw parallels between the content of the lecture and students' experiences outside of class. For example, a botanist might begin a presentation on vascular plants by asking, "How many of you have ever tried to grow a plant and failed to water it sufficiently?" An economist might ask, "Has anyone ever wondered how much beer is consumed each weekend in the US?" as a prelude to a microeconomics lecture on the interaction of supply and demand.

- Make sure students know the significance of the material you will present them. The one question that is in the mind of every learner is, "Why do I have to know this stuff?" Make sure you answer that question very early in any presentation.

> **AN EXPERT OPINION**
>
> Brian Furio, an associate professor of communication, suggests the use of some of the following statements: "Some of you have found this—" "Think about when you—" and "Perhaps you can remember—".

Continuing the Lecture

Now that you have their attention and they are focused on the material you wish to share, it's time to concentrate on how you will maintain that interest. For me, a good lecture is like competitive ballroom dancing: the material must be carefully choreographed according to rhythm, flow, and pacing.

Here are some tips and ideas that will ensure the success of any lecture you present:

- Never, *never* cover more than three points in any single lecture! Many adjunct professors make the mistake of trying to include too much in a lecture. Overloading students with material limits their ability to process and comprehend that material. Remember: Three points. Stop.

- Show, demonstrate, or model how a professional in the field deals with a concept or idea. Don't just tell students about a principle or immutable fact, provide them with a concrete example of how professionals use that information.

- Tell students how you have dealt with a particular piece of information. How did you wrestle with a concept when you were a college student? What challenges did you overcome in learning something? What kinds of questions did you have early in your career?

- Provide students with periodic summaries. Every so often, offer a mini-summary (one to two minutes) of the material discussed. This allows them to catch up to your pacing and check on their comprehension.

- Whenever possible, use analogies. Relate new information to what students already know. For example, a geologist might say, "Plate tectonics is like two slabs of wax sliding around on a hot plate." A political scientist might say, "Political conventions in the early twentieth century were like fraternity parties on Saturday night. There was always something happening in every room."

- Always try to relate something in class to something in students' frame of reference or personal life. This lays a factual background, builds in enthusiasm for discussions, and motivates students to think more deeply.

- Insert criterion checks into the presentation every twelve to fifteen minutes or so. A criterion check is a point in a lecture at which the teacher stops and checks to see if students understand the material up to that point. These can be used to see if students understand the points made up to that point. I like to drop one of the following questions periodically into my lectures:
  - "What's one thing you still wonder about?"
  - "Thumbs up, thumbs down. Did any of that make sense to you?"
  - "If you had to summarize that information in just six words, what would you say?"
  - "What is an unanswered question you still have?"
- Don't make the classic mistake of asking, "Does anyone have any questions?" You will *always* be faced with a sea of blank faces as a result. Instead, do something like the following: "Write down a question you have about the material up to this point. Share your question with a partner sitting by you. In a minute, I'll call on random teams to share their questions."
- Consider a wide variety of visuals for any presentation. PowerPoint presentations, YouTube videos, webinars, and the like are all important. Remember that this generation of students is primarily visual; use that to your advantage.
- Include some "compare and contrast" examples in your lecture. Present two sides of an argument and ask students to defend one. Share a controversy in the field and ask students to pose a solution. Explain a point of contention and invite students to defend or attack the point. Here are some leading questions you can ask:
  - "How many of you agree with _____?"
  - "Why would anyone disagree with this point?"

- "How many of you believe that _____?"
- "Who's right?" "Who's wrong?"

- Provide students with periodic "markers" throughout a lecture. These include signposts to let them know what is ahead; *transitions* to let them know when you are finishing one topic and beginning another; and *summaries* to let them know what was just covered.

- Vary your pacing. A good lecture is not a linear event moving in a straight line from Point A to Point B. Change your tone of voice, provide information from various sources, use audiovisuals or computer technology, invite student participation, and show, don't just tell.

- Most important, don't read your lecture! Your students will lose interest and so will you.

- Whenever possible, stress the need for students to have a sense of ownership in the material. Statements like, 'What do you get from this?' and 'Why would this be useful?' give students a little bit of buy-in to any presentation.

Concluding the Lecture

A lecture that is well done is a lecture that is well finished. Don't let the scheduled end of the period signal the end of your presentation. The conclusion must be as well-planned as every other element of the lecture. The last five minutes of a lecture can be just as important as anything discussed in the body of the lecture.

Here are some ideas and suggestions for your consideration:

- Invite students to get together in various ad hoc groups to summarize the lecture's main points. Invite the groups to share their conclusions.

- Provide a brief summary of the two to three main points of the lecture. Present this information in a visual format.

- Ask each student to write a one-minute summary of the lecture. Collect these and quickly review selected entries for the class. Use the remaining ones to assist you in planning for a follow-up lecture.

- Invite students to take on the role of an instructor. Ask each one to write down three questions they would ask if they had delivered the lecture. Encourage students to share some of their questions.

- End the lecture with a provocative question or set-up. For example, a physicist might say, "Now that we've studied Bernoulli's Principle in some detail, we'll see how we can use it to create the ideal paper airplane in tomorrow's class." An ethnomusicologist might ask, "Anybody wonder how the African music we studied today influenced early rock and roll? Come back on Friday, and I'll show you."

- Invite students to compare their notes with each other for one to two minutes. Call on selected pairs to share their reviews.

- Provide a visual or graphic organizer to students that encapsulate the main points of the lecture on one page.

- Be sure to leave students with an answer to their perennial question—"Why do I have to know this stuff?"

Sample Lecture Plan

Lectures are as varied as the people who deliver them. However, if you are looking for a format that will assist you in constructing a well-rounded lecture, you may wish to consider the plan below. Its beauty is in its simplicity and its adaptability to any discipline and any topic. You should feel free to modify this outline in line with your own preferences or specific topics. [Note: This plan is based on a class period of one hour.]

A. Beginning
   Time: five minutes
   Content: anecdote, question, story, vignette, graphic organizer, music

B. Middle
   Block One
      Time: fifteen minutes
      Content: Principle #1, Idea #1, Concept #1
      Students: one-minute paper - What have you learned so far? (for example)
   Block Two
      Time: fifteen minutes
      Content: Principle #2, Idea #2, Concept #2
      Students: Q & A (for example)
   Block Three
      Time: fifteen minutes
      Content: Principle #3, Idea #3, Concept #3
      Students: Debate (for example)
      Demonstration, graphics, website

C. End
   Time: ten minutes
   Content: summarization activity, provocative question
   Students: one-question quiz

Tips and Tactics

Here is a random collection of tips and suggestions collected from some of the best teachers around the country. They are designed to help you craft lectures that are educationally sound and intellectually stimulating for your students as well as yourself.

- Consider using a conversational tone rather than a dictatorial one. Help students feel as though you are having a personal conversation with them.

- A good lecture doesn't mean non-stop talking. Pause frequently. Provide opportunities for students to process what you say.

> **RESEARCH POINT**
>
> In one interesting research study of several college courses, it was proven that, when professors paused at three separate junctures in any lecture (for two minutes each) and allowed students to discuss and/or process the material, the students retained more information than when they sat through a non-stop lecture without any "processing breaks." Another study confirmed these results and also found that both short-term and long-term memory was positively affected with the "pause procedure." This may confirm the old adage "Less is more!"

- Use stories and anecdotes wherever possible. Wrap your facts around stories and students will remember the information more.

- Demonstrate enthusiasm for your topic. Let your excitement about a topic rub off on your students. Enthusiasm fosters comprehension.

- Try to make eye contact with each student at least once in every lecture.

- Invite students to become part of the lecture. "What do you think?" "How does this relate to _____?" "What do you like about _____?" "Tell me your thoughts about _____."

- Vary the pace, intensity and the cadence of your lecture. A bland monotone creates a psychological distance between speaker and listener. Use examples, models, visual cues, and demonstrations when you can. Physical objects and tangible items help students remember important concepts.

- Relate, relate, relate. Always relate material in your lecture to information students already know. Help students make intellectual connections between what they do know and what they can know.

- The best lectures end a little early (it's a psychological reward for the listeners). On the other hand, don't go past the end of the period; students won't remember (or care about) what you say.

- Remember, just because you're talking doesn't mean students are listening—or learning!

Good lectures don't just happen, they are planned, systematic, and structured. Quite simply, they are much more than the dispersal of information. They are a viable way of mentally engaging students in the dynamics of a subject or point of view.

CHAPTER 12:

Teaching Large Classes

Let's assume that you've just walked into your first college course—an 8:00 *Introduction to Psychology* class. It's a cavernous lecture hall with endless rows of theatre seats. Filling those seats are 243 undergraduates; those in the front rows are awake, those in the back are quietly dozing. Elsewhere there is an atmosphere of controlled chaos: some students are shaking off the effects of last night's fraternity party, several are having intense cell phone conversations, others are doodling, many are consuming a less than nutritious breakfast of a latte and a donut, and a good number would probably prefer to be somewhere else. If this was Berkeley, there would be a wandering dog or two for added effect.

How do you teach all these students? How do you make your presentation engaging and meaningful? Simply put, how do you keep them awake for the next fifty or seventy-five minutes? These are questions that, each year, strike fear into the hearts of new adjunct professors. Let's take a look at some answers and how you can address (and teach) large groups of students for maximum effect and maximum learning.

You may remember your days as an undergraduate student in a large lecture hall. You were one of scores (or perhaps hundreds) of other students (typically freshmen and sophomores) all taking a required liberal arts course. The professor may have seemed distant (physically and psychologically) and you may have felt distinctly disconnected with the instructor, the material, or the information being presented. You may have felt that you were nothing more than a number—a small cog in a very large machine. Now, it's your turn to teach one or more of these enormous courses. How can you do it successfully while still maintaining your sanity? Let's take a look at some suggestions.

Organization is Crucial

Large classes take lots of extra planning. It is virtually impossible to teach a large group of individuals "off the cuff." Don't make the mistake of walking into a large lecture hall without a complete and detailed set of notes about what you are going to teach and how students will learn that material. If you are armed with nothing more than a few "war stories" from your days as an undergraduate student or a practitioner in the field, you will be setting yourself up for failure. I can't stress enough the need for planning (indeed, over-planning) to ensure that students' time (and yours) is well spent. For the most part, students don't like these large impersonal formats; don't add to their "uncomfortableness" by being less than prepared.

Here are a few tips:

- Review the chapter on effective lecturing (Chapter 11, page 139). What applies in small classes also holds true for large sections, too.

- Let students know that you are organized and prepared for them. Remember that you model the same kinds of behaviors that you expect of them. Take the first three minutes of a class to briefly outline the information, activities, objectives, and procedures for the class. If comfortable, use the same style as the one-minute "promos" delivered by your local news station ("This afternoon a noted celebrity donated $500,000 to a local cause. Tune in at 11:00 for all the details.").

- If you use PowerPoint, keep in mind that the minimum font size for any PowerPoint slide is twenty-four points—no less!

- If possible, provide students with a set of lecture notes as they enter the room. This can be a detailed outline of the topics and concepts to be shared in class. I prefer to provide students with a set of questions that will be answered in the day's presentation. In front of each question is a small box that can be checked off when the question has been addressed. I've also found these useful at the end of class when I invite students to tell me about any unanswered questions that remain on their respective lists.

- Post a study guide for each lecture on your class website. You may elect to have this guide posted in advance of the class or immediately after the class. There are advantages to both. If done in advance, students can see the primary points to be covered and can draft appropriate questions that they want answered. If done after class, the guide can help students "fill in the blanks" for any information that was missed during class. The downside of this approach is that students may feel that they don't need to attend class; merely look at the notes each week. You can address this concern by posting an abbreviated form of the material.

AN EXPERT OPINION

Jessica Nolan, an associate professor of biology, posits an interesting notion that guides her courses. She says, "Concepts lead to class discussions, while facts lead to more lecture."

Active Student Involvement

Nothing does more to disinterest students in a topic or a course than knowing that every one of their large class sessions will be done in the same format or style. If students expect that every class will be a long-winded lecture, then they will be considerably less involved in the dynamics of the course and considerably less motivated to learn the material.

1. **Variety is the Spice.** As shared in previous chapters, variety is the spice of life. This is equally true in large classes as it is in smaller seminar-type classes. Here are some techniques you can use in your large sections:

    - Start the class with a question ("Someone once said that 'Art defines a culture.' What does that mean? Turn to the person sitting next to you and create a response. You have two minutes."). By letting students know that they will be intellectually engaged right at the beginning of class, they will be more prone to staying engaged throughout the class.

    - If possible, bring a small group of students to the front of the room or on stage. Divide this group into two camps: the "pros" and the "cons." Encourage the two groups to debate a concept or principle. This will be an unscripted debate, but if students are provided with guide sheets or handouts describing how a debate "works" this can be a valuable teaching tool, particularly if used several times throughout the semester. Students will tend to pay (more) attention when their fellow students are "on stage."

    - Invite colleagues or outside experts into the class to debate an issue or concern with you. Each individual can take an opposing position and defend his or her thoughts. Invite selected students to comment afterwards.

- Consider using a "fishbowl" in selected classes. Randomly select six to eight students from your class roster. Invite them to discuss some of the concepts, principles, or ideas shared during the class. The remaining students are asked to observe the discussion and to record the information shared. Afterwards, they can be instructed to write a brief summary of the events. They may also wish to pose any unanswered questions—questions that you can respond to in a follow-up session.

- Make sure any presentation is divided into "blocks." You may wish to take a look at the information in Chapter 10 (page 125). It not only is relevant for small classes, but has applicability for large class sections, too. Consider using two to three teaching methodologies in every large presentation; just as you would for a smaller class. One former colleague makes a point to insert some key phrases at the end of each "block." Here are some he especially likes: "The real key component is—" "This is important because—" "Here's the critical part/element—" and "The one thing you want to remember is—"

- The conventions for many professional organizations schedule poster sessions. These are informal opportunities for one or two persons to discuss their latest research, investigations, or observations about a specific topic. There is usually a board or wall on which charts, graphs, or other display items can be posted. The presenter may give a brief talk and then be available for questions from interested conferees. This technique would also be appropriate for large class sessions, too. Students will need some instructions and directions in order for it to be successful. A few poster sessions can be scheduled throughout the semester.

2. **Write On.** If you are faced with 243 students, you are also faced with the task of grading any work they submit as part of your course assignments. You would probably not want to assign five

or six writing assignments to a large section since the time necessary to grade all that work would be simply unimaginable.

Since grading written work almost becomes prohibitive in a large section of students, you may wish to consider some of the following alternatives:

- I've often used the "One-Minute Paper" as a writing tool in large sections. At some appropriate place in the presentation, invite students to each take out a sheet of paper. Ask them to respond to a question, issue, concern, or piece of information in sixty seconds or less. When they have finished writing, invite students to submit their papers to you for review. Or, you may want to have students exchange their papers with each other for written or verbal comments or review.

- Consider the "One Page Only" paper. Invite students to respond to a question raised in class. They may use only one side (single or double-space) of a single sheet of paper for their response. These become very easy to read because the length of each response is limited to 250 – 500 words.

- The "Thirty Percent Rule" is another way of addressing a large number of potential written assignments in a large class section. Provide a brief writing assignment to the class, but announce that you will randomly select thirty percent (or any other percentage of your choice) of the papers to review and grade. By reading just a limited number of papers, you will get a generic idea of how all the students think about a topic or how they interpret a principle or concern. You will also reduce your reading time. The common factors can then be shared and discussed with the class as a whole. This strategy releases students from the burden of having every paper graded and also provides you with important information on how they are thinking about a topic.

- Invite students to exchange, read and review each other's papers. Provide students with a standardized rubric each of them can use to "grade" their classmate's work. Students may wish to share their reviews in a scheduled follow-up session or submit them to you for evaluation.

The trick is to have a balance between the number of papers you want to assign, the number of students in a class, and the number of hours you will have available to evaluate that written work. There is no magic formula. However, as the examples above prove, there are a variety of ways in which you can deal with written work without sacrificing your course goals or the learning opportunities for students.

3. **To Test, To Test.** Evaluating student performance in a large class session can be both problematic as well as demanding. Imagine trying to read, review, and grade five or six essay questions for a mid-term exam given to a class of 243 students. It would be a physical, psychological, and mental impossibility. However, with some modifications and a little creativity, you can affect an evaluation system that is respectful of your time and the need to effectively evaluate students' performance – even in large class sessions.

   - Reconsider your use of "pop quizzes." It may seem like "pop quizzes" are easy to construct, easy to administer, and easy to grade, but the negatives far outweigh the positives. Chief among those negative factors is the fact that these random assessments do nothing to effect good relationships between professors and their students. Second, these types of assessments are often viewed as punitive measures by students—something done to test content rather that teach concepts. Third, any quiz or exam given to a large section must be carefully planned out and designed. The questions must be carefully executed, time must be allocated for the preparation and duplication process, and a sufficient amount of grading time must be allocated. "Pop quizzes" are often viewed as something that is done to students at their expense, rather than as a teaching or learning tool carefully woven into the course design.

- As indicated above, take the time necessary to carefully plan and construct any objective questions for a test. Just as you would with a smaller section, include a selection of question types from different levels of cognition (see Chapter 13, page 169). The use of a multiple choice exam provides you with the opportunity to grade it using scan sheets and appropriate software.

- Provide students with an essay exam composed of several different questions. Invite them to each select one question to which they will respond. Or, the questions can be randomly assigned according to last name, seat, birthday or some other device. The advantage is that students will prepare by studying all the necessary information, but won't know in advance the question they will need to answer. You have the advantage of grading only one question per student, while still obtaining information about all the concepts learned up to that point in the course.

- Provide students with an objective test (multiple choice questions, for example). Include one essay question at the end. Tell students that they have the option of answering the essay question if their grade is on the borderline between two grades. Or, tell all students to answer the essay question and that you will read any student's individual response only if it will significantly raise their test or course grade.

- Two weeks before the end of the semester provide students with a "take-home" final exam. Tell students that they may elect to complete the "take-home" exam only if they would like to have it factored into their final grade for the course. Students who are "comfortable" with their grade for a course need not take the final if they so choose.

- You may find it advantageous for students to take exams in a group format. Divide the class into several different groups. Provide each group with an exam and invite them to work together to provide appropriate answers. Be clear that all group members will share in the final grade for the exam. Besides significantly reducing your work load, this technique provides meaningful discussions between students (which alerts you to any misperceptions or inappropriate conclusions) and fosters cooperative learning techniques.

4. **Outside Reading Assignments.** One of the other factors you must consider when teaching a class of many students is the utilization of outside reading resources: those resources in addition to the course textbook. One of the challenges is the simple availability of sufficient copies of those resources for every student in the course. Three hundred copies of a monograph by a leading researcher in your field would be problematic for the college library to obtain or provide. As a result, the need for outside reading assignments must be carefully considered in the planning for any large course.

Here are a few considerations you may wish to think about relative to outside readings.

- Choose your textbook carefully. Does it provide students with a balanced approach to your subject or does it need to be supplemented with outside readings? Those readings may include additional materials purchased by students or materials that can be made available through the resources of the college library. If in doubt, always take time to talk with the college librarians about the practicality of assigned library readings vs. purchased materials.

- Consider providing students with a list of specific websites or electronic articles in lieu of printed materials.

- Many college libraries have an electronic reserve system which posts copies of specific reading materials on the library's computer. Students can access the material in the library or other locations on or off campus.

- Consider the use of course packets. There are several commercial firms who will gather together articles and other publications (along with the necessary copyrights) and duplicate them in a packet for students to purchase along with the textbook. As a professor, you can specify which articles, monographs, handouts, conference proceedings or other items you want in these packets. Many research institutions have their own procedures for producing these packets in-house. Check with your department chairperson or appropriate dean to determine the procedures in place at your specific institution.

- Consider setting up a class website on which you can post selected articles (or the Internet links to those articles). This allows large numbers of students the option of accessing that information at their convenience.

5. **The Anonymity Factor.** Large classes are often the rule at large institutions. They are the administrative method of choice for teaching required courses to large masses of students. But, they come with a price. That is, many students lose their individual identity in these classes. They become anonymous, disengaged, and often disconnected.

> ### RESEARCH POINT
>
> Social psychologists have drawn parallels between the size of a group and the degree of anonymity experienced by any single individual within that group. In short, the larger the group, the more disconnected a person feels. In college classes, there is a direct correlation between group size and students' sense of self (larger classes = more anonymity).

Large college classes promote anonymity. It is easy for some students to "hide" in a large class than in a small seminar. Admittedly, some students prefer this sense of disconnectedness, yet we know that anonymity tends to create lower levels of motivation, less involvement in the subject matter, and more opportunities for uncivil behavior (see Chapter 16). Students' feelings of anonymity determine, in large measure, their engagement (and ultimate success) in a course.

With large classes, it will be a challenge to establish and maintain "connections" with your students. Yet, the efforts can be well worth it, particularly in terms of student engagement, participation, and identity. Here are a few suggestions:

- If you are in a large lecture hall, see if a wireless microphone is available. Take several opportunities to walk up and down the aisles looking at students, asking specific questions, and listening carefully to their responses. Moving away from the podium or stage and down into the audience has long been used by performers to significantly shorten the distance between themselves and their audience.

- Come to class a few minutes early and walk among students. Greet them by name, welcome them to the day's class, and spend a few moments talking about the "big game" last weekend, a cultural event on campus, or some bit of national or regional news. Don't begin a class by walking in and immediately perching yourself and your notes behind a podium.

- Create a seating chart that has student names (and photos, when available). When you pose questions to the class, make sure they are asked of specific students and randomly distributed throughout the room (front, back, left, right, and center).

- Provide an opportunity in each class for student pairs or triads to work together. Ask a question and invite students to turn to one or two neighbors to discuss a possible response. You may wish to invite these small groups to define some terminology, create a question that they would like answered, or to recapitulate a portion of the class for others. Randomly call on selected groups to share their response with the whole class.

- Offer opportunities for students to engage in buzz sessions or small discussion groups. Pose a problem and invite students to tackle it in groups. Circulate among the groups (if possible) and listen in on their conversations.

- Ask students to create "snowball" groups. Ask a question and invite two students to discuss a possible response. Invite those two students to join with another two students to arrive at a mutually satisfactory response. Then, ask one four-person team to join with another four-person team to create an answer acceptable to all eight individuals. Randomly call on two to three eight-person teams to share and defend their responses.

- Invite students to participate in informal discussion groups after class. Provide some coffee and donuts. Encourage students to set the agenda (which may or may not be class-related).

- Once a week, set up an informal buzz session. Send out invitations to students randomly selected from your class list (Note: Send out at least twice as many invitations as the number of students you expect).

- As students arrive, randomly pass out five to ten simple class evaluation sheets such as the one below. Meet with the students after class to discuss their observations. If time is a factor, you may wish to respond to their comments via a group e-mail. Consider incorporating their views and opinions into a subsequent class.

- Many large classes are supplemented with regularly scheduled seminars or discussion groups. These are often led by teaching

CLASS REACTION FORM	
Name:_____	E-mail:_____
Course:_____	Date:_____

Please complete this form by the conclusion of today's class. You may hand it to me or drop it in the box in the back of the hall. Please be honest in your assessment. I may wish to contact you for further details or information. Thank you in advance.

1. One point or piece of information that was particularly clear:

2. One question that I still have about the topic:

3. Something else I'd like to know:

assistants. Plan to stop by these sessions occasionally to chat with students or listen in on their conversations.

- Assist students in setting up study groups outside of class. Use your institution's technology to establish chat rooms, a calendar of available meeting rooms and times, instant messaging groups, or video conferencing sessions across campus.

- As practical, provide opportunities for breakout groups to work on a problem or a specific task. Divide the class into groups of fifteen to twenty students each. Invite them to use corners of the room, a hallway, a nearby empty classroom, or some other space to meet. Each group then reports on their deliberations (to the whole class) after a specified period of time. The trick to making these sessions work is to keep the time frame limited and tight (fifteen minutes maximum). Plan to circulate among the groups during their deliberations.

Here are three essential points that you should keep in mind as you begin designing a course for a large number of students:

1. Don't turn the course into an endless series of impersonal lectures.

2. Provide students with multiple opportunities to become actively engaged in the dynamics of the course. Use a variety of teaching methodologies (re-read Chapter 10, page 125).

3. Connect with students as often as you can. Meet with them before and after class in both planned and unplanned sessions.

Courses with large numbers of students can be both an intellectual challenge for you as well as a psychological one for your students. They are not easy courses to teach. But, with prior planning and an attention to community building, they can develop into effective instructional venues no matter what your topic or discipline.

CHAPTER 13:

Questions— Your Most Powerful Teaching Tool

Allow me to take you back in time to either middle school or high school. Imagine, if you will, an American history class. The teacher ("Miss Boring") is leading the class in a discussion of The Underground Railroad.

"Who can tell me what the Underground Railroad was?" Miss Boring asks the class.

No response.

"Doesn't anybody remember what we talked about two days ago?" she inquires.

Still no response.

"Once again, what was the Underground Railroad?" she asks.

By this time, most of the eyes are at "half-mast" as students are struggling to stay awake, even though the period started a mere five minutes ago,

"Okay, Sarah, can you tell me a famous person associated with the Underground Railroad?"

"I dunno," Sarah replied.

"Jackson, what about you?"

"I can't remember,' Jackson mumbles while texting his girlfriend.

"Ashton, can you tell us one significant fact related to the Underground Railroad?" Miss Boring asks.

The question catches Ashton unawares, as he is doodling in the margin of his history book. "I really don't know, " he replies.

"Justine, how about you?'

"Harriett What's-her-name," she guesses.

"Well, almost," Miss Boring replies.

The painful and tortuous scenario continues until Miss Boring, frustrated at all the "non-answers," finally tells everyone that Harriett Tubman was one of the pivotal figures in the Underground Railroad movement. Some of the students dutifully write the name in their notebooks, while others force themselves to stay awake for the next round of (boring) questions.

This classroom scene might be more prevalent than we like to admit. It depicts a teacher asking inane questions, students with little or no involvement in the lesson, and a kind of verbal ping-pong in which the teacher keeps asking low-level questions of various students until one student "gets" the right answer or until the teacher is forced to "give" the answer to a class of uninterested and uninvolved students.

As you might imagine, no instruction has taken place. The only objective in this scene is to obtain an answer to a predetermined question. It's a guessing game between students and the teacher. Students try to guess at the answers imbedded in the teacher's head. If they get it, the game moves on to the next question; if they don't get it, the teacher keeps asking until someone does or until the teacher gives the correct answer.

Unfortunately, most of the questioning that takes place in college classrooms is trivial, with the emphasis on memory and information retrieval. Seldom are students given opportunities to think about what they're reading or doing, and rarely are they invited to generate their own questions for discovery. Yet good questioning is one of the most significant teaching skills you can acquire. And take it from me: it is also one of the most challenging!

Why Ask Questions?

Teachers ask questions for several reasons. These include:

1. Tapping into background knowledge (to find out what students know before the lesson begins) with questions such as "Before we begin the lesson, why do you think plants are useful to humans?" This is critical because you always want to know both the depth and breadth of background knowledge students bring to a lesson.

2. Evaluating student progress or performance during a lesson with questions such as "How would you summarize what we have discussed so far on the Trojan Wars?" These are often called criterion checks and are a way of monitoring how well students are understanding a lesson. Stop every ten to fifteen minutes and ask students a question about how well they comprehend the material.

3. Evaluating student understanding at the end of a lesson with questions such as "What are the three types of rocks?" Unfortunately, this may be the most overused function of questions. Yes, you need to know if students mastered the objectives of the lesson, but to always end a lesson with a barrage of short-term memory questions is a sure way to make your lessons dull and boring.

4. Getting students involved in the lesson. Questions can be used as effective motivational tools that assist students in becoming actively involved in the dynamics of a lesson. For example, "Now that we have discussed latitude and longitude, how can we use those terms on this map of the world?"

5. Stimulating students to ask their own questions. When students self-generate questions, they will be more inclined to pursue the

answers to those questions simply because they own the queries. For example, "How many different questions can you come up with regarding the destruction of the Amazon rain forest?"

6. Moving student thinking to a higher level. It doesn't make any difference what subject you are teaching; all students can benefit from the use of higher-level thinking questions. By the way, stay tuned, and I'll share one of the most powerful teaching statements a little later in this chapter.

A Taxonomy of Questions

Here's something important you need to consider. That is, the goal of questioning is not to determine whether students have learned something (as would be the case in tests, quizzes, and exams), but rather to guide students to help them learn necessary information and material. Questions should be used to teach students, rather than to just test students!

Teachers frequently spend a great deal of classroom time testing students through questions. In fact, observations of professors in all subject areas reveal that most spend more than ninety percent of their instructional time testing students (through questioning). And most of the questions teachers ask are factual questions that rely on short-term memory.

Although questions are widely used and serve many functions, teachers tend to overuse factual questions such as "What is the chemical symbol for salt?" And approximately eighty percent of the questions teachers ask tend to be factual, literal, or knowledge-based questions. The result is a classroom in which there is little creative thinking taking place.

It's been my experience that one all-important factor is key in the successful college classroom:

> Students tend to read and think based on the kinds of questions they anticipate receiving from the teacher.

If students are constantly bombarded with questions that require only low levels of intellectual involvement (or no involvement whatsoever), they will tend to think accordingly. Conversely, students who are given questions based on higher levels of thinking will tend to think more creatively and divergently.

In 1956, educator Benjamin Bloom developed a classification system (we now refer to as Bloom's Taxonomy) to assist teachers in recognizing their various levels of question-asking (among other things). The system (revised in 2001) contains six levels, which are arranged in hierarchical form, moving from the lowest level of cognition (thinking) to the highest level of cognition (or from the least complex to the most complex). The six levels are: Remembering, Comprehending, Applying, Analyzing, Evaluating, and Creating. Let's take a look:

1. **Remembering.** This is the lowest level of questions and requires students to recall information. Knowledge questions usually require students to identify information in basically the same form it was presented. Some examples of knowledge questions include:

    - "What is the biggest city in Japan?"

    - "Who wrote War and Peace?"

    - "How many ounces in a pound?"

    Words often used in knowledge questions include *know, who, define, what, name, where, list,* and *when.*

    Observations have shown that teachers significantly overuse remembering questions. In fact, during the course of an average one-hour class, most instructors will ask upwards of forty to fifty remembering-based questions.

> **RESEARCH POINT**
>
> In one study of college professors, it was found that eighty-nine percent of all the questions asked by instructors were simple recall.

2. **Comprehending.** Simply stated, comprehension is the way in which ideas are organized into categories. Comprehension questions are those that ask students to take several bits of information and put them into a single category or grouping. These questions go beyond simple recall and require students to combine data together. Some examples of comprehending questions include:

    - "How would you illustrate the water cycle?"

    - "What is the main idea of this story?"

    - "If I put these three blocks together, what shape do they form?"

    Words often used in comprehending questions include describe, use your own words, outline, explain, discuss, and compare.

3. **Applying.** At this level of questioning, teachers ask students to take information they already know and apply it to a new situation. In other words, they must use their knowledge to determine a correct response. Some examples of applying questions include:

    - "How would you use your knowledge of latitude and longitude to locate the Maldives?"

    - "What happens when you multiply each of these numbers by nine?"

    - "If you had eight inches of water in your basement and a hose, how would you use the hose to get the water out?"

    Words often used in applying questions include apply, manipulate, put to use, e*mploy, dramatize, demonstrate, interpret,* and *choose.*

4. **Analyzing.** An analyzing question is one that asks a student to break down something into its component parts. To analyze requires students to identify reasons, causes, or motives and reach conclusions or generalizations. Some examples of analysis questions include:

> **AN EXPERT OPINION**
>
> As stated earlier, I strongly suggested that you should never end a presentation by asking, "Are there any questions?" This is the surest way to turn off students (You can also be assured that absolutely no one will raise their hand.). Instead, say something like, "Take five minutes and write down two questions you have about the lesson. Share those questions and discuss possible answers with a partner."

- "What are some of the factors that cause rust?"
- "Why did the United States go to war with England?"
- "Why do you think the author wrote this book?"
- "Why do we call all these animals 'mammals?'"

Words often used in analyzing questions include *analyze, why, take apart, diagram, draw conclusions, simplify, distinguish,* and *survey.*

5. **Evaluating.** Evaluating requires an individual to make a judgment about something. We are asked to judge the value of an idea, a candidate, a work of art, or a solution to a problem. When students are engaged in decision-making and problem-solving, they should be thinking at this level. Evaluation questions do not have single right answers. Some examples of evaluating questions include:

- "What do you think about your work so far?"
- "Which of Chekov's stories did you like the best?"
- "Why do you think the pioneers left the Oregon Trail at that point?"
- "Why do you think Benjamin Franklin was so close to the French?"

Words often used in evaluating questions include *judge, rate, assess, evaluate, What is the best value, criticize,* and *compare.*

6. Creating. Creating questions challenge students to engage in creative and original thinking. These questions invite students to produce original ideas and solve problems. There's always a variety of potential responses to synthesis questions. Some examples of creating questions include:

- "How would you assemble these items to create a windmill?"
- "How would your life be different if you could breathe under water?"
- "Construct a tower one foot tall using only four blocks."
- "Put these words together to form a complete sentence."

Words often used in creating questions include *compose, construct, design, revise, create, formulate, produce,* and *plan.*

What's It All About

OK, what does all this mean? Several things, actually! It means you can ask your students several different kinds of questions. If you only focus on one type of question, your students might not be exposed to higher levels of thinking necessary to a complete understanding of a topic. If, for example, you only ask students remembering questions, then your students might think that learning (a specific topic) is nothing more than the ability to memorize a select number of facts.

You can use this taxonomy to help craft a wide range of questions from low-level thinking questions to high-level thinking questions. If variety is the spice of life, you should sprinkle a variety of question types throughout every lesson, regardless of the topic or the level (freshmen, seniors) you teach.

Remember, students tend to read and think based on the types of questions they anticipate receiving from the teacher. In other words, students will tend to approach any subject as a knowledge-based subject if they are presented with an overabundance of knowledge-level questions throughout a lesson. On the other hand, students will tend to approach a topic at higher levels of thinking if they are presented with an abundance of questions at higher levels of thinking.

Dynamic Questioning Strategies

Questioning can certainly be much more than a teacher asking a question and a student answering that question correctly (or incorrectly). As my students would point out, that is "so old school!" It also sends the wrong message to students that teachers are in control of the information simply because they are in control of the questions. More important is the concept that questioning is a way to enlarge, expand, and diversify our thinking in new and creative ways. We can look at ideas in fascinating and interesting ways; we can expand our intellectual horizons; and we can develop higher levels of comprehension at any grade and in any subject area.

Following are some of my favorite questioning strategies. Consider these strategies as part of your teaching retinue and, you too will see some magical (intellectual) events taking place in your classroom.

1. **Wait Time.** Listen in on several college classrooms, and you'll probably hear professors asking question after question. With so many questions coming at them, students have little time to think. Looking at it another way: the more questions that are asked, the less thinking occurs. Classroom observations reveal that teachers typically wait less than one second for students to respond to a question. Teachers often conclude that students don't know the answer to a question if they don't respond quickly. And when they do respond, they usually use remembering-level responses.

   Those same observations also reveal that if a student manages to get a response in, most teachers tend to ask another question within an average time span of nine-tenths of a second! In classrooms where students are bombarded with questions (this is the norm, not the exception), students have little time to think.

Is this a problem? Yes! But here's an interesting solution: increase the time between asking a question and having students respond to that question from the typical one second to five seconds. This is known as "wait time." Believe it or not, this simple act produces significant and profound changes in the classroom, including:

- The length of student responses increases 400 to 800 percent.
- The number of unsolicited but appropriate responses increases.
- Failure to respond decreases.
- Student confidence increases.
- Students ask more questions.
- Student achievement increases significantly.

Wait time provides students with time to think and time to create an appropriate response. Imagine if you went to your local coffee shop, ordered a vanilla latte (with whole milk and no foam), and the clerk reached under the counter and handed one to you im-

AN EXPERT OPINION

Here's a super tip I frequently shared with new colleagues: when you ask a question, don't preface it with a student's name. For example, "Marsha, what are some of the reasons why Leonardo da Vinci is considered a genius?" As soon as you say one student's name, all the other brains in the room immediately shut down. Often, the other students will be saying to themselves, "We don't have to think now because Marsha is going to answer the question for us."

Instead, ask the question, wait, and then ask for a response (For example, "What are some of the reasons why Leonardo da Vinci is considered a genius?" [five second pause] "Marsha?") Interestingly, you'll discover a heightened level of involvement. Everyone has to think about a response because nobody knows who will be called on to respond. And, the responses you receive will be considerably better and more thoughtful.

mediately. Wouldn't you be just a little suspicious of the quality of that brew? You expect that, after you place your order, the coffee shop employee would take some time to brew your beverage and serve it to you a few minutes later when it's done. You're willing to wait because you know you'll be getting a beverage that has gone through an extensive brewing process rather than one that has been whipped out of an assembly line.

Wait time is the same thing. After you ask a question, let it percolate in students' heads for a while (a minimum of five seconds is recommended). And after a student responds, let the response percolate as well. Believe me, you'll wind up with a much better "brew" in your classroom.

Adding wait time to your teaching repertoire will, perhaps more than any other teaching strategy, have the greatest impact on student performance. However, it's only fair to tell you that it looks simpler than it is. It may be for you, as it has always been for me, one of the greatest teaching challenges you will ever face simply because teachers are uncomfortable with classroom silence. We tend to abhor it, often believing that learning can't really be going on in a quiet classroom. But with practice, you'll begin to see its incredible benefits!

2. **Expanding.** Remember Miss Boring from the beginning of the chapter? Miss Boring and thousands of other teachers engage in a practice that I refer to as "verbal ping-pong." Here's how it goes:

- Teacher asks a question.
- Student responds.
- Teacher asks a question.
- Another student responds.
- Teacher asks a question.

- Another student responds.
- And so on and so on.

Sounds pretty exciting, doesn't it? But it happens all the time. When a student answers a question, there's absolutely no response from a teacher. Most teachers tend to accept student answers without any sort of elaboration or expansion. In short, we become "satisfied" with any correct response a student shares and then quickly move on to the next query. There is virtually no intellectual stimulation!

If all we do after getting an answer to a question is mumble "Uh-huh" or "Okay" and then move on to the next question, our students get the message that the sole object of those questions is to identify correct responses (a focus on the lowest level of cognition). Equally important, this "verbal ping-ponging" inhibits both the quality of responses as well as higher-level thinking abilities. A much more powerful response is to use the student's answer as part of a series of follow-up questions. Here's a scenario:

- Teacher: What do you believe was the central message of "The Gettysburg Address?"
- Student: I think Lincoln wanted to emphasize the indivisibility of the Union.
- Teacher: So you think Lincoln wanted to project the country as a unified entity?
- Student: Yes. He was saying that, in spite of the Civil War, we should, or we would, continue to exist as one nation.
- Teacher: Are you saying, then, that the United States—at least according to Lincoln—was far stronger than its civil challenges?
- Student: Yes, but, I also think that he wanted to assure the American public that the nation could move beyond those challenges towards a stronger future.

Chapter 13: Questions—Your Most Powerful Teaching Tool   **181**

Notice what happened here. For each response the student provided, the teacher used some of the student's words to craft a follow-up response or question. This process accomplished several things:

- It recognized that the teacher was actually listening to the student.
- It provided the teacher with an opportunity to help the student clarify her or his thinking.
- It provided a motivation to keep the conversation going.
- It celebrated the student's participation in the lesson.

What results is an emphasis on, not just answering a question, but an active process of thinking, expanding, and elaborating on the answer(s). Students get the idea that answering questions is not simply about right answers, it is also an opportunity to engage in an active dialogue with someone to further comprehension about a topic or area of study.

3. **Prompting.** Prompting involves assisting students in thinking beyond their responses to a question. It stimulates and encourages students to investigate and rationalize their answers and can enhance classroom dialogue. Prompting questions such as these should be dropped into a discussion periodically:

    - "How did you know it was _____?"
    - "What do you know that isn't right?"
    - "What do you think this should be?"
    - "Why do you think your answer is correct?"
    - "What do you think will happen next?"

Notice that these questions do not have right or wrong answers. Rather, they are designed to help students think about, defend, and rationalize their responses. Best of all, they ask for students' opinions and reactions. This is a sure way to increase student involvement and understanding of any topic.

4. **Probing.** Good teachers invite students as active participants in the dynamics of a lesson by probing. Simply stated, probing is a series of teacher statements or questions that encourage students to elaborate on their answers to previous questions. Probing is a way of shifting an individual conversation or class discussion to a higher level.

   Good teachers use some of these probing questions frequently throughout a lesson:

   - *Clarification:* "What do you mean by that?"

   - *Obtaining more information:* "What's another word for that?"

   - *Making connections:* "Is this like anything else you're familiar with?"

   - *Comparison:* "How is your idea similar to or different from _____'s?"

   - *Expansion:* "Is there any other information you can add to that?"

   - *Validation:* "Why do you believe your response is correct?"

5. **Reducing the "Dunno" Syndrome.** There's something that happens in almost every college classroom almost every day. Questions are asked and students (who are either bored, frustrated, distracted, or unprepared) answer "I don't know" or "Dunno." It's a common enough occurrence in any classroom that it is quite easy to recognize (I am certain that you and I and hundreds of millions of other students have used this "cop out" more than once sometime in our educational careers.).

   When students respond with "I don't know" they are effectively saying that they don't want to make any kind of intellectual investment in the topic under discussion. It's a convenient way of escaping from any intellectual pursuit—a way of telling the teacher, "I'm not responsible and I don't want to get involved." In many ways, the student is telling the teacher, "I'm done here, go ahead and move on to someone else."

I find this common occurrence unacceptable. I don't ask questions to waste students' time, rather I ask questions to help students understand the ramifications of a concept, expand their thinking horizons, and engage in a supportive conversation that is both respectful and educational. To do that, I don't allow students to escape from a question, I always pursue some form of dialogue—some form of intellectual discovery. "I don't know" is never an acceptable response. Here's a scenario:

- **Professor** (to Becky): What do you think are some of the consequence of oil pollution?

- **Becky:** I dunno

- **Professor** (to Stewart): Stewart, what's your thinking about the effects of oil pollution?

- **Stewart:** Well, it certainly alters the environment for wildlife. Animals can't find the food they need to survive, and their habitats are often damaged.

- **Professor** (back to Becky): Now, Becky, what do you think about oil pollution?

- **Becky:** It's dangerous for animals. They often can't find food or a place to live.

- **Professor:** How would you feel if you couldn't find any food or didn't have a place to live?

- **Becky:** I'd be pretty bummed out. I'd probably have to move out of the area.

In this scenario, Becky responded to the initial question with an "I don't know." The professor then turned to another student and invited him to respond to the same inquiry. Then, the professor came back to Becky and asked the same question (although in a different format). Becky knew that she wasn't going to "escape." If necessary, the professor could have turned to yet another student, asked for a response, and, once again returned to Becky.

What is important about this questioning sequence is the fact that students realize that their mental presence in a subject is not optional, it is required. As college professors, we need to provide opportunities for ALL students to become engaged in learning a planned topic. What you will discover, as I did many years ago, is that over time the number of "I don't knows" decreases significantly to the point where they almost become non-existent.

Here's another scenario (from an Introduction to Philosophy course):

- **Professor** (to Terry): Why do you think Aristotle achieved much of his fame after his death?

- **Terry:** I don't know.

- **Professor** (reworking the question): If you could be famous for something, what would it be?

- **Terry:** I guess my running.

- **Professor:** Why running?

- **Terry:** Because I spend a lot of time working out, trying to lower my personal best in the 5,000 meters.

- **Professor:** Was there something Aristotle spent a lot of time on?

- **Terry:** Yeah, he spent a lot of time working with Alexander the Great.

- **Professor:** So, what is one thing that made Aristotle so famous?

- **Terry:** He taught Alexander the Great.

Notice in the sequence above that the teacher didn't give up on Terry. It would be quite easy whenever getting an "I don't know" response to end the conversation with one student and move on to another student. Don't do it! Rework, revise, or reconfigure your original question in a way that taps into something you know the student enjoys or is familiar with. Use that background knowledge to help the student eventually arrive at an appropriate response to the original question.

Here's something else you may have noticed. In both of the scenarios above, the questions asked by the two teachers were all at higher levels of cognition. They were not, as is often typical in most classrooms, primarily Remembering questions. And, here's why that is so important: By focusing more on higher level cognitive questions, you give yourself more options for ensuring student responses than you would if using a preponderance of low-level or Remembering questions. In other words, you limit your opportunities for engaging students with low-level queries; you significantly increase those opportunities with questions higher on the taxonomy.

6. **Everybody In.** I'm going to suggest something radical—something that will go against the status quo. Yet, it's a procedure that can produce some dramatic and dynamic results. Simply, when I ask a question, I don't ask for a show of hands. In fact, I frequently discourage the common practice of "raising your hand to answer a question." Here's why. Often (as you might imagine) it's always the same students who raise their hands in any classroom. And, it's always the same students whom the teacher recognizes to answer those questions. As a result, students quickly learn that it is possible to "hide" in the classroom simply by never raising their hands during any inquiry process. They never have to participate.

Instead, I want everyone in the room to accept the responsibility of answering any and all questions that might be posed. In short, there are no "innocent bystanders." I want everyone to be intellectually engaged and ready to contribute at a moment's notice. Here's a typical scenario:

- **Teacher:** What do you think the "Founding Fathers" would have thought about how the second amendment is being interpreted today?

- (pause for five seconds)

- **Teacher:** Kayla, what do you think?

Notice that the teacher didn't ask for any hands to be raised. She asked the question and allowed it to seep into everyone's brain. Then, she called on a random student. In other words, everybody was "asked" to consider and process the question. Then, after a short period of time, one individual, selected arbitrarily, was invited to answer. You will quickly notice that this is a reaffirmation of "Wait Time," a strategy that will dramatically and positively influence the dynamics of your lessons.

AN EXPERT OPINION

At the beginning of a course, I invite students to each write their name on a colored craft stick or tongue depressor (available at my local arts and crafts store). I then collect all those sticks and place them in a small glass jar. When I ask a question of the class, I allow the question to percolate for a while and then I randomly select one of the craft sticks from the jar. The student whose name is on that stick gets "first crack" at answering the question. Then another stick is selected—and another—and so on. Not only did this help me quickly learn student names early in the semester, but it also ensured that the student answering process was completely random and by chance. Students didn't have to raise their hands, but they were all potential "subjects" for a teacher/student interaction.

Something to Think About

There is a long-standing "tradition" among teachers to use questions as a way of testing students—finding out what they read or learned. But, the real value of questions is as a teaching tool—one that helps students comprehend and master material. That comes about when you place a value on:

- Using questions as a natural and normal part of EVERY classroom lesson

- Helping students understand that questions are always a part of good lesson

- Asking higher-level questions more so than lower-level queries

- Providing opportunities for all students to take part in the cognitive processes required to answer those questions

- Working to eliminate any and all "I don't knows"

Always include questions in any kind of classroom presentation—old material or new material. Help students understand that questions are always a part of learning. Just as the kinds of questions are important; so too, is how we process information after a question has been asked. You want to let students know that learners—good learners—are always responding to questions. The ultimate goal is students who begin asking their own self-initiated questions as a result of the models you provide in the classroom.

CHAPTER 14:

Discussions: The Right Way

Let's imagine that it is Monday morning and that there was a major athletic competition on campus the previous weekend. Students are discussing the event. Some are commenting on the results. Others have something to say about the athletes. A few may be talking about key circumstances, key plays, or key decisions. There is discussion about the coach, the weather, and a dozen other factors that may have taken place prior to, during, and after the event.

What is taking place? In this discussion, there is a sharing of information in a supportive environment. Students can all relate to a common experience. Sometimes there is disagreement; sometimes there is acclimation. Students are reviewing the event based on their experiences with previous contests or events. Questions are posed, problems are aired, interpretations are made, points are established, and emotions may, at times, run high. It's not the final score of the event that is critical here (unless it's a conference championship); rather it is everyone's perception, interpretation, and input that makes this an active dialogue. The same thing can be part of any class as well. Let's take a look.

In our earlier discussion of constructivism we made a distinction between a more traditional view of college teaching as a transmission of knowledge (giving knowledge to students who then attempt to absorb it) and a view of teaching (students use what they already know along with their prior experiences to help them incorporate and understand new material). Let's analyze the scenario at the beginning of this chapter as a form of constructivism:

- Students use what they already know. Students all watched the same athletic contest.

- Students have prior experiences. Students have a basic knowledge of the sport being discussed (football, basketball, field hockey).

- Students incorporate new material. Students share their own views of the recent contest and listen to the views of others who also watched the same contest.

- Students understand new material. Students' positions about the contest are strengthened, realigned, modified, or thrown out when compared with other interpretations.

In many ways, the discussion about last Saturday's football game is emblematic of constructivist classrooms. In both cases, students are trying to assimilate new information with what they already know and understand. This process can be promoted in our college courses when discussions are incorporated as a regular feature.

Classroom discussion offers students incredible learning benefits.

RESEARCH POINT

Research conducted by numerous investigators over the past several decades has revealed that students pay attention and think more actively when engaged in discussion than when exposed to lectures.

Here are a few:

- Students learn to weigh different types of evidence in reaching a conclusion.
- Students are able to think more deeply about a topic or subject.
- Students are able to evaluate the strength of their own position on an issue or concern.
- Students are provided with a safe environment in which to articulate their beliefs.
- Students can engage in higher level thinking activities that offer multiple perspectives on an issue.
- Students can tackle problems and seek multiple solutions.
- Students' interest and curiosity about a subject can be heightened and expanded.
- Students are engaged in active listening opportunities.
- Students have opportunities to learn from others.

> **RESEARCH POINT**
>
> A significant body of research has demonstrated the value of classroom discussion in improving student attitudes toward learning, enhancing learning and retention of material, and promoting the development of critical thinking skills.

Good classroom discussions don't just happen, they must be planned. While you can never be sure of the ultimate destination of every discussion, you should develop a course of action to ensure that students reap the greatest benefits from the process. There are three stages to consider (By now, this design will look very familiar to you.).

The three stages are:

1. Before the discussion

2. During the discussion

3. After the discussion

Let's look at each stage in a little more detail.

Before the Discussion.

Good discussions take planning. Organizing your thoughts and helping students organize theirs will help guarantee that important concepts and necessary information are shared in a supportive arena that promotes learning through dialogue. The groundwork you lay before a discussion is directly related to the success students enjoy while participating in a classroom discussion. Here are a few considerations.

As you begin planning for your course—laying out the topics, arranging textbook readings, scheduling exams, etc.—you should also plan for structured discussions. A structured discussion is one in which the instructor takes a strong leadership role. The topic is selected beforehand, the questions are carefully planned, and the goals are very specific. In a structured discussion, there is a specific idea or conclusion you want students to reach.

Here are some ideas:

- List structured discussion sessions (and the individual topics) in the course syllabus.

- Include a note in your syllabus about the importance of these discussions. This lets students know ahead of time the value you place on their involvement.

- Along with the topic of each structured discussion list one or two pre-planned questions that will be the focus of each discussion. Again, this prepares students in advance.

Make discussions a regular feature of your course. Schedule them on the syllabus (once a week, for example). Let students know in advance about these interactive experiences. As a result, they will be better prepared for them.

1. **Classroom Design.** The design and configuration of the classroom will either facilitate or hamper discussions. The worst possible configuration is the classic straight rows and straight columns. Here, students are merely conversing with you, rather than interacting with each other. You will see the quality and involvement of students escalate when you provide a configuration in which they can physically see each other or be in close physical proximity. The room configuration also enhances the involvement of those who may be reluctant to participate in discussions.

   Consider the following configurations (which can be set up in advance of a class or "on the fly" in the middle of a class session):

   - The desks are arranged in mini-groups of four to five each with all the desks facing inward.

   - A U-shaped design in which all the desks or chairs are set up in a horseshoe-shaped arrangement.

   - Individual work tables with chairs arranged around all four sides.

   - Desks or chairs arranged around the perimeter of the room, all facing inward.

AN EXPERT OPINION

According to Angela McGlynn, a professor of psychology, "The classroom seating arrangement will influence both the atmosphere of the class and students' willingness to enter into discussions. Without an atmosphere of trust, safety, and connection, our attempts to lead rich classroom discussions are bound to fall short."

2. **Start Early.** Good discussions don't just happen just because you've put students into a small group and given them a question to analyze. There must be a sense of shared responsibility as well as an element of psychological comfort. Here's how you can make that happen.

    - On the first class session, organize students into groups and invite them to introduce themselves to each other. Keep this "getting to know you" session relaxed and informal.

    - In the second and third class session, provide small groups with an opportunity to tackle a question with which they will all have an opinion or an experience. For example, "Should everyone go to college?" "What's the best thing to do on the weekend around here?" or "Why do we have to take this course?" These broad topics may not have anything specific to do with course content, but they help students establish important bonds that will pay dividends throughout the semester.

    - Early in the semester, invite students to discuss (in small groups) the value of discussions. Encourage them to establish a list of "rules" or expected behaviors that will make a discussion valuable for everyone. Invite groups to come together to establish a "master class list" or a discussion protocol.

    - Inform students that how they learn is just as important as what they learn. Emphasize early (and throughout the semester) the importance of discussions as a way of mastering the necessary materials.

3. **Before Class.** There are several techniques you can put into place before each class to ensure the success of any planned or unplanned discussions. In short, good planning beforehand ensures good discussions (and outcomes) during a class.

    - Make sure students all have a common experience. This may include a textbook or article reading, a podcast, a PowerPoint presentation, a guest speaker, a demonstration, or a webinar. This ensures that everyone has the same frame of reference to draw on.

- Determine the objectives of a lesson beforehand and develop two to four discussion questions based on those objectives. Share the discussion questions with students along with the assigned reading.

- Before class, write out a series of question types as "stimulators" for classroom discussions. These can include the following:

  - *Application:* "How could we use this information in _____?"

  - *Interpretation:* "How do you feel about this position?"

  - *Making Connections:* "How is this like something else you're familiar with?"

  - *Comparison:* "How is your idea similar to or different from _____'s?"

  - *Validation:* "Why do you believe your response is correct?"

  - *Evaluation:* "Why do you think this concept is so important?"

- Prepare students in advance of any discussion. I like to give students a pre-discussion sheet similar to the following. This discussion sheet is geared to a specific reading and provided to the class several days in advance of a scheduled discussion.

> **A. Why is this reading important?**
> (Here, I provide students with a brief explanation of the importance of the reading—a new philosophy, a different perspective on an issue, a controversial topic, etc. I do not provide a summary—I don't want students to rely on my summary for their interpretation.)
>
> **B. Reading Points**
> (Here, I offer students two or three critical points in the reading that they should look for. I might pose the following: "What do you know about the author's philosophy after reading the first two paragraphs?" "Note where the author contradicts herself." "Where does the author confirm his thesis?")
>
> **C. Self Questions**
> (Here, I invite students to record approximately three to five questions that they have about the reading. I encourage them to record the questions as they are reading. As an alternate to questions, they may record responses to open-ended statements such as "I didn't understand when he—" "I was confused about—" "I thought that the most important point she made was—" "I particularly liked—")
>
> **D. Discussion Questions**
> (Here I provide students with some pre-selected discussion questions that we will address in class. All the questions are at higher cognitive levels [applying, analyzing, evaluating, creating]. Students are encouraged to record key words or phrases from the reading, their own interpretations, or notes from another source. I also provide space for additional questions [and responses] that will inevitably arise during the actual discussion.)

These discussion sheets have several advantages. Students come to class with written information as an aid to their oral discussions (their conversation is not off-the-cuff). Students sense that a discussion will not be a recitation of factual information, but rather one focused on higher cognitive thinking skills. And, the discussions are focused and purposeful—students view them as integral elements of a course, rather than as "time wasters."

- Consider establishing a set of rules or behavior expectations for any and all discussions in the class. While it would be advantageous for students to create these rules on their own, you may wish to posit the following in your course syllabus:

- Respect the opinions of others, even when they may differ from your own.
- Everyone has the right and opportunity to express an opinion.
- A discussion is a group activity rather than an individual crusade.
- Personal attacks, blaming, and condemnation are inappropriate.
- What is said here, stays here.

During the Discussion

Not only will you want to make discussions an integral part of any course or any topic, you will also want to make those discussions fruitful and productive for your students. Here are some time-tested strategies that will do just that.

1. **Visual Organizers.** I have found it very helpful to provide students with one or more visual organizers at the start of any classroom discussion. The visual organizer (projected on a screen, written on the whiteboard or a large sheet of newsprint, or distributed as a handout) may be one of the following:

    - A web of key points, terminology, or concepts
    - A taxonomy of various classes or groups of data
    - A "tree" of contrasting or related features
    - An outline (i., i., ii, a., b., c.) of important points
    - A "fill-in-the-blanks" paradigm

Here are two ways I like to use a visual organizer in my courses:

- I prepare the organizer by filling in information and details from the text in one color of ink (red, for example). Then, as we discuss the reading, students' opinions, comments, and ideas are recorded on the organizer in another color of ink (for example, green). This helps students draw positive (and visual) relationships between an author's ideas and their own.

- I fill in an organizer with a limited number of details. I tell students that the object of a forthcoming discussion is to complete the organizer with information they've garnered from the text or their interpretations of and opinions about the reading. Afterwards, we take time to discuss the "completeness" of the organizer.

2. **The "Ping Pong" Effect.** In the previous chapter, we discussed the "ping-pong effect." This happens when a teacher asks, Student A answers, teacher asks, Student B answers, teacher asks, Student C answers—and so on. In reality, there is no discussion, simply because you are the one "calling the shots." Here are some alternate strategies for you to consider:

- When a student responds, try to get other students involved ("Sandra, how do you feel about Albert's interpretation?" "Raymond, any reaction to Jasmine's opinion?")

- Establish a rule that you will ask a follow-up question only after three different students have responded to an introductory question (this is a good opportunity to practice wait time).

- Divide students into triads. In each group, one student is responsible for posing a question. The other two students must respond to the question. Then, invite the triads to share their responses amongst each other.

- Arrange students into small groups. Pose a question or problem to the entire class. Each student in a group must offer a response or reaction to the question/problem before tackling another question/problem. Many students are more comfortable in expressing their thoughts in small group settings.

> **AN EXPERT OPINION**
>
> Kay McAdams suggests that our primary role in any discussion is "to expose students to ideas, not to tell them what to think."

After the Discussion

There are several things you can do at the conclusion of a whole-class or small-group discussion that can emphasize the importance of this teaching technique to your students. Consider some of the following suggestions:

- Take a few moments to summarize the major points of the discussion. It would be valuable to do this in both an oral as well as written format.

- Give students opportunities to summarize the essential points. You may elect to do this in a whole class session or ask small groups to collectively brainstorm and then record their information on the whiteboard

- Appoint a class scribe for each class session. That individual is responsible for recording the essential points of a discussion as well as any conclusions reached. Invite the individual to duplicate her or his notes and distribute them or post them on the class Website.

- I often like to end a discussion with an intriguing question ("You know we've thoroughly analyzed the basic elements of commensalism, however tomorrow we're going to discuss a commensalistic relationship that defies both logic and common sense!")

- Be sure to celebrate the contributions of everybody. Acknowledge their opinions (even if they were different from yours or the textbook) and congratulate them for their oral participation. Let students know that their verbal engagement in the course is key to their comprehension and appreciation of course concepts.

Troubleshooting

It's inevitable. You've planned for an exciting and stimulating discussion, but students couldn't care less. You pose a fascinating question to the class, and all you get is a sea of blank faces. You've shared an intriguing problem or set up a conceptual conundrum, and a wave of silence engulfs the room. It's bound to happen, and it will happen more than once in your professional career.

Let's take a look at some of the most common discussion problems as well as some ways of dealing with those challenges.

1. **Students Are Unprepared**

    - In a preceding class, assign students a critical question (to be recorded on their cellphone or tablet). By showing up in the next class they affirm that they are ready to discuss that question.

    - Each student is required to bring one question to each class session.

    - Students are given specific roles (within a group) ahead of any discussion. One can be the leader, another the recorder, another a questioner, and another a summarizer.

    - Invite students to select a passage from the text that they would like to discuss or challenge in the next class.

2. **Students are not participating**

    - Keep the groups small. Small groups facilitate discussion simply because there are fewer persons "listening in."

    - Provide multiple opportunities for students to interact and get to know each other in a variety of ways throughout the course.

    - Invite students to tackle a problem or question in two-person teams.

- Invite students to write out a response to a question first. Then, encourage students to share their written responses in a larger group setting.

- Students respond more when they are facing each other—in a circle, for example. In this way, they receive visual feedback (smile, nod, body language) that they don't get in rows and columns.

- Use a plethora of open-ended questions. Instead of asking "What is the main idea of this article" (which puts a student on the spot if a wrong answer is given) ask "What do you think about this particular article?" Questions for which there are multiple answers are much more comfortable for students, and they engender more participation.

3. **The Discussion Monopolizer**

    - Divide and conquer. Assign discussion "monopolizers" to a variety of smaller groups.

    - Invite the class to discuss the importance of equal contributions from all class members.

    - Assign a "talker" the role of discussion recorder. Give the individual the responsibility of recording the concepts discussed and the conclusions reached.

    - Videotape a class session and invite the monopolizer to view the recording. Often, these individuals are not aware of their actions.

    - Pose a question and invite a student to respond for a maximum of two minutes. Each speaker who follows must briefly summarize the comments of the person before her or him before voicing their own opinions. And so on.

4. **Controversial topics**

    - Make sure the focus is on the facts, rather than the opinions. It's quite easy to "get emotional" when the emphasis moves from verifiable elements to personal attacks.

    - Refer to a passage in the textbook or other written resource. Keep bringing the discussion back to proven facts that are within the student's experience—textbook readings, for example.

    - If two or more individuals are engaged in a heated discussion, establish a rule that each person must briefly summarize the comments of the other before voicing her or his thoughts.

    - Sometimes, you may elect to allow a 'pitched battle" to continue. Oftentimes there is learning through conflict, particularly in a follow-up class.

    - Establish a rule that the personal pronoun "you" may never be used in discussing any controversial subject ("You always—" "You have to be the—" "I can't believe you are—").

    - Consider establishing time limits for any comments about or discussions of controversial topics. For example, each person may have a maximum of two minutes to state her or his case. This signals students that their remarks must be well-planned, concise, and to the point.

    - Above all, keep the emphasis on respect! It's alright to have a difference of opinions; however, it's not alright to use that opinion as a battering ram or personal attack weapon.

Class discussions are valuable learning opportunities. When used regularly throughout a course, they offer students multiple opportunities to process information, rather than just commit that data to memory (or not). As discussed earlier in this book, their brains will change in very positive ways!

CHAPTER 15:

Collaborative and Cooperative Groups

In a constructivist classroom, there is an assumption of responsibility on the part of students for some of the direction and depth of learning. The implication is that professors release instructional responsibilities to their students. Constructivism is when students integrate prior experiences with new information to develop extended or deeper understandings. The constructivist model places students at the center of the learning process and encourages them to think about ideas, discuss them, and make them meaningful.

There is a growing body of educational research which suggests that providing students with less content (less transmission), but more opportunities to actively engage in the material at higher levels of cognition, results in a more productive educational experience.

Let's review some of the components of a constructivist classroom:

- Less material covered; but more information uncovered
- Prior knowledge is incorporated into new information
- More emphasis on the processes of learning rather than the products
- Learning takes place in a social context
- Learning is less teacher-directed; more student-centered
- Higher-level thinking opportunities are emphasized over low-level cognitive skills
- Student-initiated goals are valued and celebrated
- Students are actively involved in self-assessment
- Learning is integrative and active
- Learning is produced, not reproduced

In a constructivist classroom, you're still responsible for delivering materials to your students. However, you also provide opportunities for students to actively process that material, to interact with the ideas, and to relate the new material to concepts previously learned. This can be effectively and successfully accomplished by incorporating collaborative and cooperative learning opportunities into your courses. These two terms have often been used interchangeably. Although they share some common elements, it's important that we make a few distinctions between the two.

Collaborative Learning

Collaborative learning is a teaching technique in which a specific learning task is defined by the professor, who then organizes students to work it out collectively. Various student groups work on specific tasks that have more than one answer or solution. The benefit is that students are exposed to multiple perspectives and multiple viewpoints. The completion of any task is the result of a collective judgment in which everyone has a voice.

The basic elements of collaborative learning are as follows:

- **Consensus Building.** In collaborative learning, students work together to reach consensus on an issue or topic. This is more than everyone simply expressing their opinion; rather it involves a concerted effort toward some level of agreement—an intellectual "give and take" to arrive at a common response.

- **Divergent Viewpoints.** The expression of divergent views and opposing arguments is celebrated, not in a hostile environment, but rather an environment that recognizes and celebrates differences. Students learn that they all have differing biases and perspectives that shape and influence their thinking.

- **Minimal Teacher Involvement.** Your primary role is that of a manager; you set the task, arrange the groups, oversee the deliberations, and synthesize afterwards. You may need to occasionally keep the groups focused on the task; but other than that, your task is to step back and let students proceed without your intervention.

- **Synthesis and Evaluation.** When student groups have completed their tasks, reconvene the whole class and synthesize the results. Each group's spokesperson shares the results of her/his group. Afterwards, invite students to examine the similarities, differences, contradictions and parallels among the recorded information. Guide students in reaching appropriate conclusions about the material.

RESEARCH POINT

A wide range of studies at various institutions indicates that students who learn through collaborative exercises have greater long-term retention of the material.

Cooperative Learning

Cooperative learning is a successful teaching strategy in which small teams, each with students of different ability levels, use a variety of learning activities to improve their understanding of a topic. Each member of a team is responsible, not only for learning what is taught, but also for helping her or his teammates learn—thus creating an atmosphere of achievement. Cooperative learning is beneficial for any subject or any topic. That means that it can be effectively used in an upper-division physics course, an introductory English course, an advanced algebra course, or a lower-division history course.

The success of cooperative learning is predicated on three interrelated factors:

- **Group goals.** Cooperative learning teams work to earn recognition for the improvement of each member of a group.

- **Individual accountability.** Each member of a team is assessed individually. Teammates work together, but the learning gains of individuals form the basis of a team score.

- **Equal opportunities for success.** Individual improvement over prior performance is more important than reaching a pre-established score (ninety percent on a test, for example). A student who moves from seventy-three percent on a test one week to eighty-one percent (eight percent improvement) the next week contributes just as much to a group as a student who moves from eighty-two percent to ninety percent (also eight percent improvement).

However, the ultimate success of cooperative learning is based on a single and very important principle: Students must be taught how to participate in a group situation. Professors cannot assume that college-level students know how to behave in group settings. Here's how to do that:

- **Positive Interdependence.** It's important that you structure learning tasks so that students come to believe that they sink or swim together. Students need to know that each group member's efforts are required for group success and that each group member has a unique contribution to make to the joint effort.

- **Heterogeneous Groups.** Groups should be comprised of three, four, or five members each. The membership within a group should be mixed according to academic abilities, ethnic backgrounds, race, and gender. It's also important that groups not be arranged according to friendships or cliques.

- **Clear Directions and/or Instructions.** Be sure to state directions or instructions in clear, precise terms. Let students know exactly what they are to do. When appropriate, inform students what they are to generate as evidence of their mastery of the material. These directions must be shared with students before they engage in cooperative learning activities.

- **A Clear Set of Learning Objectives.** You must describe exactly what students are expected to learn. Let students know that cooperative learning groups are a means to an end, rather than an end in itself. Do not use ambiguous language in describing what students will learn or the knowledge they will gain.

- **Individual and Group Accountability.** Ask group members to discuss how well they are achieving their goals or how they are maintaining effective working relationships. Help students make decisions about what behaviors to continue, what to change, and what to eliminate.

- **Sufficient Time.** Make sure there is sufficient time to learn the targeted information. Groups should stay together until the designated subject matter is learned.

When discussing cooperative and collaborative learning, it's not the terminology that is important, rather it is the overall benefits that these practices can have on students' retention and integration of course content.

1. **A sense of community.** Both approaches place a premium on learning as a social activity. Listening and reacting to different perspectives—and valuing those perspectives—is at the very heart of group work. Students' knowledge base grows exponentially.

2. **Respect for students.** Both approaches underscore a basic respect for students and their abilities to solve common problems and deal with "thorny" issues. Students' engagement in the learning process is valued and celebrated.

3. **Constructivist learning.** The two approaches emphasize a constructivist view of learning. Students learn that learning is not a passive activity (listening to and recording lectures), but rather one in which they can, and should, have an active role. The process is as important as the product.

4. **Student achievement.** The effects on student achievement are positive and long-lasting irrespective of the course or subject matter.

5. **Information retention.** When students process information in group contexts, they usually retain more of it over longer periods of time.

6. **Improved relations.** One of the most positive benefits is that students who cooperate with each other also tend to understand and appreciate each other more. This is particularly true for members of different ethnic, cultural, social, and religious groups.

7. **Interdependence.** When students work with, and rely on, other students, their interpersonal and social skills are maximized. They become more than observers, they become participants in the social order.

8. **Critical thinking skills.** More opportunities for critical thinking skills are provided and there is a significant improvement in those thinking skills.

> **RESEARCH POINT**
>
> A small but growing body of research looks at cooperative and collaborative learning from the perspective of students. According to student self-reports, the benefits include: higher levels of motivation to learn the material, opportunities for enhanced peer interactions, greater class interest and enjoyment, opportunities to process rather than simply record information, and an appreciation for divergent perspectives and outlooks.

9. **Oral communication improvement.** Students improve in their oral communication skills.

10. **Promoted social skills.** Students' social skills are enhanced and promoted.

11. **Heightened self-esteem.** Students' work is valued by team members and their individual self-esteem and respect escalates dramatically.

Group Selection (and one caution)

One of the elements that has come out of the research on college-level group work deals with how students are selected for their respective groups. Several researchers point to the advantage of having teachers select the members of a group rather than having students self-select their own groups. When students select their own groups, they tend to engage in excessive socializing and off-task discussion within those groups. It is far more advantageous to group students heterogeneously and randomly. This ensures that each group is composed of a diversity of opinions and an equal diversity of abilities, genders, races, and other factors.

There are any number of ways you can divide your students into collaborative or cooperative groups. Here are a few you may wish to consider:

- Whip around the classroom assigning each student a sequential number (one, two, three, four). All the "one's" go into one group, the "two's" in another, and so on.

- Randomly distribute colored index cards to the class. All the yellow cards form one group, purple cards another, and so on.

- Assign students to groups based on their month of birth. For example, all the "February's" will work together, all the "October's" will work together.

- Remove all the face cards from a deck of cards, shuffle the remaining cards, and distribute them to students. All the "twos" form a group, all the "nines" form another group, and so on.

- Invite students to write down a randomly selected four-letter word. Those who have a word that begins with a letter between "A" and "E" form one group, those with words between "F" and "J" form another group, and so on.

- Use the last number in each student's social security number (or cell phone number, or student identification number). All the "nines" in one group, all the "threes" in another group, and so on.

- One of my favorites is to select several simple five-piece children's puzzles from the local toy store. I remove all the pieces and mix them together in a box. When students come into class, they each select a random puzzle piece. They must then locate others who have pieces that form a complete puzzle (all the puzzles are different). When a puzzle is complete, that becomes a working group. I sometimes create an "added value" by having an initial discussion question taped to the back of each puzzle piece.

It doesn't make any difference what method you use to determine the members of each group. It is important, however, that you use a variety of methods and that you keep the selection process entirely random.

One of the biggest issues (voiced by professors and students alike) of collaborative and cooperative learning is how to deal with "nonparticipating" students (a topic we also addressed in the previous chapter). Often there will be some students who "hitchhike" on the work of others. That is, the work a group does is sometimes the result of one or two highly motivated students rather than all members equally.

Unfortunately, there is no way we can completely eliminate this situation, but there are ways in which you can minimize the likelihood of it occurring. Here are a few suggestions:

- Develop group assignments that allow you to grade both individual and group performance. For example, each group member takes a quiz; the scores are all added up to calculate a group grade which every group member receives for the task.

- Invite each member of a selected group to make an oral presentation of their discoveries and results. Let students know ahead of time that you will select one group at random (from a hat) to share their collective information.

- Ask groups members to submit a group written report to which each member must sign her or his name and to indicate the amount (percentage) of involvement of contributions they made.

- In several of my courses, I used a "Chapter Log" in which small groups recorded reactions to a textbook chapter assigned prior to class. There's an example on the next page.

Strategies for Your Classroom

To help your students master essential material via group work, you must provide a range of classroom possibilities. You can do this by using this collection of specific cooperative and collaborative learning strategies. Of course, you're not going to use all these at the same time, nor are you going

> **CHAPTER LOG**
>
> Name:_____ Date:_____
>
> Chapter Number(s):_____ Pages:_____
>
> Topic(s):_____
>
> Group members: _____   _____
>
> _____   _____
>
> End of chapter question:_____
>
> _____
>
> **My response(s) [to be completed before class]:**
>
> Group Consensus:
>
> **A significant quote from the reading is [to be completed before class]:**
>
> Page:_____ Column:_____ Line:_____
>
> Group Consensus:
>
> Overall, my participation in today's discussion was:
> ❏ Extensive   ❏ Moderate   ❏ Minimal

to use any one of these over and over again (remember, variety if the spice of life.) And keep in mind that these strategies are just part of an enormous range of instructional options you have at your disposal.

- **Jigsaw.** Groups of four, five, or six students are set up (these are called "home" groups). The material to be learned is divided into four, five, or six sections. Each team member is "assigned" to one of the subsections of material. She or he works on that material and how it will be learned. Each of these subgroups is known as an "expert" group. After students have mastered the material in their "expert" group, they each return to their "home" groups. Each "expert" then teaches the information learned to the members of her or his group. Afterwards, each student can be tested independently on both group and individual activities (and learning).

- **Panel Discussions.** Stage a panel discussion in which students are randomly assigned to several different groups. Some of the groups will be "pro," others will be "con." Each group must prepare an appropriate "argument" related to a specific topic (abortion, immigration, nuclear energy, intelligent design, foreign policy, etc.). Since students are randomly assigned to a group, they may have to wrestle with their own beliefs, particularly if assigned to a group that must take a conflicting viewpoint.

- **Trial.** As a variation of the strategy above, invite students (in groups) to conduct a mock trial. One group of students could be the prosecuting team, another the defense team, another witnesses, another the judge, and a fifth the jury. Invite them to "try" a controversial figure or issue. For example: Osama bin Laden, creationism vs. evolution, immigration policy, euthanasia.

- **STAD (Student Teams—Achievement Divisions).** Students are assigned to four-person teams. Each team is mixed according to ability, gender, race, and ethnicity. After the presentation of a teacher-directed lesson, students work in teams to master the material. Buddy work, group quizzes, or focused study questions may be part of a group's efforts. A quiz is given to all group members. Improvement scores are assigned to each individual as well as the entire team as a whole.

- **Modified Focus Group.** Provide students with a question that has different perspectives and requires collaborative effort to solve. Invite students to each list as many responses, interpretations, or reactions to the question as possible (you may want to establish a time limit). Divide the class into groups and appoint a recorder for each group. Each student, one at a time, shares an idea with the whole group. Students share, in round-robin fashion, their ideas which are recorded on a large sheet of newsprint. After everyone has shared all the items on their individual lists, the group works together to rank order of all the items on the sheet of newsprint from five (greatest importance) to one (least importance). Each groups' final rankings are reported to the entire class. The class then engages in dialogue to synthesize and analyze the information. Different perceptions and interpretations are both solicited and encouraged.

- **Think-Pair-Share.** This cooperative learning activity involves a three step structure. In the first step, students think silently about a question asked by the teacher. Individuals pair up during the second step and exchange thoughts. During the third step, the pairs share their responses with other pairs, other teams, or the entire group.

- **Constructive Controversy.** Divide your class into groups of four students each. Within each group further divide students into two separate pairs. Each pair within a group is assigned to opposing sides of a controversial issue. Each pair is responsible for gathering appropriate information in support of their "position." Each pair within a team presents its "argument" to the other pair. The intent is not to create a debate, but rather for students to begin appreciating the different sides of a single issue. You may wish to invite pairs to switch roles and "argue" the opposing point of view. Comprehension of the material can be assessed individually or as a group effort to master the content.

- **Numbered Heads.** The class is divided into teams of four students each. Each member of the team is given a number: "One," "Two," "Three," or "Four." Ask questions of the entire class and have groups work together to answer the question so that all of them can verbally respond to the question. Then call out a random number ("Three"); each "number Three" will give the answer.

- **Three-Step Interview.** Have each member of a team choose another member to be a partner. During the first step, have individuals interview their partners by asking clarifying questions. During the second step, have partners reverse the roles. In the final step, have members share their partner's response with the team.

- **Reader's Roundtable.** Divide the class into several small groups. Assign all the groups the same piece of reading (e.g. a monograph, a textbook chapter, an article). Each group is responsible for dividing the reading into several parts—one part for each member of the group. Each member reads her or his assigned section and explains it to the team. Then, each team shares an overall interpretation with the entire class. In this activity, it would be important to discuss the differences in interpretation with class members.

- **Three-Minute Review.** Occasionally during a lecture or discussion, stop and give teams three minutes to review what has been said and ask clarifying questions. Invite each team to arrive at a summary statement (a main idea) of what was presented, then write these on the whiteboard. Take time to discuss any differences among teams. At the end of the lesson, invite teams to review the summary statements and to arrive at the most appropriate ones for sections of the lesson or the entire lesson all together.

- **Case Studies.** Case studies are used in medical colleges, law schools, and business courses. They provide students with opportunities to answer the question, "What would you do?" To conduct a case study, select a brief article from the newspaper, a section of text from an outdated textbook, a video clip from a national news program, or create your own case study (story) that engage students in creative decision-making (Note: There is a variety of Internet sites that provide a range of case studies for classroom use). Invite students, in various teams, to work out appropriate decisions or solutions using material learned in the course.

- **Other Options.** Here are a few more options for you to consider in your various courses:

  - Team interviews (of students or faculty)
  - Group surveys (of community members)
  - Focus group sessions (on specific issues)
  - Public displays and exhibits
  - Discipline-specific research projects (of professionals in the field)

As you become more familiar with cooperative and collaborative learning, you might want to create your own learning activities. Even better, challenge your students to invent and design variations of these suggestions for use in the classroom.

Teaching Constructively

The effective use of cooperative and collaborative learning is often built upon a four-step process. Consider the following four elements as you begin to design and implement constructivist learning into your teaching routines:

1. **Presentation of Content.** Cooperative and collaborative learning are not self-instruction models, but rather ways for students to interact with previously presented material. In short, cooperative and collaborative learning comes after you have taught something to your students.

2. **Teamwork.** This is the time—after you've taught new material—when students are engaged in a cooperative or collaborative learning activity. The strategy is selected and explained to the entire class. Students are divided into various teams and provided sufficient time to complete their assigned duties.

3. **Facilitation**. You role is primarily that of a facilitator. You are there to help groups define their goals, engage in meaningful dialogue, and work towards pre-established goals. Your primary responsibility is not to tell them what to think, but rather to provide them with the forum in which they can engage in productive and active deliberations.

4. **Director not Dictator.** Utilizing collaborative and cooperative strategies in your courses means releasing responsibility to your students. This may be uncomfortable, particularly if you've been exclusively exposed to more traditional college teaching protocols. This "loss of control" can be both frightening and exciting. But, to use a familiar educational maxim, your primary responsibility in any collaborative venture should be that of a "guide on the side, not a sage on the stage."

Integrating collaborative and cooperative groups into your courses can open up new worlds of discovery and application for all your students. Students will also begin to understand the relationship of course content to their daily lives as well as to their chosen majors. Learning will escalate dramatically and interest will soar exponentially.

PART FOUR:

Challenges and Possibilities

CHAPTER 16:

Problem Students (and their solution)

Imagine the following classroom scenarios: You walk into the room and a student approaches you and tells you to "take a hike" (or other words which can't be printed here) after getting a less than memorable paper back. A small group of students talks during your entire presentation. A third student has his hand raised for every question you ask in class. Another student is busy texting all his friends about the hot date he had on Saturday night. A fifth student comes up to you after class and says how much she "loves your course" (it's the eighteenth time this semester she said it). A sixth student tells you that her grandmother is sick back home, and she must miss the next two weeks of class (Can she turn in all her assigned papers when she returns?).

Class situations such as the ones above may be out of the ordinary. But it is certain that one or more of the students profiled above will find her or his way into your courses. How do you deal with some of these "problem students?" Let's take a look at some of the common "problems" encountered and how they can be addressed.

Earlier in this book, I talked about the value of establishing a "community of learners" in your courses. Simply put, when students feel a connection with other students and the professor, their likelihood of academic achievement mushrooms accordingly. Conversely, when students feel disenfranchised or disconnected from the class, their academic performance suffers, as does their self-concept.

The key to any successful academic venture is to create a community in which all participants and their contributions are valued. Will that eliminate all the problems that students bring to those classes? No! But, it will provide you with a structural foundation upon which you can approach and deal with some of the most common problems in a supportive and encouraging environment. In short, students are not the enemy. True, they bring their own unique characteristics and personality dynamics to a classroom (just as we bring ours). It's not a matter of isolating those behaviors from the mainstream, but rather of working to involve those students into the culture of the classroom.

Let's take a look at some of those challenges.

Unprepared Students

It is quite common to have unprepared students in your classes. These may be students who neglect to read the assigned chapters in the textbook, fail to turn in papers on time, are unprepared for class discussions or group work, or who seem disconnected from the other students in the course.

In my own work with students and in conversations with other professors, I've discovered some practical and universal ideas that will help you deal with unprepared students. Here are some suggested approaches.

- Make sure that the assigned readings, scheduled exams, and other course requirements are clearly and sufficiently detailed in the course syllabus. Unprepared students are often those who don't know the precise expectations of the course. If necessary, list each day of the semester and the readings, quizzes, exams, papers due for each particular date. My own preference is to list each week of the semester in a spreadsheet and the specific assignments and responsibilities scheduled for that time frame.

Here's a portion of a course schedule I included in each of my syllabi:

WEEK OF	TOPIC	TEXTBOOK READING	OUTSIDE READING	TUESDAY	THURSDAY
Oct. 30	Multiple Intelligences	Pages 10 – 12	Gardner article	The 8 Intelligences	Focus groups
Nov. 6	Differentiated Instruction; Constructivism (review)	Pages 37 – 56	Chapter 3 Tomlinson book (on reserve)	Definitions, experiences, practices. Paper #3 due	quiz #2; lesson planning
Nov. 13	Concepts and generalizations	Pages 102 – 124	(none)	Creating pyramids	Webinar; roundtable presentations (Students #4 – 6)

- Sometimes, at the beginning of the semester, I will tell students that each day they come to class, I will provide them with a "One Question Quiz" on the assigned reading for that class. When students arrive to class, there is a slip of paper with a single question on each desk—a question that can only be answered after having read the assigned pages in the text. They have three to four minutes to answer the question. These are collected and factored into each student's final grade. Later in the semester, instead of having these for every day, I may reduce this to a weekly event. The message, however, is very clear. The assigned material must be read in order to respond to the "One Question Quiz" each class. Students cannot be unprepared.

- Start each class with focus groups. Let students know that when they arrive to class they will be working with other students on a specific topic or problem-solving experience. Each student must be prepared in order to effectively contribute to the group. Walk around the room and monitor each group's activities. Consider some of the cooperative learning strategies in Chapter 15 (page 203).

Inattentive students

Typically, inattentiveness in students arises as a result of one of two factors. If the material is too complex or confusing, many students tend to "zone out" and disconnect from the class. They often engage in "back of the room" conversations, texting, catnaps, doodling, or other inappropriate behaviors. Or, students may not be aware of, or practiced in, appropriate social graces or expectations. Here are some suggestions for you to consider:

- Be clear about your expectations for classroom behavior on the first day of class. State those expectations verbally and be sure they are backed up in writing throughout the syllabus.

- Always have a physical presence throughout a classroom. If students know that you will always be "parked" behind a podium for the duration of every class, they will have more of a tendency to "disconnect" from the class—particularly those in the back of the room. Move around the room, call on students from every quadrant of the class, speak from the front, sides, and back of the room. Your physical presence throughout the classroom is a major deterrent to inattentiveness.

- Examine the material you are sharing with students. Is it too complex? Is it confusing? Is there too much theory and not enough practical applications? If inattentiveness is a persistent problem in your courses, it may a result of the material rather than a fault of the students.

- It is strongly suggested that you provide for at least one activity in each class in which students work in small groups. I like to randomize the groups each time so that the same students are not always working together. I'll assign random numbers to individuals (All the "Three's" will form a group."), or assign students to groups based on birthdays, the color of their shoes, or some type of random sorting. If there are several inattentive individuals in a class, this ensures that they would be equitably distributed throughout the groups. These students then become responsible to the members of a group and their successful completion of a specific task. I always make it a point to "travel" around the room to monitor each group's progress as well as the contributions of each member.

- Use low-profile intervention. When you spot an inattentive student, use the student's name in part of your presentation. For example, "As an example, let's imagine that Darren is John Scopes. How does he rationalize the teaching of evolution during this time period?" Darren, who has been whispering to a fellow student, hears his name and is drawn back into the lesson. Sprinkling these interventions periodically throughout a course helps keep everyone "on their toes."

Aggressive Students

It is not unusual for some students to want to challenge their professors. They may have some previous knowledge about a topic and want to assert their beliefs or opinions into a particular discussion. Or, they may simply be confrontational individuals who relish the thought of engaging in a "verbal battle." Doing so—particularly with a person in authority (a college professor)—often gives them a sense of power and control.

> **AN EXPERT OPINION**
>
> Robert Totenberg, a professor of anthropology, says, "Anger is often a mask for fear. If you respond to the fear instead of the anger, you can diffuse it. Always allow [the student] a way to gracefully retreat from the confrontation."

If you have an aggressive or challenging student in your class, there are two things you must never do. One, do not ignore the behavior. Doing so only adds "fuel to the fire" and raises the intensity of the individual's argument and frustration. Second, never verbally attack the student, particularly in front of other students. You will immediately lose any credibility and will come off as dictatorial, unsympathetic, and dogmatic. Rather, here are some suggested tips for dealing with aggressive students:

- Take the time to listen carefully to the student's argument. Provide the student with an opportunity to get her or his position out "into the open" where it can be addressed and/or discussed.

- Acknowledge the student's anger ("You seem to be quite upset by this."). This acknowledgement alone will diffuse some of the anger, let the student know that you are listening to her or him, and begin to build a common ground on which an ensuing discussion can begin.

- As appropriate, bring other students into the situation. For example, "Marcia is quite upset about my position on this issue. Does anyone else feel this way?" Invite others to express their feelings or perceptions. True, Marcia may gain additional allies, but even more important, her anger is dissipated among members of her peer group. This strategy also gives you additional time to ponder an appropriate response. In many cases, you can turn the experience into an interesting class discussion by posing a series of leading questions ("Are there other feelings we're not expressing here?" "Would others look at this in the same way?" "How could we organize these thoughts on the whiteboard?")

- Whenever a student becomes angry and/or verbally adamant about a certain point I usually invite her or him to come up to the front of the room. (The physical act of walking to the front of the room tends to dissipate some of the anger and allows the student a little time to re-think or re-consider the initial argument.) While the student is coming forward, I locate two chairs and place them side by side in the front of the room. I invite the student to sit down (It's much harder to be aggressive when sitting down than when standing up). I'll invite the student to restate her or his case (another way to defuse the anger) and then ask if I could restate my position. Then I'll invite other students to enter in on either side of the "debate." Irrespective of the position they choose (mine or the angry student) a conversation has been started which can lead to new observations or new insights. I've found this to be an important way of modeling critical thinking; that is, informed people must be able to look at all the evidence—both pro and con—in reaching a decision. Listening to and considering divergent views on a topic is academic growth at its finest. In addition, the act of sitting side by side not only reduces the physical distance between individuals, it also reduces the emotional distance.

- If it seems that a student's anger is directed at you rather than at your ideas (for example, the student believes that your course requirements are excessive or you assigned a grade on a paper that was unfair or even that you are incompetent) invite the student to meet with you personally to discuss the situation. Here are some specific tips:

  - Listen carefully and respectfully.

  - Don't prejudge. Encourage the student to state her or his case or rationale completely before making any comments or decisions.

  - Never demean the student or her or his opinion.

  - Don't assume an authoritarian or defensive position. Let the student know that it may be possible to reach a mutually agreeable decision.

  - By the same token, let the student know that you have a responsibility to be fair and equitable to everyone. Your final decision may not be the one the student wants to hear, but it will be based on an assessment of all the evidence.

  - If applicable, let the student know that you would be willing to re-visit the concern at any time. Promote an "open door" policy.

- Thank the student for the meeting and for taking time out of her or his busy schedule to discuss the issue.

The key to dealing with angry or aggressive students is to become an "active listener." In active listening, you respond to a student by using some of the student's remarks, thoughts, or ideas in any feedback. Here are two examples:

- **Student #1:** "You know, I think this whole thing about birth control is way off base. What gives those religious zealots the right to determine how I should live my life?"
- **You:** "So, Sarah, you think that religion is dictating how you should live your life. Is that right?"
- **Student #2:** "You know, your grading policy really sucks! Nobody's ever going to get an 'A' in this class."
- **You:** "Karl, you seem upset by the fact that my grading procedures appears harsh and unfair. Would you care to elaborate?"

Discouraged Students

Frequently, students begin the semester with a great deal of enthusiasm and energy. However, as the assignments begin to pile up, the requirements become more demanding, and the pressures escalate, some students experience a sense of discouragement. They may miss classes, submit papers after the due dates, or maintain a lethargic attitude in class.

While this is not unusual, there are some surprisingly effective measures you can implement to deal with this "condition:"

- If there is a particularly challenging assignment that you give students each semester, invite a student from a previous class to write an open note or text specifically on how she or he was able to tackle that specific assignments, what was learned, the personal benefits, and perhaps one or two study techniques. Read this letter to students in the current class immediately after you make the assignment or midway through the period of time students would be working on that assignment. You will probably notice an immediate and significant improvement in students' overall attitude toward the assignment. When students hear that their contemporaries have successfully "made the grade," they are inspired to do the same.

- Consider bringing in a student from the previous semester and inviting that person to describe their experiences of frustration and self-doubt and how they surmounted them and survived. This "pep talk" alerts students to the fact that the situation is a temporary problem and one that can be successfully addressed.

- If you notice that a student is persistently discouraged and "down," invite that individual to meet with you after class. Take time to find out the root cause of the discouragement. It may have nothing to do with you or the course, but may involve family issues, personal crises, or work-related problems. Be sure to have contact information readily available about the campus counseling center, tutoring bureau, mental heath center, campus ministry, or learning disabilities office. Make the referrals as appropriate and follow-up with the student within a week to see if the necessary contacts have been made.

Attention-seeking Students

You've probably seen them. They're the ones who always have something to say; the ones who always have their hand in the air when a question is asked; and the ones who are always hogging the instructor's time both before and after class. Not surprisingly, you can expect them to show up in your courses, too. Interestingly, some students have "marked" adjunct professors for extra attention because they think that the novices won't have the "thick skin" of more experienced faculty members and that they'll be easier to influence. Be forewarned!

Here are a few ideas for your consideration.

- I sometimes tell students that, in order to be fair and equitable to everyone, whenever I ask a question, I won't ask for hands. I'll merely direct the question to a specific individual in the class. In this way I can rotate the questions around the room and ensure that everyone has an opportunity to contribute during a single class. Also, since students don't have the luxury of deciding if they do or do not want to respond to a question, they must all pay attention since they don't know who will be called on.

- The old maxim "divide and conquer" is another effective technique in handing attention seeking students. Since attention seekers want attention from the largest audience possible, reduce the size of the audience. Every other class or so, I make sure that there is at least one activity in which students must work in pairs (or perhaps triads). I'll often put each attention seeker in a position of authority—she or he is the recorder for the group's activities, deliberations, or decisions.

- After about the third week of the semester, present students with a mini-lecture on importance of having everyone contribute to the class. Solicit suggestions and ideas from students on how to facilitate that process for the remainder of the course. Students will often come up with practical and useful ideas that will dissipate the influence of attention seekers. I sometimes convert their ideas into a chart which can be reviewed on an as-needed basis throughout the semester.

- As a last resort, invite a colleague to videotape one or two class sessions. Invite the attention seekers to view the videotape and comment on their "performance." Ask them to discuss how their actions may be influencing the opportunities for all students to participate in the dynamics of the class.

"The Fault, Dear Brutus—"

Many interesting observations have been made about students' behavior in college classes, and what we see is that the instructor's behavior often contributes to a climate that inadvertently fosters and creates problems through certain types of management procedures.

How many of the following teacher behaviors that create problems—rather than solve them—have you experienced or seen (in elementary school, high school, or college):

- **Extreme Negativity.** The instructor's comments to the class are frequently couched in negative and/or highly authoritarian terms. ("It's obvious that nobody knows anything about Kreb's Cycle. It looks like many of you will fail the midterm on Thursday.")

- **Excessive Authoritarian Climate.** These instructors desire to be the absolute and complete authority figure in a course. All decisions are theirs. ("It's my way or the highway!")

- **Overreacting.** This instructor creates mountains out of molehills by escalating minor infractions into major ones. ("I'm tired of your inattentiveness. From now on, if you are caught not paying attention in class, you will be asked to leave the room.")

- **Mass Punishment.** These instructors hope peer pressure will result in a change or behavior for a few select students. ("It's obvious that the two of you just can't stop talking, so I'm going to have to make up the time by eliminating the video I had planned for today.")

- **Lack of Instructional Goals.** Often instructors will attempt to engage students without a clearly defined or clearly understood (by students) goals for the lesson. ("Okay, is there anything anyone wants to talk about before we begin?")

- **Repeating Or Reviewing Already Understood Material.** In an effort to make sure students are exposed to important material, professors might constantly repeat material over and over again in the same way. There is no challenge. ("All right, I want you to look up the definitions for these twenty words, write them in your notebooks, and then record them again on this wall chart.")

- **Dealing With a Single Student At Length.** This teacher often disrupts her or his own instructional rhythm by spending an inordinate amount of time on one student. ("I can't believe that, once again, you are late for class, Jennifer. I've talked to you over and over about your tardiness." [Five minutes of lecture ensue.])

A combination of these teacher behaviors can create and promote significant student problems in any classroom. Be aware that avoiding these behaviors will go a long way toward creating a climate of trust and caring that will significantly reduce any potential misbehavior.

Classroom Management Tips

Classroom management is not about getting students to do what you want them to do. That's what dictators do, and you're not a dictator, you're an educator. Classroom management is providing an environment in which positive teaching and positive learning can occur simultaneously. Classroom management is not control from the outside; it's order from within.

In conversations with colleagues, I've discovered some practical and universal ideas that will help you achieve positive classroom management in your courses. Tap into the experience of these pros and turn your classroom into a place where students learn and enjoy the process.

- **Meet and Greet.** Interact with your students on a personal level every day. Greet them by name, interject a positive comment or observation, and welcome them into the classroom. I make it a practice to come to each class at least five or six minutes early. I can chat with students about vacation plans, a recent athletic competition, a musical group on campus, or even the weather. These small conversations help establish the classroom as a positive and supportive environment. They also personalize the professor/student relationship and make discipline problems less likely.

- **Get students focused before you begin.** Be sure you have their attention before you begin. Don't try to talk over students, you'll be initiating a competition to see who can speak louder and also let them know that it's okay to talk while you're talking.

- **Use positive presence.** Don't park yourself in the front of the room for an entire class period. Move around the room continuously, and get in and around your students. Make frequent eye contact, and smile with students. Monitor students with your physical presence.

- **Use a "start" messages rather than a "stop" message.** For example, "Stop talking in the back. We need to get started." A better message is "Please turn to page eleven of Thompson's monograph on commercial banking systems." The effect is tremendous. It establishes a productive, businesslike tone for the lesson. The focus is not on the (negative) behavior, but the importance of the lesson.

> **RESEARCH POINT**
>
> The research is overwhelmingly clear: Model the behavior you want students to produce. If you exhibit respectfulness, trust, enthusiasm, interest, and courtesy in your dealings with students, they will return the favor in kind.

- **Verbal reprimands should be private, brief, and as immediate as possible.** The more private a reprimand, the less likely you will be challenged. The more immediate the reprimand, the less likely the students will feel you condone her or his behavior. And keep reprimands brief. The more you talk, the more you distract from the lesson and "reward" a student for inappropriate behavior

- **Be consistent.** Although this is easier said than done, the key to effective classroom management in your courses is consistency. Make these principles part of your daily action plan:

- If you have a rule, enforce that rule.

- Don't hand out lots of warnings without following through on consequences. Lots of warnings tell students that you won't enforce a rule.

- Be fair and impartial. The rules are there for everyone, and that includes blondes as well as redheads, athletes as well as non-athletes, tall people as well as short people, people from California as well as people from Florida, eighteen-year-olds as well as forty-year-olds, and happy people as well as grumpy people.

Yup, you can count on getting "problem students" in one or more of your courses! They are as inevitable as taxes and death! But, by taking a pro-active stance, a positive outlook, and an emphasis on building a "community of learners," you can significantly reduce their behavior as well as their disruptions to your classes.

CHAPTER 17:

Teaching Nontraditional Students

During my tenure as a full-time professor, there was one event I looked forward to with great anticipation. That was the opportunity to work with nontraditional students. By definition, a nontraditional student is one outside the normal age range (eighteen to twenty-two years old) of a "regular" or traditional college student. In most cases, they were older students who had decided to start a career path a little later in life or those who attended college when they were younger, dropped out (usually to raise a family), and then re-enrolled to complete a degree. Many nontraditional students are in their thirties, forties, or older. For the most part, they are more mature, more self-directed, more academically inclined, and more motivated to learn.

These students were exciting to teach for one simple reason. They brought incredible learning experiences to every class and every discussion. They had lived the history we were studying in history courses and they had experienced the political drama we were discussing in government courses. In short, the life experiences of the thirty- to fifty-year-old students provided a stimulus for learning unavailable to younger students. Nontraditional learners may be a separate "breed," but they are no less exciting to teach. This chapter explores ways you can make that excitement part of your work with these dynamic students.

> **RESEARCH POINT**
>
> The US Department of Education has estimated that approximately forty percent of all college students in the United States are "nontraditional" students. In short, about six million undergraduate students are twenty-five years old or older.

Social Characteristics

Most nontraditional students have a wealth of life experiences. They also have a depth of social experiences that far exceeds those of typical college students. The background of experiences in "the real world" is both extensive and personal. Some of their social experiences may be negative, others may be positive. Here's what you need to know to use these experiences to your advantage:

- Many individuals may have less than favorable memories of their days in formal school settings. Keep discussions or references to these to an absolute minimum (if at all). Focus on present-day experiences and reasons why a particular course will benefit them now. The emphasis should be on the present, not the past. ("I bet you're all ready to learn something about retirement planning, so let's not waste any time!").

- Some individuals are active participants, others prefer to be passive. Be sure to provide learning opportunities for both types.

- Adult learners are often shy or reluctant to discuss their weaknesses or education gaps with others. Acknowledge this, but emphasize how the class or course will provide them with new skills.

- Learn as much as you can about the past experiences of each of the participants in a class. Use this information in stimulating discussions or in shaping the presentation of materials ("Justin, I recall you were a nurse in Afghanistan. How were those experiences similar to, or different from the CPR techniques we're learning now?").

- A significant body of research has shown that, when adult learners are provided with regular, systematic, and frequent opportunities to relate the course content to their backgrounds of experiences, the learning becomes more meaningful and lasting. Adult learners want, and need, a connection to what they already know.

- Group work should be informal and relaxed. I like to think of adult education as something similar to a group of friends gathering in my living room to chat about the latest movie or discuss a current political situation. An emphasis on informality makes learning more productive, particularly for adult learners.

Emotional Characteristics

Nontraditional learners are often afraid of learning. That fear may come from negative school experiences, non-support from parents or caregivers, or the length of time since they were in a formalized educational setting. It is always important to remember that, just like traditional college students, adult learners learn best in emotionally supportive environments. That is, environments in which their self-esteem or self-worth is valued and enhanced.

> **AN EXPERT OPINION**
>
> According to William Draves, president of the Learning Resources Network, "In helping [an adult] learn, the teacher must be able to create a positive emotional climate, and the key to that state is one's self-image."

Here are a few tips that will help you create that positive emotional climate in an adult or continuing education course:

- Be an active listener. Encourage students to contribute their ideas, reactions, frustrations or insecurities. Listen to what they have to say (without interruption) and use their words in your response ("Your comments about the 'decline of democratic principles' are quite interesting. Would you care to elaborate?")

- Always provide positive feedback to learners. Don't ridicule a person's beliefs (which may have developed over many years), but acknowledge each person's contribution ("That's a most interesting perspective, Betty. Would anyone like to ask Betty a question about her views on day trading?")

- Many adult learners express their inadequacies or deficiencies in learning new things. Let them know that you are their partner in the learning process ("Stephen, I sense your frustration regarding perspective in your paintings, but let me show you a handy little trick.").

- Adult learners are often sensitive about making mistakes, especially in front of their peer group. If someone is doing something wrong, discuss the situation rather than the individual. Focus on what was done, not the person who did it ("Francis, it looks like there are too many adjectives in this sentence. Let's see what we can do to eliminate a few unnecessary ones.").

- The research on adult learning is unequivocal on one specific point—verbal and/or nonverbal punishment is counterproductive to learning. Adult students learn best when they feel supported and secure. Negative words or actions (directed at the individual) undermine a student's learning potential.

- Adult learners respond better to "I" messages than comments beginning with "You." Instead of saying, "You aren't doing this right" convey an "I" message such as, "I sometimes get tripped up on this step, too. Let me demonstrate a technique I've learned."

- Use humor whenever and wherever possible. This doesn't mean that you have to be a comic, but rather means that you should feel comfortable lightening a class or injecting a joke into the conversation every now and again. Humor relaxes people, especially adults; creates a positive learning environment; and stimulates discussion and enjoyment of a learning task.

Motivational Characteristics

Nontraditional learners, just like traditional college students, need to be motivated throughout a class or course. One of the best ways we can do that is to provide learners with consistent and honest encouragement. Here's how I define encouragement, particularly as it applies to adult learners:

- Recognizes the effort of the doer. ("You worked really hard on your quilt pattern.")

- Promotes self-evaluation. ("How do you feel about your backstroke so far?")

- Emphasizes effort and progress of a task. ("Look at all the improvement you've made on your PowerPoint design.")

- Emphasizes appreciation of contributions and assets. ("Your efforts helped us have a successful poster presentation.")

Encouragement, in large quantities, can be a powerful element in any successful academic endeavor. But you must remember some major considerations if your verbal comments are to be effective:

- You must use encouragement consistently. It cannot be used every once in a while or randomly. And it cannot be used just for the good students and not the underachieving students. It must be a regular element for every student in every learning activity.

- You must be honest with the encouragement. It must acknowledge the learner's true achievement, rather than any fake or made-up accomplishments.

- You must be specific with the encouragement. General statements such as "Good," "Great," or "Cool" are too general to have any meaning—particularly for "nontrads". Provide a very specific reference for an adult student. ("You must feel very proud about the progress you're making learning Spanish verbs.")

- You must give immediate feedback. It has to occur soon after the event or task is completed, or it will be meaningless.

Personal Characteristics

All nontraditional students come to class with certain mental needs. Here are some of the most significant and how you can provide for them:

- **Problem-solving.** Adults want to solve problems; they want to become a better painter, they want to invest in the stock market, they want to learn Greek for an upcoming trip, or they want to learn how to dance for a forthcoming social engagement. Provide them with basic information; but, more important, offer them opportunities to use the new information in real-life situations.

- **Familiarity.** It is highly recommended that you choose the familiar rather than the unusual (when selecting samples or examples). Whenever possible, tap into what students already know and build on it.

- **Perspective.** Unlike children, adults want answers, and they want them right now! Keep the focus of your course narrow and specific. Short-term solutions will be more readily embraced by your adult students than will long-term philosophical treatises.

- **Concreteness.** Work with the concrete rather than the abstract. Whenever possible, use three-dimensional examples rather than theoretical presentations.

- **Simplicity.** Divide your topic into small steps. Move from the simple to the more complex. Provide opportunities for students to build on previously learned steps in incremental stages.

- **Immediacy.** If you teach a course that has multiple sessions or classes, be sure students take away at least one new skill each session. Don't hold out the promise of future skills; adult learners respond best to immediate self-improvement.

Planning for Nontraditional Students

It is inevitable that you will have nontrads in your college courses—particularly if you are teaching late afternoon, evening, or weekend classes. Interestingly, it is projected that the percentage of students over the age of twenty-five will increase by more than twenty percent in the next five years. In order to assist you in planning courses that will inevitably have a mix of both traditional and nontraditional students, you may want to consider the following three topics:

1. Course Preparation
2. Teaching Considerations
3. Communication Strategies

Let's take a look at these in a little more detail.

Course Preparation

Knowing you will have nontrads in most (if not all) of your courses demands some extra attention to how you want to shape your classes. Here are some suggestions for your consideration:

- Consider assessing their background knowledge about the course in advance of any formal instruction. Try to determine what they know about the material in your discipline beforehand. You may discover that some students have an enormous amount of background knowledge, while others have barely a clue about the subject. One-on-one conversations, informal assessments, or an open discussion during the first class may yield data essential to ensuring the academic success of older students.

- How will you connect the content of your course to the "real world?" Nontraditional students need to see and understand the connections between what they are learning and what is going on in the world outside a college classroom. If you're teaching a Human A&P course, how does that information relate to the adult body? If you're teaching a law course, how does that information relate to legal issues typically encountered by an average adult? Your ability to relate content to experiences will ensure that basic concepts are understood by your nontraditional students.

- Whenever feasible, invite community representatives to visit your class and share their experiences in a specific field. This will give your nontrads an opportunity to see how other adults (similar to them) have used course concepts to achieve success in their chosen field. It will also add validity to your classes by connecting theory with practice.

- Consider using optional or "replacement' assignments for your nontrads. For example, instead of writing a detailed library research paper, invite your older students to interview someone in the field for her perspectives on an issue or concern. The information gathered can be shared in a group discussion or formal class presentation. Your awareness of the skills they bring to the class will help you design appropriate activities.

- Make sure your course objectives are clear, precise, and specific. Adult students appreciate it when they know exactly what will be taught and what they are expected to learn. This needs to be established very early in the course and followed throughout the course. In short, don't change the course midway through the semester; you may discover a higher-than-average dropout rate.

Teaching Considerations

Teaching a class with a range of student skill sets and ages is always a challenge, but it's a challenge I loved. That's simply because there was the possibility of many perspectives, many viewpoints, and many different experiences. This always made for exciting and dynamic courses. Here are some considerations for your classes:

- One "rule of thumb" I always used relative to nontraditional students was to ensure there was an opportunity for small group work in every class. I included this group work as an essential component of every topic covered. Groups were always random and changing; they were seldom the same from one day to the next. The mix of students always ensured that everyone got to know their fellow classmates and that all viewpoints or philosophies were encouraged. It was usually an eye-opening experience for many traditional students when they interacted with older classmates and learned about their thoughts and views.

- Consider providing students with outside readings assignments (in the textbook, for example) over an extended period of time. Older students, who often have part-time jobs, family obligations, and day care issues are often strapped for time. Giving them multiple and extended opportunities outside of class to read materials ensures that class time can be devoted to a detailed discussion of those materials.

- One technique I often used was to distribute blank index cards to all students five minutes before the end of any class. I invited students to respond to one of the following statements:

- "One thing I didn't understand was—"
- "I really need more information about—"
- "I would like to learn more about—"
- "I'm really confused about—"
- "Can we spend more time discussing—"
- "My favorite part of today's lesson was—"
- "The one thing I will take away from today's lesson is—"
- "I really liked—"

I would review the responses prior to the next class and make any necessary adjustments or add additional material or explanations. This criterion check was especially useful for nontrads because it offered an anonymous way to tap into their learning progress without fear of embarrassment.

- Consider a variety of assessment protocols for your class. Nontrads may feel inhibited when all of their exams are essay questions or multiple-choice questions. Consider using a range of examination options for both quizzes as well as final exams. I would often provide students with several different assessment tools (essay, multiple-choice, true/false, fill in the blank, etc.) and then offer them the additional option of determining the point value for each of their selections. That is, each individual student had the option of selecting the assessment tool in keeping with their personal learning style, in addition to selecting the value of each of their responses. I quickly discovered that all students, and especially nontraditional students, experienced greater success on exams when they assumed some control over how they would be assessed.

- Encourage all the students in a class to establish study groups outside of normal class hours. This may not be possible for every nontraditional student (due to their often busy and complicated personal lives), but it opens a door for those students by engaging them in a supportive group that furthers their knowledge and stimulates the building of a community of learners.

Communication Strategies

Nontraditional students need to know that they are integral members of any class—not a separate class of individuals who are "different" from more traditional college students. This can be accomplished when you devote considerable effort to ensuring open lines of communication. Consider the following:

- Early in the course, you will undoubtedly discuss the assignments and expectations for the class. Make sure there is a written version of those standards available for students as well. Most likely, these will be detailed in the course syllabus (see Chapter 6, page 65). Nontraditional students appreciate an opportunity to review standards outside of class time.

- Show respect by learning students' names and by using those names in your comments and responses ("LaKeisha mentioned that segregation was more of a political affirmation than a social fear. What are your thoughts about that statement—Franklin?"). Not only does this help students build a classroom community, it also signals that nontraditional students deserve and get the same level of attention as everyone else in the class.

- If you have office hours, make sure your nontraditional students are encouraged to visit you during those times. Older students may feel intimidated talking with you when youngers students are around (say, immediately after class), but will feel more comfortable in a one-on-one situation at a time other than class.

- "Pump up" the confidence of your nontraditional students with occasional comments in class ("I think Nora is really on to something in her analysis of *Pride and Prejudice*. Thanks so much for sharing, Nora."). Nontrads are often self-conscious about talking in class. You can encourage more discussion when you celebrate or salute their verbal contributions whenever possible.

- Don't single out nontraditional students based solely on their ethnicity or cultural background ("Jesús, do you think that is true of all Hispanics?"). Doing so unfairly singles them out and places them in a most uncomfortable situation. Just because I, for example, happen to have English ancestors in my distant past certainly doesn't mean I can speak for all the people of England. The same holds true for your students.

- Take a look at the following statements and see if you notice a commonality:
  - "Hmmm, I never looked at it in that way."
  - "I really like your analysis. How did you think of that?"
  - "Your answer shows a lot of thought and insight!"
  - "Wow! What a neat way of looking at this!"

A quick analysis will reveal that these comments (particularly to nontraditional students) affirm their contributions to the class and place a value on their participation. When nontrads know that there is a high likelihood that they will be the recipient of a positive response from you, they will be more likely to want to assume an active role in the conversations that are an essential element of any lesson. Actively listening to, and agreeing with, your students is an excellent way of building a strong community that includes students of every age.

Including nontraditional students in the dynamics of your course can be a "value-added" component of an effective learning experience—for your traditional students as well as for yourself. Nontrads offer unique learning opportunities and varying perspectives that cannot be found in a textbook or syllabus. I think you will discover, as I did, that your course will be filled with a new energy and excitement when you actively engage your nontraditional students in every aspect of a course.

CHAPTER 18:

Diverse Students; Diverse Populations

It was a lesson well-learned. For the first several weeks of the semester, I shared my ideas, presented the latest research, and engaged students in an array of interactive activities. Yet, there was one student who never made eye contact with me. Try as I might, I couldn't make a visual connection with her. So, I asked if she could see me after class. During the course of our conversation I mentioned the fact that she never seemed to look at me during a class. It was then that she politely informed me that in Japan (her native country) it is considered rude to stare at a person of higher rank, such as a college professor

The demographics of college enrollment over the past several decades have shown a significant increase in the ethnic, gender, and cultural diversity of students enrolling in colleges both large and small. Ensuring that everyone has equal access to the educational experience in an atmosphere of respect, trust, and appreciation is sometimes a challenge—particularly for white, European American professors. This chapter offers some considerations and practices that may be appropriate for your classroom.

Since the advent of the civil rights movement in the 1960's, we have seen a significant increase in the diversity of students in college classrooms. Typically, under-represented groups of people were enrolling in college classes all across the country in significant numbers. The educational opportunities for Asian Americans, Chicanos, African Americans, Native Americans, LGBTQ, women, and various socio-economic groups (among others) were increasing dramatically. At the same time this culturally, ethnically, and gender diverse population sometimes was at odds with the backgrounds of the teachers they faced in the college classroom.

> **RESEARCH POINT**
>
> According to the Institute for the Study of Social Change, discrimination often takes the form of facial expressions, in not being acknowledged, in how white students "take over a class," and speak past students of color, or in small everyday slights in which minorities perceive that their value and perspective are not appreciated or respected. These behaviors have an understandable effect on students' personal, academic, and professional development.

Although the educational opportunities were increasing, many of these students were subjected to subtle, inadvertent, and unconscious forms of discrimination and stereotyping while they were on campus.

This chapter is designed to help you work with the wide diversity of students in your classes. However, according to Professor Richard Suinn of Colorado State University, it is imperative that college teachers avoid what he calls the *deficit model*. He defines this model as the view that inadequate performance from an ethnic person automatically means the student is academically deficient, unmotivated, uninterested, or poorly prepared.

Know Thyself

Our behavior, speech, and attitudes are often reflections of our beliefs. For example, what we say in class may, in very subtle ways, be indicative of stereotypes, biases, or patterns of discrimination. Your background, your upbringing, and your life experiences color your perceptions and treatment of other individuals. Here are some factors you need to consider.

Be aware of any "grouping" practices that you use. For example, do you assume that males are the only ones who are qualified for scientific careers? Do you assume that all African Americans are in an ethnic studies program? Do you assume that people with foreign accents are unable to write comprehensive and coherent papers?

By the same token, be aware that even within groups, people are different, and they often like to celebrate their differences and individuality. For example, just because you have several Asian American students in your class, don't assume that they all socialize together. Just because you have several African Americans in the class, don't assume that they all belong to the Black Student Union on campus. And, just because there are several Chicanos in your course, don't assume that they all celebrate *El Dia de los Muertos* every year. Sometimes, it's important to look past the cultural or ethnic label and recognize each and every individual.

The nonverbal behaviors you exhibit both in class and outside of class will have an impact on students from various ethnic and cultural groups. Cultural norms and expectations vary among different groups and may have an effect on their learning potential according to your awareness and respect of those norms. For example, the preferred personal space between two people often varies according to culture or tradition. In some cultures closeness is valued; in others a "comfortable distance" is preferred. According to several studies, African Americans and Hispanics tend to stand closer to someone they are conversing with than do white Americans. On the other hand, Asians tend to prefer a greater distance between conversants.

- Self-fulfilling Prophecies. There is an old maxim that says that students tend to perform as we expect them to perform (this is sometimes referred to as the "Pygmalion Theory" after George Bernard Shaw's play of the same name). That is, when we expect more from our students, they will learn more. Conversely, when we have lowered expectations, students will learn at lower levels. Thus, if we believe that African-Americans, or second-language-learners, or overweight people, or LGBTQ students won't be able to learn a subject as well as mainstream students, then our expectations will be fulfilled in their lowered achievement rates.

> **RESEARCH POINT**
>
> The research on this issue is clear and definitive! An instructor's expectations often become self-fulfilling prophecies. That is, students who sense that more is expected of them tend to outperform students who believe that less is expected of them, regardless of the student's actual abilities.

One of the themes promoted throughout this book is the value of knowing each and every one of your students. Knowing students' names, the background of experiences they bring to a specific course, and factors that will help them achieve academic success are critical to their scholastic progress. This is equally (if not more) true with students from various ethnic and cultural groups.

Here are a few ideas for your consideration:

- Make an effort to learn as much as you can about the history and culture of groups other than your own.

- Read books and articles written by people of a specific ethnic group, sexual orientation, or culture.

- Talk with students informally after class and ask them to share some of their cultural beliefs and traditions.

- Speak with colleagues from other departments on campus—particularly those who may be from cultural groups different than your own.

- Check out websites to learn about the history, traditions, beliefs, and culture of a specific group.

- Contact cultural centers and religious organizations in your town. Ask for printed information or opportunities to chat with members.

- Attend cultural celebrations in your area. Take time to talk with people, enjoy the food, and listen in on conversations.

- Attend campus-wide activities that celebrate diversity or ethnic heritage.

- **Don't Generalize.** While it may be tempting to ask a Japanese-American student to discuss her feelings about the internment of all Japanese-Americans during World War II, be careful that you do not single out one member of a cultural or ethnic group as a "representative" of that group. It would be a mistake to assume that one member of a minority group is an authority or expert on a culturally-related topic. Just as there is a variety of opinions and viewpoints among white Anglo-Saxon males, so too is there an equal variety of viewpoints and opinions among the members of any other ethnic or cultural group.

  - *Respect Differences:* Some students are not active participants in debates, confrontations, or arguments. That may be more the result of cultural expectations and behaviors than it is of their non-participation. They may be processing the information without the need to be actively engaged. Some students, depending on their cultural norms, may not ask questions or become verbally challenging because to do so would be rude and disrespectful. Know that students (of any culture) learn in different ways—not necessarily in the ways commonly practiced by white European Americans.

  - *Respect Language:* Students from other countries may not be as fluent in English as native speakers. They may need assistance in both oral and written language via ESL (English as a Second

Language) or ELL (English Language Learner) courses offered on campus. You may wish to check with the instructors in these on-campus courses for advice on the grading or papers, exams, and other assignments.

- *Meeting with Students:* Plan to meet with students informally after (or before) class. Invite students to meet with you for a cup of coffee at the Student Union, ask them to discuss course topics before or after a class, or talk with them informally as you cross the campus or stroll over to the faculty lunchroom. Regular and constant contact with students outside of class does much to ensure good teacher-student relationships as well as a mutual understanding of culture and traditions. These times may be group endeavors or private one-on-one sessions with specific individuals.

> **RESEARCH POINT**
>
> One recent study provided evidence that frequent and rewarding informal contact with faculty members is the strongest predictor of whether or not a student will voluntarily withdraw from a college.

- *Challenge Inappropriate Comments:* Some students may make comments about certain ethnic, cultural, sexual, or racial groups out of habit or ignorance. Don't allow these comments to pass unnoticed. Make sure students know that discriminatory comments are both unacceptable as well as inappropriate. Immediately give the student an "I message." An I-message is composed of three parts:

  1. Include a description of the student's behavior. ("When you use that racial slur . . .")

  2. Relate the effect this behavior has on you and other students. (". . . I and the other students become very upset . . .")

3. Let the student know the feeling it generates in you. ("... because we know it is both inappropriate and unacceptable.")

- **Take Advantage of the Diversity.** Knowing the culture, ethnicity, sexual orientations, and origins of the students in your course can help you in shaping selected assignments and requirements. Specifically, you can design assignments that tackle the under-representation or discriminatory practices in several academic endeavors. For example:

  - In a history course, invite students to examine the roles of males, females, and LGBTQ people in a specific historical event (The pioneering and controversial gender reassignment surgery of Christine Jorgenson in the early 1950s was splashed across the front pages of newspapers for many months.).

  - In a sociology course, invite students to look at racial discrimination from the perspective of non-whites (Reading the 1853 memoir *Twelve Years a Slave* by Solomon Northup puts a new perspective on slavery in the US).

  - In an anatomy and physiology course, invite students to look at the contributions of African Americans (The tragically ironic story of Dr. Charles Drew would be appropriate to share.).

  - In a mathematics course, invite students to examine the contributions of Middle Eastern civilizations (Interesting fact: The first recorded zero appeared in Mesopotamia around three BC).

Know Your Course

At this point, you may be wondering if you need to design a course that will be "all things to all people." That would probably be an overwhelming challenge and one that might lead to more frustration for you and less satisfaction for your students. What is more important here is that your course design be one that is respectful of each individual and one that also celebrates the "mix" of students in that course. Here are a few ideas for your consideration.

- **Select Appropriate Texts.** In reviewing possible textbooks for your course (see Chapter 5, page 51) check for any cultural, gender, or ethnic biases. Make sure the language is not gender specific (a preponderance of the word "he"), that all ethnic groups are fairly and equitably represented, and that no single culture is held as an example of all minority groups (for example, "Native Americans, just like every other minority group in this country, once . . ."). Be aware of any stereotypes—those that may be overt as well as those that may be more subtle (for example, "It is well-known that all Chicanos . . .").

- **Partner with Students.** In many cultures, modesty and humility are valued much more than centering attention on oneself or in "showing off" one's comprehension of a topic or subject under discussion. Many cultures also have an ingrained respect for people in power or authority, such as teachers. Being aware of the cultural values held by students in your class can be helpful in designing in-class activities, particularly discussion. For example, instead of asking a student to "Tell us everything you know about the Portuguese empire in the New World" which would place a student on the spot, you may want to recast the request as follows:

    - "Work with a partner on an appropriate response, then share that in a small group."

    - "Can you help me with some of the details about this topic? At my age, I sometimes forget a few."

    - "Can you write four critical facts on the whiteboard, after which I'll write three critical facts?"

- **Guest Speakers.** Consider bringing a variety of guest speakers into your course. Speakers may include colleagues from your department or other departments on campus. Consider individuals from the local community as well as various social agencies.

- **Establish Trust.** One of the most important things you can do in any course is to establish an atmosphere of trust. That is, students need to feel comfortable in sharing their thoughts and opinions without recrimination or negative comments from the teacher or other students. One way to do this is by choosing your questions carefully. Questions should be framed in such a way that students do not feel threatened or challenged, but rather that their eventual responses will be valued and respected. Here are a few examples:

- "So that I can remember where we left off in the last class, can someone remind me what we said about remote sensing?" (Establishes a partnership)

- "I like your interpretation of the differentiated roles of men and women in World War II. How did those roles affect post-war America? (Celebrates a student's response)

- "You said that the American secondary school today is rooted more in tradition than in innovation. Does that hold true for other educational institutions?" (Recognizes the contribution of the student by using her/his words in the response and follow-up question)

- "Your response shows an excellent grasp of Merriman's thesis about social contracts. How might that affect us here in this class?" (Honors the response)

- Gender Sensitivity. There has been an increasing body of research which conclusively demonstrates that college instructors respond differently to male and female students irrespective of the gender of the instructor. Both male and female professors tend to call on male students more, tend to acknowledge male students more than female students, and tend to provide more positive responses to the contributions of males students than to those of female students.

  Your gender bias often shows up in the pronouns you use in class. Relying exclusively on masculine pronouns (he, his, him) is not only inappropriate, but demeaning for your female students. Strive for a balance between feminine and masculine pronouns in your lectures, presentations, discussions, and written documents (e.g. course syllabus).

- **Differential Treatment.** Do you demonstrate any biases in the classroom? Do you provide differential treatment of various cultural or ethnic groups? Do you give preference to one group of students over another? If you're not sure of the responses to these questions, ask a colleague to videotape one of your class sessions. Afterwards, sit down with the colleague and examine your habits, language, directions, comments, questions, and in-class attitudes. What do you notice? Is there room for improvement? Are any changes necessary?

- **Assess the Climate.** As part of the course evaluation process, invite students to comment on the climate in the classroom. Invite them to share anything that makes them or other members of the class uncomfortable or uneasy. Are there things that you do (or don't do) that may be construed as culturally insensitive or inappropriate? You may wish to include one or more of the following questions on an end-of-the-semester course evaluation form:

    - Is the instructor fair and equitable in her/his treatment of all students?

    - Does the instructor show preference to any single student or group of students?

    - Does the instructor demonstrate biases (for or against) any race, culture, or ethnic or gender group?

    - How comfortable are you with the instructor? With other students?

    - What does the instructor do to make you feel comfortable in class?

    - Is the instructor respectful of each individual?

Know Your Institution

Colleges come in all shapes and sizes: no two are alike. One of the best ways to respond to the diversity of students in your classes is to learn as much as possible about your institution—its history, its traditions, and the social and cultural environment in which it operates. In a way, you are a reflection of the institution you work for; know your territory and you can also know your students.

- **Check Out the Catalog.** Read the college catalog—particularly its mission statement—and get to know its philosophy and its goals. What does the college (the administration and the board of trustees) believe? What are their operational guidelines? What is their philosophy about the education of all students? Having that information in hand will help you craft a course that is sensitive to and respectful of all students, irrespective of their culture, gender, or ethnic group.

- **College Services and Resources.** One of the first things you may wish to do upon your arrival on campus is to find out everything you can about the various support services for students. Is there a tutoring service or academic support center on campus? What services does the academic advising office provide students? What types of cultural or ethnic student groups, organizations, or clubs are on campus? Does the college have a minority affairs officer or a minority recruitment officer? Is there a women's study program or major on campus?

- **In Your Department.** How is your department responding to or addressing issues of diversity? You may wish to suggest that selected topics be included in departmental meetings. For example, are course requirements equitable for all students? Are course prerequisites fair and just? What type of orientation program is provided for new students, new majors, and transfer students? What are the graduation rates and job placement data for majors? What types of extracurricular activities and support services are available for students? How does your department interface with the English as a Second Language program?

- **In the Community.** While learning about the college, it would also be valuable to learn as much as you can about the community in which the college exists. What has been the historical relationship between the college and the local community? What is the current atmosphere between the community and the college? It would also be valuable to seek out and investigate any ethnic, cultural, or racial support groups, clubs, or organizations in the local community.

A Final Thought

In Chapter 3 (page 27), we discussed the seven principles of good teaching. The first of those principles was "Student-Faculty Contact." In other words, the more opportunities there are for all students and their teachers to get together (in class and outside of class), the more each student will invest in her or his own learning. Showing a predisposition towards, or a preference for, one group of students to the exclusion of another negates the educational benefits of this principle. Exhibiting disrespect or inappropriate verbal responses to students of non-western European-American backgrounds creates an environment of power rather than one of pedagogy. In short, teaching college is not about how much you know, but rather it's about how well you interact with students—all students!

CHAPTER 18:

Evaluation of Students

Truth be told, there is a "gremlin" lurking in the back of every college course. It's the gremlin of evaluation. That is to say, it is how we determine if our students have been able to accomplish the goals we established for them. That it is a gremlin indicates that it hovers over the course, provides anxiety for teachers and students alike, and is often the ultimate perception of the difficulty (or utility) of a course in the life of a college student.

Too often, evaluation is viewed as something punitive; a practice that does not celebrate effective teaching or honor good learning. Frequently, it sends a chilling message that the product is more important than the process. It is often viewed as an ingrained system of rewards and punishments that may have little connection to two primary goals: helping us become more effective teachers and helping students become better learners. Let's take a closer look at this ever-present gremlin.

Evaluation is, most likely, not a new concept for you; however, in most previous situations, you were probably the one being tested. As you move into your adjunct teaching position, you will now assume the responsibilities of an evaluator. You will be required to determine how well your students are learning, gauge their performance, and measure the appropriateness of the content and the effectiveness of the methods and techniques utilized in your classroom.

Effective evaluation is not simply something that is done at the conclusion of a unit of study or at the end of the semester. Effective evaluation is integrated into all aspects of a course, providing both teachers and students with relevant and useful data to gauge progress and determine the effectiveness of materials and procedures.

Here are some factors to consider for your own courses:

- Effective evaluation is a continuous, on-going process. Much more than determining the products of learning, it is rather a way of gauging learning over time. Learning and evaluation are never completed; they are always evolving and developing.

- A variety of evaluative tools are necessary to provide the most accurate evaluation of students' learning and progress. Dependence on one type of tool to the exclusion of others deprives students of valuable learning opportunities and robs you of measures that help both students and the courses you teach grow.

- Evaluation must be a collaborative activity between professors and students. Students must be able to assume an active role in evaluation so that they can begin to develop individual responsibilities for development and self-monitoring.

- Evaluation needs to be authentic. It must be based on the natural activities and processes students do in the classroom and in their everyday lives. For example, relying solely on formalized testing procedures may send a signal to students that learning is simply a search for "right answers."

Evaluation is intrinsically more complex that writing a test, giving it to a group of students, scoring it, and handing it back with some sort of letter grade. Indeed, it involves a combination of procedures and designs that not only gauge students' work but help them grow in the process.

For traditional college instructors, evaluation has meant little more than giving "two midterms and a final exam." Instructors lament the time necessary to construct those measures (as well as the time required to grade the instruments). And, students moan and groan about the time needed to "cram" a plethora of information in their heads in order to regurgitate it on a pencil-and-paper test (one they will scarcely recall a day or two later). The traditional means of evaluation seems to be onerous for all parties involved.

Part of the reason for this view is that evaluation has been viewed very narrowly by many college instructors. Simply stated, that view is that student success in a course is equated with an accumulation of points (more points accumulated = higher grade). The accumulation of knowledge is prized more than the use of that knowledge (it's also easier to measure).

Yet, in reviewing the literature on evaluation and in talking with outstanding professors around the country a predominant theme appears over and over. That is, evaluation should be used to help students learn, not to sort them into categories (e.g. A's, B's, C's, etc.). The overall consensus is that well-crafted evaluative measures are a means to an end, not the end itself.

AN EXPERT OPINION

In interview after interview, I discovered that the two basic questions every outstanding college teacher asked (relative to student evaluation) were, "Is this something that will help my students become better learners and thinkers?" and "Is this something that will tell me how well I have helped my students learn?"

Performance-based Evaluation

You are probably most familiar with this type of evaluation, also known as product evaluation. Typically, it involves some sort of pencil-and-paper test or quiz on the material learned—specifically, how much of the material was learned. The objective, in many cases, is to gauge how much of the course content has been committed to memory and how much of that memory can be reproduced on a written exam. The number of correct responses is tallied and a grade emerges. The more one memorizes, the higher the grade.

One of the inherent dangers of performance-based evaluation is that it often takes place at the conclusion of a unit or course. This tends to underscore learning as simply an accumulation of facts and figures to be memorized and regurgitated on terminal instruments.

Here are some of the typical "indicators" of performance-based evaluation:

- An over-reliance on product-oriented tests (e.g. multiple-choice, true/false, short-answer completion, matching)
- Points off for late papers
- Provision of "extra credit" assignments for students with marginal grades
- Ability testing
- An accumulation of points
- Class participation rewarded with points

Learning-centered Evaluation

Learning-centered evaluation is markedly different from performance-based evaluation both procedurally and philosophically. Basically, it means that learning is viewed developmentally rather than the simple acquisition of knowledge. That is to say, learning is a process—a reflection of intellectual growth and development over time. It is not the facts learned that is important, but rather what students are able to do with the content (in intellectual increments) over time.

This form of evaluation concentrates, not so much on what students have learned, but instead on how they learn or how they pursue learning. Learning-centered evaluation may include the development of teacher or student-initiated projects (for example, "Construct a timeline of pertinent scientific discoveries leading up to the creation of the polio vaccine.") in which students pursue a particular area of interest. It may also include measures in which the teacher provides materials and procedures for using those materials and then observes how students perform on the specified tasks. The objective in this form of evaluation is not on whether students have learned a series of right answers, but more so on how they go about learning.

Here are some practices found in courses that embrace learning-centered evaluation:

- Base-line information is collected on students at the start of the semester
- Students can submit multiple drafts of a written assignment
- Students are involved in self-evaluation activities
- Due dates for outside work are flexible
- A de-emphasis on the accumulation of points
- Students use knowledge in productive exercises both in and out of class

In short, learning-centered evaluation is centered on two fundamental principles:

1. Evaluation is used to help students learn—to progress from unknown to application
2. Intellectual development is highlighted over information accumulation

A learning-centered approach to evaluation can provide both you and your students with valuable and useful information to gauge progress and assess the effectiveness of the instruction. In so doing, you can help your students assume an active role in the evaluation process and can help make your courses more of a collaborative effort, instead of one in which you assume all the responsibilities for teaching and evaluating.

While there are many forms of learning-centered evaluation, I will concentrate on just a few. I do not mean to imply that these are the only forms and formats, but rather that they have been proven over time to yield important data for teachers and students alike. Consider these (or modifications thereof) for your own courses. You should also be willing to attempt other evaluative measures in keeping with your philosophy of teaching and your students' developing abilities and attitudes.

Effective evaluation is not based on the traditional model of "I know what is best for my students." Rather, it is founded on the principle of knowing where students are starting from and taking them to where you would like them to be. That means, quite simply, that you need to know your students' backgrounds. It means that you need to take the time early in the semester to discover as much as possible about your students. In doing so, you are creating a course that is responsive to their needs, rather than one managed by the dictates of content.

Good adjunct professors use a variety of techniques and strategies to assess their students at the start of a course. Here are a few you may wish to consider:

- Survey students on what they believe are their strengths and weaknesses relative to the objectives of the course ("How comfortable are you in using algorithms?" "What is your level of expertise in staining slides?")

- Provide students with a list of the eight to ten major objectives of the course. Invite students to indicate their level of interest in each of those objectives.

- Offer students the opportunity to write a brief essay on what they hope to gain as a result of their involvement in the course. Divide the class into various groups and ask each group to arrive at a consensus of opinion.

- Talk with students informally outside of class (student union, off-campus site) about their goals and expectations for the course.

- Give students a pre-test on important vocabulary, significant concepts, or relevant data (the information you would like them to know at the conclusion of the course).

- After several weeks of teaching the course, invite students to form groups and respond to the following questions: What have you learned so far in this course? How has the instructor helped you to learn that material? What modifications in the course design or delivery would you like to suggest?

Knowing your students (and continuing to know your students throughout the length of the course) is an essential prerequisite of effective teaching and, ultimately, effective evaluation. Evaluation is focused on how students change (intellectually, socially, individually). To know if students have changed, you also need to know what they started with.

Standards and Criteria

One of the most important elements of good evaluation is to have clear standards and appropriate criteria for those standards. That is to say, what should students know at the end of the course and how will you (and they) know how well they learned it. A **standard** is a description of what students should know and be able to do. Here's an appropriate standard for an English Composition course: "Students will write a persuasive piece that includes a clearly stated position or opinion." A **criterion** is a level of performance that determines to what level the standard has been mastered. For example: Very Good, Good, Adequate, Poor, Unacceptable.

> **RESEARCH POINT**
>
> In one study of 140 college teachers, only eight percent were able to identify the key criteria and standards by which they evaluated the quality of student learning.

The use of standards and criteria for those standards seems to be a rather obvious element for any course. Yet, surveys of professors around the country indicate that this essential course component is barely addressed or is nonexistent. This may stem from the traditional model of college teaching as lecturing ("information dump"), recording (taking copious notes), and testing (recalling information on "two midterms and a final.").

In other words, evaluation is not something done to students, but rather a means to help them grow and develop. When students are compared against each other (Whoever gets the most points gets an "A.") then evaluation is often haphazard, arbitrary, and punitive. Grades should not be used to rank students, but rather they should represent clearly stated levels of achievement. In short, students must meet certain standards of excellence that are well-defined, articulated, and shared in advance. If an assignment is returned to students and they comment, "How did I get this grade? or "Where did this grade come from?" then it is certain that the standards and criteria of the course are either minimal or nonexistent.

How can you do a better job of clarifying the criteria and standards for your courses? Here's a suggested plan of action:

1. Divide your course content into logical segments, topics, or concepts.

2. For each one, write one to three standards (what you want students to know or be able to do).

3. For each standard, construct a rating scale that includes descriptive statements of good to poor versions of students' performance (How well do you want students to know or do the standards?)

4. Provide students with your established standards and the criteria by which they will be assessed.

Effective Assessment Tools

Just as a carpenter has many tools in her toolbox; so too do college teachers have a wide variety of assessment options to use with students. Here, I would like to share a variety of assessment tools for you to consider as part of your teaching repertoire. This is not meant as an exhaustive list, but rather a collection of some of the most useful and informative instruments available.

1. **Rubrics.** A rubric is a one-page document that describes varying levels of performance, from high to low, for a specific assignment. Rubrics let students know the expectations for an assignment before they begin work on that assignment. They clearly define what a student must include in a piece of work to achieve a certain score. As such, they may be general in nature (all the homework assignments in math) or specific (an assignment that focuses on the use of details in an expository writing paper). Here's an abbreviated example of a rubric that might be used to assess written papers in an English class.

	4 POINTS	3 POINTS	2 POINTS	1 POINTS
ACCURACY	Factual data is accurate	Most data is accurate	Some information is accurate	Little accurate information
ORGANIZATION	Material is presented logically	Material is reasonably logical	Material is minimally organized	Little or no organization is evident
CREATIVITY	High level of creativity and originality is evident	Moderate level of creativity and originality is evident	Some creativity and originality	Little or no creativity and originality
FOCUS	Project is focused and detailed	Project is moderately focused and detailed	Project is minimally focused and detailed	Project shows little focus; unclear ideas

You can easily create a rubric for any assignment or instructional activity. Here are some steps to follow:

1. Determine the criteria by which you will grade a specific assignment.

2. What are the levels of mastery you want in that assignment? You can do this by determining to best and worst levels, and then determining the levels in between.

3. Create a rubric using the format in the sample above.

4. IMPORTANT: Show students models of both acceptable and unacceptable assignments. For example, show a paper that would get a high score and the rubric used to determine that score. Make sure students understand how each of the criteria was satisfied in the rubric.

5. You may wish to distribute several random papers and invite students (in groups, perhaps) to assess the assignment using a prepared rubric.

RESEARCH POINT

There are several websites that allow you to customize your own rubrics. These sites also have a plethora of prepared rubrics that you can use for any subject, any assignment, and any activity in any grade (Yup, there are hundreds of them ready for you to use). Some are available in both English and Spanish:

4Teachers (www.4teachers.org)

Educator's Network (www.rubrics4teachers.com)

2. **Anticipation Guides.** Anticipation guides alert students to some of the major concepts in textual material before it is read. As such, students have an opportunity to share ideas and opinions as well as activate their prior knowledge about a topic before they read about that subject. It is also a helpful technique for eliciting students' misconceptions about a subject. Students become actively involved in the dynamics of reading a specified selection because they have an opportunity to talk about the topic before reading about it.

- Read the textual material and attempt to select the major concepts, ideas, or facts in the text. For example, in a selection on "Weather" the following concepts could be identified:
  - There are many different types of clouds.
  - Different examples of severe weather include tornadoes, hurricanes, and thunderstorms.
  - Precipitation occurs in the form of rain, snow, sleet, and hailstones.
  - Many types of weather occur along "fronts."
- Create five to ten statements (not questions) that reflect common misconceptions about the subject, are ambiguous, or are indicative of students' prior knowledge. Statements are written on the white board or photocopied and distributed.
- Give students plenty of opportunities to agree or disagree with each statement. Whole class or small group discussions would be appropriate. After discussions, let each individual student record a positive or negative response to each statement. Initiate discussions focusing on reasons for individual responses.
- Direct students to read the text, keeping in mind the statements and their individual or group reactions to those statements.
- After reading the selection, engage the class in a discussion on how the textual information may have changed their opinions. Provide students with an opportunity to record their reactions to each statement based upon what they read in the text. It is not important that a consensus to be reached, nor that students agree with everything the author states. Rather, it is more important for students to engage in an active dialogue—a conversation which allows them to react to the relationships between prior knowledge and current knowledge.

As part of an "Oceanography" unit, students had expressed an interest in learning about some of the dangers facing the world's oceans. The effects of a recent oil spill off the New Jersey coast had received front page coverage in the *New York Times* and had sparked students' curiosity about how oil spills and other environmental hazards affected the local flora and fauna. In preparation for their study of ocean pollution, the instructor prepared the following Anticipation Guide:

DIRECTIONS: Look at the sentences on this page. The statements are numbered from 1 to 6. Read each sentence; if you think that what it says is right, print "Yes" on the line under the word "BEFORE." If you think the sentence is wrong, print "No" on the line under the word "BEFORE." Do the same thing for each sentence. Remember how to do this, because you will do it again after you read the selection.

BEFORE   AFTER

_____   _____   1. There is only one way to clean up an oil spill.

_____   _____   2. An oil spill is dangerous to sea and land creatures, but not birds.

_____   _____   3. Untreated sewage is dumped directly into the ocean.

_____   _____   4. Bottom-feeding fish eat cigarette butts.

_____   _____   5. Laundry detergent is a pollutant.

_____   _____   6. The oceans of the world are in serious danger.

Working as a class, students responded to each of the statements on the Anticipation Guide. Class discussion centered on reasons for their choices and predictions about what they might discover in the forthcoming chapter. The instructor then provided multiple copies of a newspaper article to students and invited them to read and locate confirming data related to each of the identified statements. Afterwards, students completed the "AFTER" column of the guide and shared their reasons for placing "Yes" or "No" on each line. Follow-up discussions revealed some differences of opinion, yet the conversation was lively as well as supportive. Students found that they each brought different perspectives to the article, yet they could all benefit from those differences in a mutually stimulating learning environment.

3. **Group Quiz.** Here's an assessment tool that will reap untold benefits, not only in terms of your overall assessment of student progress in a class or subject, but also in terms of other essential factors critical to a well-run classroom environment. In fact, I've been using this strategy for many years with incredible success. It is appropriate for use with students in any course and will help clarify (for them) critical concepts in your course while promoting an active learning environment.

Called a "Group Quiz," here's how it works. Assign a specific reading assignment to your students. This can be a homework assignment or an in-class reading assignment. Let students know that after they have read the assigned text, they will take a ten-item multiple-choice quiz.

Prepare a ten-item multiple-choice quiz on the reading selection with four choices for each of the ten questions. Type up the quiz, duplicate it, and distribute it to all the students in the room.

- **Phase A:** Invite each student to complete the quiz by circling the correct answer to each question according to what they read or understood from the assigned work.

- **Phase B:** After everyone has completed Phase A, assemble the students into various groups of about four to five students each. The groups can be permanent groups or are assembled as ad-hoc groups on the spot. Distribute a Quiz Record Sheet to each group (see the sample on page 277) and invite them to work together using their own individual quizzes as starting points to collectively determine an appropriate answer for each question. They may not use any notes or the actual text.

All responses are recorded on individual Quiz Record Sheets (one for each group). The initial responses for each group is recorded by hand in the "5 Points" column. After the answers to all ten questions have been recorded by a group, one person raises her or his hand and invites you (the teacher) to score the responses. If a response is correct, it is left intact. However, if a response to a question is incorrect an "X" is put over it. If a group gets all ten questions correct, they receive 50 points (5 points per question, ten questions).

However, if an answer is incorrect (an "X" was placed over the answer recorded on the sheet) the sheet is returned to the group and they are encouraged to select a response from the remaining items for that question. That new response is recorded in the "3 Points" column. Once again the sheets are handed in and immediately scored. If, again, a recorded response is incorrect an "X" is placed over it and the sheet is returned. The next response is then recorded in the "1 Point" column. If that answer is incorrect, the last (and the correct) answer is recorded in the final ("0 Points") column.

The overall scores for each group is tallied and recorded.

EXAMPLE:

You are teaching a freshman Biology class and are in the midst of a series of lessons on invertebrates. One of the "classic" invertebrates studied during these lessons are clams. You assign the following reading selection (from a popular nonfiction book) to your students to read as a homework assignment. You tell your students that the first thing they will do in class tomorrow will be to take a Group Quiz on the material in the assigned reading (NOTE: While they are doing the reading, you are putting together the ten-item Group Quiz for tomorrow's class.)

> While clams are not endowed with a brain, they have what is often referred to as a "simplified brain," known to biologists as ganglia. While most creatures have a single brain, many spe-

cies of clams have two coordinated ganglia. One, known as the pedal ganglia, is responsible for controlling the clam's foot. The other, known as the visceral ganglia, regulates the clam's internal organs.

Ask a zoologist for a definition of ganglia and he or she will tell you that it is "a biological tissue mass, or a mass of nerve cell bodies." Human brains, such as yours and mine, are capable of thought and reason; however, ganglia are only capable of controlling the most rudimentary of biological functions: moving the foot, for example, or moving food along the digestive tract. In short, clams cannot think, they can only do. It's a classic case of stimulus/response—no pondering, no thought, and no contemplation. Clams are essentially creatures without reason; organisms without a conscience.

Although clams do not possess thinking organs, they have the capacity to sense their surroundings. For example, many species of clams have a series of tentacles with chemoreceptor cells used to taste the surrounding water. By tasting the water a clam can determine if food is nearby or if a fellow clam is in the immediate area.

Another notable sensory organ is the clam's osphradium, a patch of sensory cells located below the posterior adductor muscle (the muscle that opens and closes a clam's two shells). A clam sometimes uses this organ to taste the water or measure its turbidity (the cloudiness or haziness of water due to particulate matter [dirt] suspended in the water).

Clams and their relatives also have an additional sensory feature, a collection of organs known as statocysts. These organs help the clam sense and correct its orientation, that is, is it right side up or upside down? And, if it is right side up, is it tilted to one side or the other? This orientation is critical in helping ensure that the clam is able to feed efficiently.[1]

1 Excerpted from: Fredericks, Anthony D. *The Secret Life of Clams: The Mysteries and Magic of Our Favorite Shellfish* (New York: Skyhorse Press, 2014), pp. 110-111. Used by permission of the author.

Following are the first four questions (of the ten-question Group Quiz) you have developed for the assigned reading above. These questions have been typed and are distributed to every student in the class.

1. The clam's osphradium is used to:

    A. Measure the cloudiness of the surrounding water

    B. Taste the water

    C. Both A & B

    D. Neither A or B

2. The pedal ganglia controls the clam's

    A. Brain

    B. Foot

    C. Stomach

    D. Reproductive organs

3. In order to feed efficiently clams rely on their

    A. Statocysts

    B. Visceral organs

    C. Brains

    D. Posterior adductor muscles

4. "A mass of nerve cell bodies" refers to a clam's

    A. Shells

    B. Ganglia

    C. Particulate matter

    D. Foot

Each group records its answers on a Quiz Record Sheet. A partial one is illustrated below:

	5 POINTS	3 POINTS	1 POINTS	0 POINTS
1.				
2.				
3.				
4.				

Group Quiz Number _____

Group members: _____ _____

_____ _____

_____ _____

Group Name: _____

As detailed above, when the group completes answering all of the questions (recorded in the "5 Points" column), they submit the sheet to you. You quickly score it on the spot (By the way, for the four questions above the correct answers are: 1, C; 2, B; 3, A; 4, B). An "X" is marked over any incorrect answers (by you) and the sheet is returned to the group for them to make some decisions on more appropriate responses.

Group Quiz scores are recorded over the length of the school term and become part of the final grade. My own experience has shown that this is one of the most enjoyable assessment exercises students have experienced. It is non-stressful, engaging, and offers valid information necessary for you to ensure a well-focused lesson or unit. Other teachers from around the country have also seen some very positive benefits of this tool. Here are some of their insights:

1. This is an excellent way to ensure that students read the material assigned. They cannot actively participate in group discussions unless they have read the assigned text. Initially, some may be reluctant to do so, but if you make these a normal and regular part of your academic program (in my classes about twenty percent of the final grade is the results of these quizzes) you will notice, over time, more and more students reading the necessary material.

2. These Group Quizzes also serve as a way to determine the background knowledge of the class for a forthcoming topic. By giving a Group Quiz before launching into a formal lesson plan, you can determine if students have sufficient prior knowledge to handle the material. If a significant majority of the class "bombs" the quiz, then you may need to revise a forthcoming lesson; on the other hand, if most groups "ace" the quiz, then you can feel comfortable in the fact that they are sufficiently prepared to handle the material.

3. The quizzes promote a sense of classroom community. Students are working together in a coordinated fashion to arrive at answers that are beneficial to the entire group. The individual groups are not competing against one another, they are only competing with themselves. When I debrief with students at the end of a course, the one element they always mention is the value of the Group Quizzes in helping to form friendships, solidify class camaraderie, and cement a spirit of cooperation.

4. The Quizzes are never viewed as punitive in nature. Students see them as what they are—a way to actively assess their reading knowledge and comprehension about a specific topic. These are not something "done by the teacher," but, rather are instruments that help clarify important concepts and clearly identify specific objectives for a lesson.

5. Most important, students don't see themselves as academic combatants. In many traditional classrooms students are evaluated on tests that rank order them from high to low; good to bad. Students (as did you) quickly learn how they rank on the scholastic ladder. In many cases, they are permanently categorized. Group Quizzes, however, place more of the emphasis on a shared intellectual responsibility—an academic cohesiveness that is significantly more cooperative than combative. The result, I'm happy to report, is students more (successfully) engaged in their own learning.

4. **Journal Entry Sheet.** Whenever students work together in cooperative groups it may be appropriate for a designated member of each group to complete a survey form similar to the one below. Copies of completed sheets can be included as entries in each group member's personal folder.

Journal Entry Sheet

Topic/Subject: _____

Date: _____

What we knew: _____

_____

_____

What we discovered: _____

_____

Books or media where information was found: _____

_____

The most interesting fact we learned: _____

_____

Signed: _____ (Group Recorder)

Some Final Thoughts

Here is a final collection of thoughts, ideas, and suggestions for your consideration:

- Grading on the Curve. I would like to suggest that you don't use this evaluative technique. In studies of outstanding college teachers, it was discovered that the majority graded on pre-established standards, rather than on a curve. These exceptional teachers believed that grading on a curve made their classrooms more competitive, rather than cooperative. It also sent a signal to students that the accumulation of points was much more important that the accumulation and use of knowledge. Cumulative evaluation measures places a premium on deep learning, rather than the superficial (and quixotic) learning promoted via competitive, or curved, grading.

- Evaluation as a process. Keep in mind that the best kind of evaluation is that which offers opportunities for growth—teacher growth, student growth, and program growth. It is one thing to assess and evaluate student performance, it is quite another to do something with that information. If all you do is administer an endless bank of tests, quizzes, and written assignments and do little with the results, then your evaluation is close to worthless. The data you gather from all forms of evaluation should be used productively; that is, to help students develop the skills, processes, and attitudes that help make learning an important part of their lives.

- Evaluation as an integral part of the learning process. Evaluation must be sensitive to the needs, attitudes, and abilities of individual students as well as the class as a whole. Be careful that you do not over-rely on one or two forms of evaluation just because they are easy or convenient for you. Be aware that evaluation involves some part of a student's self-esteem and that affective factors are an important ingredient in evaluation. In other words, what you evaluate is just as important as how you evaluate.

Learning to become an effective evaluator takes time. It is not easily learned, nor easily practiced. It is, however, an essential element of the effective and successful college classroom.

CHAPTER 20:

Issues and Concerns

I wish I could tell you that being an adjunct professor was as simple as sharing your love and passion for a subject with an eager and enthusiastic group of undergraduates who wait patiently for your "words of wisdom" with affection, sincerity, and desire. I wish I could tell you that; but you probably know better.

College students come with a varied set of expectations, experiences, and goals. They also come to your courses with their own ideas about how the teaching/learning paradigm works. After all, they are products of twelve or more years of education; they have some ideas about how the "system" should operate. Unfortunately, there is sometimes a conflict between their beliefs and yours. Let's take a look at some of the more common ones and how you can effectively address them.

Expectations vs. Reality

Many college students come to class with a set of expectations that have been shaped by their experiences in high school, their family, their peer group, or the media. Sometimes those expectations are in agreement with yours; at other times they are in disagreement. When students are engaged, when a class runs smoothly, or when students adhere to the demands of the course, we can say that student expectations are in agreement with teacher expectations. When there is discord between student and teacher expectations, then some sort of conflict may ensue.

Steven Richardson, vice president for academic affairs at Winona (MN) State University makes the case that traditional-age college students are still "apprentice" adults, and therefore not fully mature. It becomes necessary for us, as college professors, to establish appropriate models of behavior and to make our expectations for class conduct and course requirements explicit, well-defined, and clear.

Richardson proposes a set of guidelines through which college teachers can establish appropriate models of behavior and classroom decorum. I've presented these below with some additional annotations:

- Make behavioral expectations clear in your syllabus. Be sure to use positive, constructive language, not threats of reprisal. Students respond best to clear, concise language that leaves little or no room for doubt (or interpretation).

- It is most valuable to talk about yourself and let students know what you value. "Apprentice" adults need models to emulate. You can offer a positive model simply by sharing your beliefs and values in a comfortable arena.

- Learn as much as you can about your students. Find out about their hopes and dreams. In doing so, you show that you are interested in them as human beings, rather than simply as students.

- Earn trust by being trustworthy. Be consistent in applying your expectations to students. In other words: do what you say, and say what you do.

- Establish a classroom environment in which learning is promoted as a process, rather than as a product. When students' investment in a course is celebrated and valued, then they will have a stake in the success of that course for themselves and for others.

- The traditional lecture format—which promotes a one-way transmission of knowledge—may be counterproductive to appropriate classroom behavior. Interactive styles of instruction (e.g. cooperative learning, constructivism, active discussions) are more likely to engage students and significantly reduce inappropriate behaviors.

- Cooperative projects and group discussions provide opportunities for students to establish personal expectations. Additionally, when students are engaged with other students in productive exercises then learning mushrooms and behavior is aligned with group goals.

- It is vitally important that we, as college professors, model the behaviors we expect of our students. Students take their cues from those in front of them—adult teachers. If you're enthused, they will be enthused. If you are honest with them, they will want to be honest with you.

- Do not ignore minor events in the classroom. A combination of minor events can add up to a major situation or crisis. As Barney Fife (on the old "Andy Griffith" show) would say, "Nip it in the bud!"

- Be willing to adjust your own behavior. Don't set yourself up as a "perfect" example; show students your human side, too. Provide students with opportunities to learn from your example. I find that self-disclosure is a way of bonding with the audience. It's a way of connecting with students while personalizing instruction."

- Plan time to talk with colleagues in your department or other departments. What expectations do they have for students? How do they articulate those expectations? What do they do when there is a mismatch between their expectations and those of their students?

> **AN EXPERT OPINION**
>
> Ed Ransford, a professor of sociology, says, "Let a little of your personal self out. Don't get gushy, but there's no need to be totally objective all the time." Brian Furio, an associate professor of communications, seconds that when he says, "I find that self-disclosure is a way of bonding with the audience. It's a way of connecting with students while personalizing instruction."

Stating Your Expectations

Typically, you will want to put your expectations for the course in your syllabus. You may choose the option of developing a separate document which focuses specifically on your expectations. Many institutions have a set of expectations which are provided to faculty members as required elements of any course syllabus.

In stating your expectations for the course it's important that they include the following:

- Clear and concise language. This is not the time to pontificate.

- A positive tone. Students will quickly "read between the lines" to determine if you have their best interests in mind.

- A democratic atmosphere. Let students know that their involvement and participation are valued.

- You are in charge. You will need to strike a delicate balance and let students know that you are in charge, but without sounding authoritarian.

Now, let's take a look at some common course expectations and how you can effectively communicate them to students.

Attendance

In my experience there are two "camps" with respect to the issue of attendance. One group of professors says that it is the student's responsibility to attend class. They pay the tuition and they can, therefore, make the necessary decisions about whether or not they wish to be in class. They should be prepared to suffer any consequences with respect to their non-attendance or non-participation in the regularly scheduled events of the course. In short, it is not the duty of the professor to "force" students to attend.

The other camp says that students need guidelines and expectations that are clearly stated and clearly enumerated. Without those guidelines, students may get a feeling that attendance is not important and that their engagement in the course is not valued. The opinion of many professors is that an attendance policy places a value on students' participation in every aspect of a course. My personal philosophy is that students are more inclined to attend class when attendance is valued (and recorded) and when there are some consequences tied to their attendance. An attendance policy establishes a model of behavior and expectations that contributes to academic success.

Listed below is the attendance policy statement I included in every course syllabus. Feel free to use or modify this example in your own syllabi:

> "Class attendance is both mandatory and necessary. Valuable information and ideas are presented and shared during each class session, and it is to your benefit as well as the benefit of your classmates to be present for each and every class. In fact, it is your primary academic responsibility to attend all classes. Roll will be taken periodically throughout the semester. Your final grade for the course may be affected as follows:
>
> » 3 unexcused absences = deduction of 1 full grade
>
> » 4 unexcused absences = deduction of 2 full grades
>
> » 5 unexcused absences = deduction of 3 full grades
>
> Excused absences (for health or family emergencies) must be verified with a physician's note or a memo from the Student Affairs Office. Materials, assigned work, and information missed due to absence are your responsibility and will need to be made up on your own time. Each student is responsible for making sure all course requirements are completed and on time. The instructor is not responsible for reminding students of missing work."

This example incorporates several elements that you should consider in your own attendance policy:

- There is a rationale for this policy. I let students know that their attendance is tied to their success in the course.

- Use of the word "may" (fifth sentence). This gives allows me to keep my options open. If there are some unique or special circumstances (death in the family, severe illness), then I've given myself some leeway.

- The responsibility for making up missed work is the student's, not mine.

- Specific consequences are clearly stated. Students are aware, from the first day of class, what may happen as a result of non-attendance.

While students may say that an attendance policy is unnecessary or demeaning at the college level, the experiences of several colleagues has shown that there is a positive correlation between a clearly stated policy and student success. On end-of-the-semester evaluations, students will often state that the attendance policy (as stated in the syllabus) was a motivation to come to class regularly.

Tardiness

There is often a direct correlation between the time a class is offered and the level of tardiness exhibited by students. The level of tardiness increases with early morning classes (sleeping in until the last minute) and late afternoon classes (part-time or full-time work schedules). It tends to decrease in classes held between 10:00 and 2:00.

You may wish to consider including a statement about tardiness in your course syllabus. Doing so will send a message that all of the time in the class is important and that all students are expected for the entire duration of each class.

Here is the tardiness statement I included in my syllabi. As with the attendance policy above, consider this (or a modification thereof) for your own use as well.

> "LATE POLICY: It is the practice and tradition of the instructor to begin class at the scheduled start time. All students are expected to be seated and ready for instruction at the start of each class. Any student who arrives late (during or after the opening activity) should see the instructor after class to change the absence (as indicated on the periodic attendance sheet) to a lateness. Two "latenesses" equal one absence."

Academic Integrity

It is a sad fact of academia that students cheat. In fact, many new professors might be quite surprised at the level of cheating that takes place in higher education. Here are a few eye-opening statistics to consider:

- Numerous studies have found that from forty to ninety percent of all students cheat on classroom tests.

- Several studies have shown that between seventy-five and ninety-eight percent of college students surveyed each year report having cheated in high school.

- In one survey of 6,000 students at thirty-one institutions, sixty-seven percent of students reported having engaged in one or more questionable academic behaviors.

- In another study, seventy-eight percent of all college students reported that they had engaged in at least one type of cheating.

- In one study, eighty-four percent of the college students surveyed admitted to cheating on a written assignment.

- In one national survey of over 2,000 undergraduates, more than fifty percent admitted to cheating and half of those individuals admitted to cheating more than once.

To obtain the data above, I did a Google search. When I entered "cheating in college," I was surprised to discover 58,000,000 web pages on this topic! I suspect that by the time you read this, there will be many more added to this collection.

There are several reasons why college students cheat. For many students, a combination of factors is at play. Here is what the research indicates as the primary factors that influence student cheating:

- Peer pressure or peer influence (in many studies, this is reported as the number one reason)
- Low self-esteem or self-confidence
- An overwhelming belief that they won't get caught
- A feeling that the professor doesn't care or doesn't place a high enough value on academic honesty
- Unclear or ineffective policies (by the institution or individual professors)
- The rewards outweigh the potential consequences
- It's easy

There are probably as many different ways to cheat as there are college students. The methods and procedures are becoming more and more sophisticated via technological advances and innovations. Here is a list (definitely not a finite one) of some of the ways in which undergraduate students cheat:

- Downloading Internet articles and submitting them as their own (through "cut and paste")
- Paying someone to take an exam
- Paying someone to write a required paper
- Downloading test answers on a PDA, cell phone, or other device

- Facts and formulas written on various articles of clothing (prior to an exam)
- Looking at someone else's paper during an exam
- Copying material from another source (including other students) and submitting it as their own
- Providing answers to someone during an exam
- Stealing an exam
- Presenting another person's work as one's own
- Falsifying bibliographic entries or data
- Making false statements

The prevalence of cheating on college campuses makes it seems like a virulent disease—one impossible to totally eradicate. Yet, there are practices and measures we can implement in our courses that will significantly reduce the "need" to cheat by students and establish at atmosphere that values honesty and academic integrity. I have found that the incidence of cheating is directly related to the classroom culture that is established at the beginning of the semester and promoted throughout the semester. In its simplest terms this is a culture of "we," rather than the traditional culture of "us" versus "them."

Here are some suggestions and ideas on preventing cheating. They have been culled from a number of sources, colleagues, and colleges. I've also included my own practices. What is most interesting is that these recommendations have remained fairly consistent over the years and between investigators of this phenomenon.

- Establish a clear policy on cheating and make that policy known to students on your syllabus and in discussions with the class during the first week of a course. Many colleges have an institutional policy which is required on all syllabi. Here is the policy used at my institution and which is required on every course syllabi:

> "Academic dishonesty will not be tolerated at [this college]. Academic dishonesty refers to actions such as, but not limited to, cheating, plagiarism, fabricating research, falsifying academic documents, etc., and includes all situations where students make use of the work of others and claim such work as their own. Thus, it is expected that all assigned work for this course will be entirely original. In cases of academic dishonesty, the student involved may receive a grade of "0" for the course, and the matter will be reported to the Department Chairman and the Dean of Academic Affairs."

- The greater the psychological distance between the instructor and the student, the greater the inclination for cheating. That is, if the professor is seen as simply a mechanical dispenser of information or if students feel that they are nothing more than student ID numbers, the likelihood of cheating will mushroom accordingly. The more "community" you can build into your classroom and the more personal interaction you foster between yourself and your students, the less likely they will want to cheat. For example, I make a point to identify and briefly talk with one new student before or after each class. In one class, I complimented a young lady on her ever-present smile. In another class, I thanked a young man who contributed an in-depth response to a question asked during class. In still another class, I talked with a soccer player about an upcoming contest with a conference rival. You may argue that these are only single students, but each of these individuals will share her or his conversation with other classmates and peers thus spreading the interpersonal bonds I hope to promote.

- Provide multiple opportunities for students to demonstrate their mastery of course materials. The traditional "two quizzes and a final" places undue pressure on students to achieve in a very limited number of assessments. Although each course and each discipline will be different, work to have a balance of quizzes, tests, papers, projects and other assignments so that students can demonstrate their knowledge in array of evaluative measures.

- Consider the length of your exams or assigned papers. A test with 150 multiple-choice questions or a paper requiring a minimum of twenty-five references or fifty pages will seem extreme to students. They will view these assignments as both excessive and punitive and may "retaliate" with some form of academic dishonesty.

- Examine your grading policies to ensure that they are consistent, fair, and equitable. Whenever possible, de-emphasize grades and provide students with opportunities for self-evaluation.

- Foster the principle of academic integrity regularly. While it's important to discuss academic honesty at the beginning of the course, it's also appropriate to bring up the topic periodically throughout the semester. You may elect to have a brief statement included on an exam or quiz. Invite students to talk about academic honesty prior to a final exam. Re-emphasize your standards about 1/3 of the way into the course and invite student comments. Frequently refer to the academic integrity statements on your course syllabus.

- Think about methods that significantly reduce any tendencies to cheat. Use multiple forms of an exam, reassign seats for a final examination, stagger the seating pattern throughout the classroom or lecture hall for mid-term exams, create exams with scrambled questions, rotate the assignments for a course from semester to semester, physically move around the room during an exam, or invite monitors to help you proctor an exam.

- I have discovered that cheating tends to escalate when the emphasis on written assignments or exams is on low-level thinking. This includes memorizing facts, simple recall of information, or knowledge-based responses (see Chapter 13). When the emphasis on papers and tests shifts to higher levels of cognition (application, analysis, synthesis, and evaluation), the potential for cheating tends to diminish.

- Try to get to students who are struggling academically early in the semester. Take the time to discover the reasons for their academic problems and counsel them as necessary. Refer them to the academic assistance center or tutoring center on campus.

- Meet with small groups of students regularly. Set up discussion groups in your class and talk with them periodically. For larger classes where teaching assistants meet with students, plan to drop in every so often to chat with students. Small group encounters allow you to meet with students on a more personal basis and address any concerns or issues they may have.

- Consider the use of technology as a deterrent to cheating. There are a number of web-based anti-plagiarism services available such as www.turnitin.com. These programs automatically compare student papers with text on the Internet and in published work. Cheat-proof software is being used by many colleges. These programs prevent cheating on computer-based tests by blocking students from using other applications, such as e-mail and Web browsers. Other colleges are using thumbprint scanners and digital cameras to thwart test-taker impersonations.

- Finally, promote and adhere to your institution's policies on academic integrity. Regularly talk with students about those policies, disseminate them on printed materials (including tests and syllabi), and clarify your expectations for student behavior throughout the semester.

It is an unfortunate "fact of life" that cheating is a common occurrence on college campuses. Students will sometimes resort to extreme measures in order to cheat. Several years ago, on our campus, one student broke into a professor's office in order to steal a forthcoming final exam. Frustrated by his inability to locate the exam, he eventually resorted to setting the office on fire. He left a trail of clues, was quickly discovered, arrested, and expelled from school.

Late Papers; Late Assignments

As long as there are college students, there will be papers turned in late or assignments that need "just a little more time." The challenge for professors is how to deal with the "lateness factor" or the excuses that seem to be attached to almost every assignment.

> **RESEARCH POINT**
>
> In one study, researchers found that about sixty-seven percent of the college students surveyed admitted to making at least one fraudulent excuse while in college. Most of the excuses were made to gain extra time in order to complete an assignment.

Unfortunately, there is no magic formula for eliminating late assignments. They are as persistent as swarms of mosquitoes at a lakeside resort in the summer. However, here are a few suggestions on how you can reduce the incidence of lateness in your courses.

- Invite students to submit written assignments in stages. That is, ask that they turn in an outline of a paper first. This submission is checked off in your grade book. Then, a few days or weeks later, they can submit a draft of the paper for your comments and suggestions. Finally, they can turn in the final paper for a grade.

- You may wish to consider including a hierarchical series of penalties for late work. These deductions should be clearly stated on the course syllabus. For example, one to two days late = one grade deduction, three to four days late = two grade deduction, etc. Or, deduct ten points for every day a paper is late.

- One strategy that I have used with considerable success is to eliminate "due dates" for all written assignments. I tell students that it is their responsibility to determine the actual due dates of specific assignments. This requires them to balance the assignments in my course with those in other courses. It also eliminates the "lateness factor" because they now have latitude to determine the amount of work necessary for each assignment. I realize that this technique won't work for every course or every instructor; but it has, over the years, promoted a sense of individual responsibility and self-initiative in students.

- Some instructors have offered a bonus for papers turned in prior to the due date. Extra points are added to a paper if it arrives one, two, or three days in advance of the due date. Besides the incentive to turn in work early, this also has the added advantage of having papers come in over a span of several days, thus allowing you to spread out the reading of those papers over an extended period of time.

- Inform students that if all their assignments are turned in on time, they will have the option of dropping their lowest grade on any single assignment. Not only will this option spur students to complete all assignments in a timely manner, but also offers them an incentive or bonus. Conversely, students who are tardy in their submissions are "penalized" by having every grade count. For this option to work, it would be necessary to have a range of writing assignments for students to tackle.

Suffice it to say, there are many challenges, and concerns that will consume your time—both in class as well as outside class hours. Your "pro-activeness", however, can help ensure that all students are treated equitably, respectfully, and honestly. In most cases they will return the favor in kind.

Chapter 20: Issues and Concerns **297**

PART FIVE:

Life as an Adjunct

CHAPTER 21:

Evaluation of Teaching

Peter Filene, a professor of history at the University of North Carolina at Chapel Hill, says that "Teaching is only as successful as the learning it produces." As we have discussed throughout this book, students bring a certain set of expectations, personalities and learning dynamics with them at the beginning of any semester or any course. Those elements shape how they learn as much as they shape what they will learn. As professors, we try to meld those factors with course content and delivery to craft a "package" that will have a lasting effect on students irrespective of their major.

But, how do we know if we are "making the grade?" How do we know if we have a significant impact on student learning, student growth or students thinking? Are we "getting through" to students—altering or shaping their interest in our discipline? Are we, as professor Filene underscores, producing learning? Let's take a look at some of the issues surrounding the evaluation of teaching and how we might approach them.

How Are You Doing?

Recently, my department chair sent me the summary results of the student evaluations of a course I taught:

- "Knows all materials thoroughly and is very informative."
- "Interest, engagement, and excitement is embedded in every lesson."
- "Always excited, many details provided for every assignment."
- "Class is very interesting and lively."
- "Takes students opinions and feelings into consideration."
- "Is willing to change assignments to help students."
- "Clear, detailed expectations from the beginning."
- "Very clear and descriptive syllabus is presented to the class."
- "Very informative and worth taking."

(Of course, immediately after reading those evaluations I purchased some filet mignons and a fine bottle of Cabernet with which I could celebrate the innate "wisdom" of my students!)

While almost anyone would be thrilled with a set of end-of-the-semester student evaluations like those above, it was important that I put them in proper perspective. Truth be told, those comments were reflective of my performance over the course of a semester moreso than they were of whether students actually learned.

If you go back and read each of the evaluation statements above, you will note that there is an emphasis, on the part of students, on what the instructor (me) did during the course of the semester moreso than on what students actually learned. That's not to say that I'm dismissing these student comments (or the bottle of Cabernet). However, I'm also aware that these statements are more reflective of my performance in the classroom—they underscore the fact that my methodology, practices, and beliefs are all acceptable to students.

What those comments don't do, unfortunately, is tell me whether or not those same students learned anything significant—whether their intellectual lives were altered in some positive way. That's certainly not the fault of the students, but may have more to do with the questions students were asked on the evaluation forms.

> **AN EXPERT OPINION**
>
> Ken Bain, director of the Center for Teaching Excellence at New York University, says that all professors need to ask themselves a critical and fundamental question: "Does the teaching help and encourage students to learn in ways that make a sustained, substantial, and positive difference in the way they think, act, or feel without doing them any major harm?"

Student Ratings

Most colleges and universities have an elaborate system of end-of-the-semester evaluations centered around student ratings of their professors. At my institution, for example, each professor has the option of selecting one of four different evaluations forms and administering it to one or more classes during the last three weeks of the semester. Students complete the forms anonymously. The evaluations are then tabulated by the department administrative assistant and distributed by each department chairperson to respective faculty members several weeks after the course is over (and all grades have been submitted).

Here is one form my institution makes available to faculty (Note: For each question, students answer a yes/no question and then record a separate response in a follow-up "comments" section:

TEACHING

1. Does the faculty member seem to exhibit a sound understanding of the range of subject matter?

2. Is the faculty member able to maintain interest during the class period?

3. Does the faculty member present material clearly and without distracting mannerisms?

4. Does the faculty member attempt to improve the course where problems arise?

5. Is the faculty member sensitive to student responses and adaptive to student needs?

6. Is the faculty member fair in evaluation of student work?

7. Did the faculty member provide an adequate syllabus for the course so you understand the operating procedures?

8. Do you feel that there are an adequate number of test given during the semester?

9. Where do you place this faculty member among all you have had at [this institution]?

COURSE

1. Were the objectives of this course made clear to you?

2. Overall, was the course of value to you?

3. Compared to other courses you have taken at [this institution], where would you place this course?

Just like mayor Ed Koch's perennial question to New Yorkers ("How am I doing?"), college professors want to know how they are doing, too. We can know that only if we ask our students the right questions. For example, the Student Observation Form (above) asks questions related to the performance of the faculty member. If a faculty member considers her or his performance to be critical, then the results generated by this form will either validate strengths or expose weaknesses in the individual's performance during the semester.

In my recent student evaluation, students seemed to feel that I was a good performer because that was the focus of the questions they were asked. However, I'm equally interested in how well my students learned during that particular course. What did I do (or not do) that had an impact on them as learners? I'm certainly not discounting the performance factor; but I think that there are other questions that need to be posed as well.

> ### AN EXPERT OPINION
>
> When I asked Terry Seip, professor of history at the University of Southern California, for his evaluation of a good course he said, "[It's when] they've had a real learning experience! It's when they see that history has value and that it relates to their real lives. It's less about my performance and more about their connections, or linkages, with history."

Student Perceptions

One of the factors that influence student ratings is the perceptions they bring to the evaluation process. That is to say, if a student is a "surface learner" (Surface learners are those individuals who like to learn the facts of a topic or subject. They equate learning with the memorization and accumulation of a large body of knowledge.), she or he will praise a professor who focuses on the memorization of facts and figures. On the other hand, that same student will give considerably lower ratings to a professor who emphasizes thinking at higher levels of cognition (analysis, synthesis, evaluation). By the same token, a "deep learner" (Deep learners are those who prefer to engage in higher-level cognitive activities: analyzing material, synthesizing information from several different sources, and evaluating the worth or utility of data from a variety of viewpoints.) will give low ratings to a professor who emphasizes memorization and regurgitation of a finite list of facts; but provide a higher rating to a professor who emphasizes the critical explorations of topic.

> **RESEARCH POINT**
>
> According to a substantial body of research, students who take a course to satisfy their general interest or as an elective, tend to give the course (or professor) slightly higher ratings. Students who take a course to satisfy a major or liberal arts requirement tend to give slightly lower ratings. By and large, students tend to be more critical of required courses and less critical of non-required courses.

So, here's the bottom line: When students rate your teaching performance, they are only assessing part of the teaching equation. It is equally important that you have information relative to your teaching effectiveness. Only then will you be able to design courses that are learner-centered, intellectually stimulating, and educationally productive. Here are some proven strategies:

Criterion Checks

A criterion check is a way of monitoring how well students understand a lesson. It is an informal evaluation technique that can be used at the end of a class or periodically throughout the length of a course. The focus is on student comprehension, not on teacher performance. A criterion check is a point in any lesson where the instructor stops and checks to see if students understand the material up to that point.

- Prepare a standardized form to be passed out to students during the last four minutes of a class. Invite students to respond to the following questions: How well do you understand this topic? How has your thinking been changed by today's activities? What can I do to make this topic more comprehensible?

- In the middle of a class, ask students to write a response to the following question on a blank index card: What did you learn so far? Collect the cards, quickly glance at them while students are engaged in a small group discussion (for example) and take a few moments to respond to the information they share.

- For a particularly difficult topic or complex concept, stop every fifteen to twenty minutes and ask students to give you a quick rating of their level of comprehension. Ask them to give you a "thumbs up," "thumbs down," or "thumbs sideways" according to how well they understand the presentation.

- At the beginning of a class, pass out blank index cards to the students. Tell them that sometime during the first half of the lesson you would like them to write down two questions about the topic that they need the answers to. Collect the cards prior to the second half of the class and take time to respond to a selection of representative questions.

Here's a form you may wish to duplicate and use in your own courses:

MID-TERM COURSE EVALUATION

Course Name/Number: _____

Semester: _____

	High/Low
1. How well are you learning the material in this course?	7 6 5 4 3 2 1
2. How would you rate your comprehension of course concepts so far?	7 6 5 4 3 2 1
3. How would you rate your effort in this course so far?	7 6 5 4 3 2 1
4. How many unanswered questions do you have right now?	7 6 5 4 3 2 1
5. How much is the instructor contributing to your learning?	7 6 5 4 3 2 1
6. What is your overall rating of this course so far?	7 6 5 4 3 2 1

End-of-Course Ratings

While performance ratings have their place, you should consider the use of instructional ratings, too. Here's a form you may wish to consider for your courses. Please feel free to modify or adjust this according to the dictates of your discipline or the individual design of your classes.

END OF COURSE EVALUATION

Course Name/Number: _____

Semester: _____

1. How well did this course influence your enjoyment of the subject?
2. How well did this course influence your comprehension of the subject?
3. In what ways did this course cause you to think or interact intellectually with the content?
4. What was the most challenging concept or principle in the course?
5. What did you do to meet that challenge?
6. Comment on how much you learned in this course.
7. Comment on how well you learned in this course.
8. How much did you contribute to the course?

You will notice that in the form above, the emphasis is placed on the students as learners, rather than on the instructor as a performer. The shift in emphasis is enormous and can provide you with valuable data, not only on a course's effectiveness, but also on the need to modify or alter a course based on student learning potential.

Peer Evaluations

Many institutions have a well-embedded peer evaluation system—particularly for adjunct professors. Peer evaluation provides you with observations, input, and suggestions from colleagues in your department or from across the campus. It has proven itself as a viable evaluation technique that yields valuable information about your teaching style as well as student performance.

Peer evaluation is when one or more of your departmental colleagues visit one or several sections of your courses. They observe you and your students and typically provide a written report of their observations. Those observations may form part of your annual review or may be used in matters related to tenure and promotion.

Peer evaluation serves several functions. These may include:

- The promotion of good teaching as a community or all-department concern. Bonds between department members are strengthened when everyone works together for a common cause: the promotion of quality teaching.

- Peer evaluation provides you with non-judgmental input and advice, especially from those faculty members who are long-time members of the department or institution.

- Peer evaluation can alert you to behaviors or practices that may have a negative effect on student learning. Often, these behaviors are not evident to the professor practicing them, but may be detected by impartial observers.

- Peer evaluation frequently turns up issues that students may ignore or be unfamiliar with. These may include communication idiosyncrasies, organizational weaknesses, inappropriate presentation methods, or lack of student attention.

- Peer evaluation can assist you in attaining a balance between professor performance and student learning. It can help you focus more on helping students understand a topic rather than the simple delivery of information to students (often in a lecture format).

Peer evaluation is handled in several different ways, depending on the practices of the institution or a particular department. Here is a typical order of events:

- Meet with the assigned evaluator before a class (one to two days in advance is recommended).

- Share your syllabus with the evaluator. Discuss how the lesson fits in with the overall direction of the course.

- Provide the evaluator with a copy of your lesson plan; what will you be covering and how will you cover it?

- Make sure the evaluator is familiar with the content of the class; its importance to student learning; how it satisfies departmental, institutional, or governmental standards; and traditions of the discipline.

- Provide an appropriate "location" for the evaluator in the classroom. Typically, this will be a desk or table in the back; however, depending on the configuration of the classroom, another location may be more practical.

- It is suggested that you take a few moments to briefly introduce the evaluator to the class. Students will feel more comfortable knowing that the individual is there to assist in the improvement of departmental teaching, not necessarily to evaluate their performance in the class.

- The evaluator will typically record notes on the various activities that take place during the class, including students' reactions to those activities.

- Sometimes, at the end of the class, the evaluator may talk with several students about what took place and their personal evaluations of the class

- Later, typically one to three days after the class, the evaluator will sit down with you to discuss her or his observations as well as suggestions for improvement. Although you may find this to be an anxious time, please keep in mind that your colleague is your ally; she or he is there to assist you in becoming the best instructor possible. They are not there to make you look bad.

You can help the people who evaluate you by giving them a list of specific behaviors or reactions to look for. For example, invite a peer evaluator (during the observation) to respond to some of the following questions:

- How does the instructor help students learn the material?
- How does the instructor foster higher level thinking by students?
- How does the instructor relate new material to previously learned material or to the "real world?"
- What expectations does the instructor have and how does she/he promote those expectations?
- How does the instructor stimulate/encourage the learning of new material?
- Is the quality of student participation and student work commensurate with the objectives of the lesson?
- How is learning fostered both in and out of class?
- Did students learn?

There is convincing evidence that professors tend to evaluate their peers according to their individual philosophies of pedagogy. That is to say, professors will evaluate more favorably those colleagues who teach the way they do and less favorably those colleagues whose teaching style is significantly different.

The success of peer evaluation is founded on several practices. Promote these as part of your own teaching and learning cycle:

- Invite a peer evaluator to visit several different classes during a semester. It's analogous to purchasing a new car. We typically test drive and check out several different models before we make a final decision. Encourage your colleague to see you "drive your car" several times before they reach a conclusion.

- Encourage peer evaluator to spend time with your students. Ask them to pose some questions to the students (see the previous section) and encourage responses.

- Return the favor. Ask if you can sit in on the classes of your peer evaluator. Indicate that you would like to get a 'feel' for her or his philosophy of teaching and how that is accomplished in their classroom.

- Plan regular and systematic meetings with a peer evaluator over the course of the semester. Peer evaluation is not a "one shot" strategy, but one that succeeds when it is done over time.

- Keep the focus on student learning. Use student ratings primarily for your instructional performance. Encourage and emphasize student learning as the critical element of peer evaluations.

Self Evaluation, Self Reflection

Throughout this book I have tried to focus on the concept of "professor as learner." That means a professor who guides rather than leads, facilitates rather than assigns, and models rather than tells. After nearly four decades of collegiate teaching experience, I've learned that the most successful professors are those who are willing to learn alongside their students—providing students with the processes and the supportive arena in which they can begin to make their own discoveries and pursue their own self-initiated investigations.

Throughout this book we have looked at all the attributes and all the qualities of good professors. But, I'd like to save the best for last. That is, a good professor is also a reflective professor. A reflective professor is one who thinks as much as acts and one who is constantly searching for self-improvement.

Professors who reflect are professors who are open to change. Reflective educators do lots of self-assessment, and, in doing so, they help their students grow both as scholars and as individuals. Here are some reflective qualities essential to your success as a college teacher:

- Be open minded to new ideas and new possibilities.

- Think about the reason and rationale for every task and assignment.

- Be willing to take responsibility for your actions. If students aren't learning, it may not be entirely their fault.

- Be open to improvement on both major and minor issues.

- Regularly assess your teaching philosophy.

- Make time for regular periods of self-questioning.

Your success as an adjunct professor should not be based solely on how well your students perform on a mid-term or final exam. It should not be based on what your students think about you as a teacher or as a human being. Rather, your success should be based primarily on how students are able to use the information you taught them in both their chosen profession as well as in their personal lives. For me, I am less concerned with my "academic popularity" and more interested in how I was able to change students for the better. If the change is positive, then I'm a "happy camper." If not, then I still have some work to do!

CHAPTER 22:

The Successful Adjunct Professor —You!

Throughout this book I have talked about the qualities, attributes and dynamics of successful college teaching. Undoubtedly, you saw some of your own college professors in the pages of this book. You saw individuals who inspired you in your graduate work, people who made an indelible impact on your interest and passion for a particular field, and educators who were inspiring as well as caring. Your current position as an adjunct professor may well have been determined by the efforts of one or two significant individuals in your educational past.

What did those people do that influenced you current career path? What attributes did they display on a regular and consistent basis? In this final chapter, we'll consider those characteristics. Most important, you will learn how you can make those attributes your own, how to become an effective adjunct professor—a teacher your students will remember long after they leave your institution.

What is it that makes some adjunct professors excellent teachers and others slightly less memorable? That's a question I've been asking for almost forty years, so I decided to go to the experts: college students. As part of my periodic survey of undergraduate students, I've frequently asked them about their criteria for effective adjunct instructors. Here's a sampling of responses from the past few years:

"Good adjunct professors . . ."

- ". . . are eager and willing to work with students."
- ". . . are knowledgeable about their subject and can present it in an organized fashion."
- ". . . display lots of enthusiasm for their discipline and for teaching."
- ". . . are willing to admit their faults, shortcomings, and mistakes."
- ". . . are able to use a variety of teaching technique to help me learn a topic."
- ". . . have a sense of humor."
- ". . . encourage student opinions (right or wrong) and provide opportunities for classroom discussions."
- ". . . have high expectations for students and work with them to achieve those standards."
- ". . . are respectful of my needs and honest with their opinions."
- ". . . are able to relate the content of the course to our lives."
- ". . . are available outside of class to discuss course issues and/or personal concerns."
- ". . . treats students as adults, not as children."

Each year, when I ask students for the number-one quality of a good adjunct professor, they all say that the most important quality is a passion for teaching. That characteristic holds true irrespective of the discipline, field or department. The bottom line: excitement about teaching was the single most significant quality of any college professor.

It's important to point out that your effectiveness as an adjunct professor is dependent on much more than your knowledge of your specific discipline. In fact, your success will be driven by characteristics and dynamics that are as much a part of who you are as they are of your classroom instruction.

Conversations with scores of post-secondary colleagues around the country indicate that good adjuncts are effective because of the interaction of five distinguishing characteristics:

1. Individual accountability
2. Student orientation
3. A critical learning environment
4. Constructivist orientation
5. Learning as a lifelong process

I invite you to consider these characteristics in terms of your own personality dynamics as well as in terms of your reasons for becoming an adjunct professor.

Individual Accountability

The reasons you are an adjunct instructor are undoubtedly many. Who you are as a person and how you would like to share your knowledge with college students are significant determinants in why your chose this position. So too, will they be significant in terms of your success in the classroom. My own experiences with fellow college teachers has taught me that the personality of a teacher is a major and predominant factor in the success of students within that teacher's influence. Here are some factors to consider:

- **Learn the Culture.** Your success in the classroom may be determined by how much you know about the institution(s) at which you teach. Learn the culture of the institution; every college has its own unique set of traditions, customs, and practices. At the very least, you should be aware of the mission of the institution, the long-range plans of the institution, and the core values that shape the daily life of the institution. Here are some specific ideas:

- Read the college catalog from cover to cover. If you don't understand something, be sure to ask.

- Watch the local newspaper for articles and information about the college. How is the institution viewed in the local community?

- Find out if there is an orientation program for adjunct faculty. Plan to attend all the sessions scheduled for just such a program and read all the materials distributed. This can be one of the most beneficial ways to learn about the college and its expectations for instructors both full-time and part-time.

- Talk to students informally about some of the traditions of the college. Who's the big rival? What do students do on the weekends? Is it a party school?

- Talk to colleagues in your department whenever possible. When time allows, have a cup of coffee or lunch with members of the department. What do they talk about? What do they think about the administration or the student body?

- Read the faculty handbook, advising manual, student handbook, and other documents prepared by the institution. Can you discern the institution's philosophy from these publications?

- If practical, attend athletic contests, visiting speakers, guest lecturers, concerts, and other extra-curricular activities.

The key is to know as much about the institution as you can. The more you know, the better you will be able to "fit into" the culture of this particular college.

- **Connect with Your Department.** In your role as an adjunct professor, it is quite easy to feel "out of touch" with the institution as well as with the members of the department in which you are teaching. Working to establish and maintain good relationships with department members can go a long way towards ensuring success—both in the classroom and outside. Consider the following:

  - Whenever possible, talk with members of the department (full-time and part-time) in a variety of informal conversations. Talk about the weather, a recent political situation, or the status of students.

  - Ask if you can attend department meetings (if your schedule allows). Listen to the various topics and challenges under discussion. If allowed, volunteer your views and perspectives.

  - If practical, volunteer your services to the department. Can you put together a newsletter or blog for the department? Can you offer some type of technological support? Because of your expertise, can you help design a new course? Do you have "contacts" out in the community that could be tapped by department members?

  - Stay in touch with your department chair. Keep that individual informed about your availability for future courses as well as your progress in teaching your current course(s). Stop by the department office every once in a while to say "Hi."

- **Get a Mentor.** One of the most effective ways you can help yourself both as a teacher and as a colleague is to find someone who is willing to act as your mentor. Not only can a mentor keep you up-to-date on classroom procedures and institutional policies, that individual can also help you feel more comfortable in the academic community. Here are some ideas to consider:

  - Find out if your institution has a mentoring program for adjunct faculty. Contact the individual (typically, another faculty member) in charge of the program and ask to be assigned a mentor.

- Talk with your department chair about the possibility of being assigned a mentor from within the department. Is there someone who would be willing to take you "under their wing" for your first semester or academic year?

- Talk with full-time department members. Is there someone who would be willing to work with you on teaching methodologies, course design, or syllabus construction?

- Consider having a mentor from another department. Not only will you obtain varied perspectives and viewpoints from an "outsider," you will gain a fresh outlook on ways to effectively teach undergraduates.

- Look into any faculty development opportunities on your campus. Many institutions have a Faculty Development Office or a special faculty committee devoted to faculty enhancement. Investigate the possibilities of working with one or more individuals associated with those endeavors.

RESEARCH POINT

Observations of successful college classrooms reveal that the professor's knowledge of the subject is of considerably less importance (to student learning) than her or his energy for teaching the subject.

Student Orientation

If you were to walk into the classroom of any outstanding college instructor, irrespective of her or his discipline or experience, one thing will become immediately clear: students are respected, trusted, and honored. These are classrooms where the professor is not lecturing from atop a marble pedestal, but rather down interacting on a personal level with students.

Students need to know that they will never be embarrassed or ridiculed. Nor will they be intimidated or shown excessive favoritism. The best teachers are those who have positive attitudes about everyone in the course. High expectations abound for each and every student and successful teachers create a learning environment in which those expectations can be realized.

Good college teachers are listeners. Good teachers know that students have much to contribute to the curriculum and to each other and provide numerous opportunities for them to do so. Or as a colleague once told me, "Good teaching often means opening your ears and closing your mouth!" Another colleague put it this way: "The connection between students and the teacher is what makes a good class. Professors should always be looking for relationships between events in students' lives and the course content. The event may be family, work, weekend parties, world news, or a campus function. Strive to make the connection and you can always make an impact."

Outstanding teachers know that students bring background knowledge, perceptions, preconceptions, and a certain degree of misinformation to any course. They do not see this as an "intellectual deficit," but rather an opportunity to build bridges of understanding between what students know (or think they know) and the concepts of a course. This is the foundation for comprehension development irrespective of course, subject, or topic. Those bridges can be initiated with some of the following:

- "What did you find most interesting about today's reading?"

- "What surprised you in the chapter you read for today?"

- "What do you think of when I say 'respiration' or 'Marxism' or 'latitude' (or any other key concept or term)?"

- "In your own words, describe a cell (or "jazz" or "surrealism" or "Particularism")."

- "Here are two positions on abortion (or "existentialism" or "global warming" or "customer service"). Which one do you favor and why?"

- "If you could say one thing to the author of this article, what would it be?"

Good college teachers raise questions without easy answers. They ask, "How do we know. . .? Why do we believe this? How does this relate to what we already know? When would you need to know this? How can we prove. . .? These teachers join their students in an intellectual partnership—an intellectual journey of discovery with tough questions and few pat answers.

Good college teachers know that they can significantly increase student engagement in the learning process by incorporating students' ideas in classroom discussions by:

- Using student ideas by repeating nouns and logical connections.
- Rephrasing student ideas in teacher words.
- Using student ideas to take the next step in problem solving.
- Drawing relationships between student ideas and information shared earlier.
- Using what students say as a summary of important concepts.

Here's how another colleague put it: "I can facilitate student learning best when I help them build scaffolds, or frameworks, that enhance their critical and creative thinking. By blending their ideas with course concepts, I help them develop new ways of thinking. There may be less content, but there's certainly more process."

Critical Learning Environment

Good adjunct professors "pepper" each class with an array of higher-level questions that help students apply, analyze, synthesize, and evaluate content. They use questions to arouse curiosity, stimulate thinking and engage students in an active model of discovery. Rather than falling into traditional models of teaching in which all the answers are provided, effective professors make good questioning their instructional priority. In short, knowledge is never static, rather it is the dynamic process coupled with knowledge that makes lessons productive and intellectually stimulating.

Good teachers provide opportunities for students to generate their own questions for discovery. However, instead of falling into the trap of providing answers to those self-initiated queries, effective teachers help students discover the answers for themselves. Self-discovery has more lasting implications and effects that simply telling students the answers.

Good professors provide opportunities for students to relate the content to their personal lives. Having a "head full of facts" is considerably less important than the ability to use that information to solve problems in one's personal or professional life. Good teachers ask students to draw their own conclusions and to defend the choices they make with the following queries:

- "Why do you think that way?"
- "What evidence do you have?"
- "How can you defend your position?"
- "Why is your thinking or position important?"
- "What unanswered questions still remain?"

AN EXPERT OPINION

One of my colleagues puts it this way: "I like to present material as a topic of debate. For example, 'Here's information some people think is true. What do you think? Let's look at this together.' When the discussion comes out of them, it's stronger learning. Also, I'm not afraid to ask questions I don't really know the answers to."

Effective teachers also know what students need, and they know how to provide for those needs. That means good lesson planning. Here are some "markers" you can use to evaluate the appropriateness of your lessons:

- Students know the purpose of the lesson.

- The background knowledge of students is assessed frequently and regularly and is used to help direct the lesson.

- Structuring comments or advance organizers are at the beginning of the lesson.

- The lesson is logical, clear, and understandable.

- Examples, illustrations, and demonstrations are used liberally.

- Group and individual activities are provided.

- Practice and feedback is regular and systematic.

- Student questions and comments are incorporated into the lesson.

- A variety of instructional activities and instructional materials are woven throughout a lesson.

- Thinking skills are emphasized, and higher order questions are used.

Constructivist Orientation

Good adjunct instructors enjoin students in a process of discovery, exploration, and inquiry. They eschew a transmission model of teaching—one in which students are merely vessels into which the professor pours all her or his vast amounts of knowledge. Rather, good teachers embrace a teaching model that provides students with responsibilities, challenges, and a measure of self-determination.

Good teachers know that learning is not simply the accumulation of knowledge (which is passive), but rather how we make sense of knowledge. Constructivism recognizes that knowledge is created in the mind of the learner. Professors help students relate new content to the knowledge they already know. In addition, students have opportunities to process and apply that knowledge in meaningful situations (sometimes called "hands-on, minds-on" learning).

Good adjunct professors promote the idea that knowledge is never a product, rather it is a process. How we learn is intrinsically more important than what we learn. For college students, this is a critical factor in the academic success they enjoy in a course as well as the intellectual experiences they can carry with them well after then course is over.

> **AN EXPERT OPINION**
>
> One colleague puts it this way: "I design my classes with interaction. It's not so much the content—I don't jam them with vast quantities of information—but rather how we process it. I want students to know how science is done; I want them to focus on the process."

Learning as a Lifelong Process

Good adjunct professors are those who keep learning, those who continually add to their knowledge base throughout their teaching career. My lifelong motto has always been: "Good teachers have as much to learn as they do to teach." Your education doesn't stop just because you have a graduate degree. It means that if you are to provide the best possible education for your students, then you need to provide yourself with a variety of lifelong learning opportunities, too.

Good adjuncts keep current, stay active, and continually seek out new answers or new questions for exploration. Your desire to find out more about effective teaching methods and dynamic new discoveries within your field can add immeasurably to your talents as a teacher and can also add to your students' appreciation of your discipline in their own lives.

Your success as an adjunct professor can be ensured when you consider and plan long term goals. Whether you are teaching one course at a single college or a multiplicity of courses at several institutions, you need to devote some time to "career planning" strategies that will continue to enhance your teaching effectiveness as well as your personal growth and development as a college instructor.

Based on conversations with adjunct instructors at several institutions, as well as faculty development plans in place at select colleges and universities, here is a self-evaluation paradigm for your consideration:

PERSONAL DEVELOPMENT PLAN

» Short-term Goals: What do you hope to accomplish in the next one to two years?

» Long-term Goals: What do you hope to accomplish in the next three to five years?

» What college/university services will help you accomplish those goals?

» What off-campus services will help you accomplish your goals?

» What funding requirements will help you accomplish your goals?

» What technology training will you need?

» What workshops or seminars are you planning to attend? In the next year? In the next two years? In the next five years?

» In what departmental activities do you plan to participate (retreats, departmental meetings, workshops)?

» What grants or other funding resources will you apply for?

» What additional education or training will you need?

» What community resources, contacts, or materials will you need?

» What professional conferences or meetings do you plan to attend?

» What travel will be necessary to maintain or upgrade your skills?

» What special writing or research opportunities will you pursue?

» What members of the department will you consult?

» How will you monitor your progress?

Creating a personal development plan can be a critical step in your journey as an adjunct professor. Besides providing specific personal and professional goals, it underscores the resources necessary for your current and continuing success. Having a "plan of action" can make you a more effective teacher and your students more successful learners.

BONUS CHAPTER:

How to Get an Adjunct Professor Position

According to some estimates, the need for adjunct professors is expected to grow by nineteen percent through the mid 2020's. This is due in large measure to increased enrollment rates in both public and private colleges in concert with ever-tightening budgets at most institutions of higher education. Most colleges depend on adjunct professors to deal with the financial constraints associated with hiring full-time professors. Adjunct instructors can bring their unique professional experiences into an academic department without a substantial outlay of financial resources on the part of the institution. Adjuncts add layers of experiences, philosophies, perspectives, and insights in a most cost-effective way for any college or university.

Suffice it to say, the role and contributions of adjunct professors is important for every institution. A college needs instructors, and these positions allow folks with a diversity of backgrounds to enhance and compliment the educational offerings for undergraduates in every academic department.

The Hard Realities

The roles and responsibilities of an adjunct professor are always changing and tentative. What seems secure today may be gone tomorrow. What looks financially stable in the present may be economically insecure in the future. What appears to be a positive contribution to the lives of young people now may be a professional challenge of superhuman proportions down the road. In short, adjunct professors have few guarantees, but many certainties. Here is what you can expect as an adjunct professor:

- You are not on the tenure-track; in short, there is no job guarantee from one semester to the next.
- You will, most likely, teach introductory freshmen courses at odd hours (evening), odd days (Saturday), and odd places (an unused office building off-campus).
- Your compensation will be lower than that of full-time professors
- There will be no health or retirement benefits.
- You will probably not have a desk or designated office space.
- You may not have administrative assistant support.
- Your schedule is always subject to change from semester to semester and even from week to week.
- You may have little or no interaction with other members of your department.
- You may feel isolated, alone, and "left to your own devises" in designing your assigned courses.

- You'll have a lot of fun.

Long before I began my position as a tenure-track faculty member, I dipped my toes in the adjunct waters. I taught courses at three different institutions while maintaining a full-time job. I taught one course once a week at an institution an hour-and-a-half away from where I worked, and by the time I got home at 11:30 on those Wednesday evenings, I was exhausted, tired, and intellectually drained. But I loved it! I was aware of all the potential negatives of adjunct teaching, but I also saw it as a unique opportunity to "taste" college teaching - something I desired for quite some time. More important, I saw the unique and distinctive ways in which I could help young people achieve their occupational dreams. It cemented my love of teaching and eventually propelled me into a thirty-year career as a full-time professor.

Are You Qualified?

Many folks interested in applying for an adjunct teaching position wonder if they have the necessary skills, talents, and qualifications for the job. Well, I've searched the literature, pored over some extensive research, interviewed colleagues and associates from coast to coast, and tapped in to the experiences of administrators at institutions both large and small. "What qualities make for a good adjunct professor?" was the universal question I posed. All that data, surprisingly, can be boiled down into fourteen distinctive elements. I've presented them for you in the self-assessment chart below. Review each one and indicate whether or not you possess that skill-set ("Yes," or "No"). If you discover a preponderance of affirmative responses, then you may also discover, as I did, that you possess the necessary qualifications to apply for and succeed as an adjunct professor.

MID-TERM COURSE EVALUATION

Qualification	Do I have this skill?
1. A passion for teaching.	YES ❏ NO ❏
2. A desire to make a difference in the lives of young people.	YES ❏ NO ❏
3. An ability to communicate effectively.	YES ❏ NO ❏
4. Specific skills and experience in my designated field.	YES ❏ NO ❏
5. A passion for my academic field.	YES ❏ NO ❏
6. A student orientation.	YES ❏ NO ❏
7. An intense love of learning.	YES ❏ NO ❏
8. Flexibility—able to "roll with the punches"	YES ❏ NO ❏
9. An ability to serve as a positive role model	YES ❏ NO ❏
10. Technological savvy (e.g. PowerPoint, Word, social me-dia)	YES ❏ NO ❏
11. Educational background (typically, a master's degree)	YES ❏ NO ❏
12. High energy level.	YES ❏ NO ❏
13. Sense of humor.	YES ❏ NO ❏
14. Enthusiasm and motivation.	YES ❏ NO ❏

How did you do? I suspect that if you are reading this book (which you got for a specific reason), then you probably have an abundance of "YES" checked off on the scale above. What does that mean? Is it easy being an adjunct professor? No! What it does mean is that, if you have a certain set of occupational or professional skills you can effectively and inspirational-ly share with college-age students, then you have the basic qualifications to be an adjunct professor. The refinement of those skills and the strategies necessary to make that educational experience productive for students are what the previous twenty-two chapters of this book are all about.

What About Teaching Experience?

One of the persistent questions that always arises whenever someone is considering an adjunct teaching position is, "What kind of teaching experience do I need in order to secure the position?" As we will soon discover, you may already have the necessary experiences that make you a highly qualified adjunct professor.

For most full-time (tenure-track) positions, professors are typically required to have a terminal degree or doctorate (e.g. Ph.D, Ed.D, D.Ed, etc.). For community college, technical college, and part-time instructors, the academic requirements are slightly different. For most of these positions, a master's degree is usually sufficient. In some cases, due to mandated accreditation requirements, instructors may also be required to have professional certifications in order to teach courses in real estate, specific medical fields, education, accounting, computer technology, or nursing (as examples). In a few cases, experience in a very specialized field in combination with an associate's degree may be sufficient for employment.

For most adjunct positions, education and experience are satisfactory requirements for a teaching position. Having prior teaching experience is a bonus not just in the classroom, but even more importantly as a skill set to share during the application and interview process. You may be surprised to learn that formal educational training or formal classroom teaching experience, while desirable, are not strict requirements for an adjunct position. In fact, it is highly likely you have some informal teaching experiences that can be highlighted on your resume, your cover letter, and during the interview process that will distinguish you as candidate worthy of serious consideration.

Following is a partial list of lifetime experiences that come under the category of "teaching experiences." Review this brief collection in terms of your own personal experiences and how those experiences could be highlighted in your application materials AND job interview to underscore your qualifications for a teaching position.

- Work as a teaching or graduate assistant in a master's program.
- Making formal presentations at your company
- Experience as a trainer in an industrial setting
- Giving a speech at your local Rotary or Kiwanis organization
- Lay preacher at your local church
- Work with a Scout troop
- Writing a training manual for new recruits in an local industry
- Guiding a hike or kayaking venture for a local environmental group
- Leading meetings, conferences, seminars, or colloquia
- Sharing information at a local school board meeting or civic group
- Speaking at a local school
- Running for public office

For the time being, let's assume you have little or no formal teaching experience. You do, however, have other experiences that demonstrate your ability to guide a group of people to learn something or do something (as indicated in the list above). How could you use that informal experience to your advantage when applying for a formal teaching position as an adjunct professor? Good question! Let's answer by sharing a sample cover letter one (fictitious) applicant included with his application materials. In spite of his lack of formal teaching experiences, this letter showcased relevant instructional skills that established him as a worthy candidate—one who would make any administrator sit up and take notice of his unique qualifications for the advertised position.

RALPH J. BURDETT
86395 Bison Road, Manville, WY 82227 • (307) 555-9999 (H) • (307) 555-6666 (C) • rjburdett@xxx.net

April 2, 20__

Dr. Leroy Smithton, Chair
Department of Biology
High Plains College
420 Cottonwood Drive
Lusk, WY 82225

Re: Adjunct Professor (Introduction to Ecology)

Dear Dr. Smithton:
"The whole art of teaching is only the art of awakening the natural curiosity of young minds for the purpose of satisfying it afterwards." —Anatole France

In a recent post on the Department of Biology blog, you stated that one of the chief responsibilities of the Department was to stimulate and encourage the natural curiosity of all High Plains students taking life science courses. As you will note in the enclosed resume, I am passionate about inquiry-based biology, higher level thinking, and purposeful question-asking. I have had several unique opportunities where I have worked with individuals in diverse educational endeavors. My goal in these ventures is to create highly interactive and inquisitive biological experiences that promote self-discovery and self-direction.

Beyond my day-to-day responsibilities as a senior research scientist with the Niobrara County Environmental Consortium, I've also been involved in a number of educational ventures including the following:

- Worked with teachers at Niobrara County High School on the annual statewide Envirothon.
- Addressed county commissioners on environmental issues and concerns.
- Led Sagebrush Grasslands Outings for the Sierra Club Wyoming Chapter.
- Developed ecology workshops and field trips for scouts in Scout Troop #346.
- Served as a consultant to the Wyoming Stock Growers Association.
- Guest speaker at Rotary International on environmental issues

As epitomized in the quote above, I continue to strive to "awaken" and "satisfy" a natural curiosity in ecological matters and initiatives—both for myself as well as for others.

Please refer to the enclosed resume for further details of my training, skills, and educational commitment. In that regard, I look forward to the opportunity of working closely with the Biology Department in addressing your immediate educational goals. Thank you for your time and attention, and I look forward to hearing from you soon.

Sincerely,
Ralph J. Burdett

It is clear that this applicant took the time to write a letter that underscores his unique educational experiences (even though he has had no formal teacher training or classroom experiences). This is a letter which highlights a commitment to teaching, rather than one apologizing for a lack of formal training. In concert with a resume that outlines his formal education (e.g. B.S. and M.S. in Biology) and work experience after graduation, this candidate has established himself as a potential instructor with much to offer undergraduate students.

Here's the bottom line: lack of formal teaching experience is not a major deterrent to getting an adjunct professor position at local college or university. That "deficit" can be compensated for with a positive attitude, a commitment to teaching college students, education and skills relevant to the position, and an availability to teach (e.g. evenings, Saturday mornings, etc.) when specific courses are offered. In my conversations with many department chairs in various disciplines at institutions across the country, the prevailing determinant in obtaining a teaching position as an adjunct instructor was the quality of both verbal and interpersonal skills an applicant displays during the interview process. Strong communication abilities can more than offset any perceived deficits in formal teaching experiences. Improving your interviewing skills will go a long way to ensuring a "Congratulations, you got the job! How soon can you start?" than anything else.

A Suggested Sequence

Let's take a look at a sequence of planned activities that will assist you in getting an adjunct professor position. You will quickly note that these suggestions are more general than they are specific. That's simply because every institution has its own procedures, rules and expectations regarding the hiring of part-time instructor. What holds true for one institution may not hold true for another. While the guidelines suggested below will work for most situations, your first-hand knowledge of your local college or university (and a specific department) will go a long way to ensuring your success in any job search.

1. **Background Information.** One of the questions many people ask is, "What is the best time to apply for an adjunct professor position?" The simple answer is, "anytime!" There is no specific hiring "season" for adjunct instructors; they are often hired throughout the year as budgets shrink and expand and as the student popula-

tion shrinks and expands. Unlike the more formal hiring "season" (late fall/early spring) for tenure-track faculty members, adjunct professors are interviewed and hired on an ongoing basis throughout the year. So, when is the best time to apply? Right now!

It's also important to remember that the hiring of adjuncts in normally not done as a function of the larger institution, but rather in response to the specific needs of an individual department. As a result, each academic department determines how many adjuncts it needs and what courses they will be assigned to teach. In many cases, this changes from semester to semester and certainly from year to year. In short, know that there is no "perfect time" to apply for an adjunct teaching position.

2. **Advance Preparation.** One of the best things you can do in advance of applying for any potential teaching positions is to make yourself known to the members of a specific academic department. Keep in mind that hiring part-time instructors is considerably more informal than hiring full-time faculty. By establishing your presence, commitment, and qualifications over an extended period of time, you can establish yourself as worthy addition to the teaching ranks long before any formal application and interview takes place. Here are a few suggestions for your consideration:

- Schedule a face-to-face meeting with a department chair. This should be an informal conversation to let that individual know who you are, some of your qualifications, and your desire to teach sometime in the near future. You may wish to drop off a copy of your curriculum vita (CV) during the conversation.

- Ask about the possibility of observing one or two classes. Since many adjuncts are assigned introductory courses, ask about the possibility of sitting in on one of the courses normally scheduled for freshmen. If possible, take some time afterwards to talk with the instructor about some of the content shared in her/his presentation.

- Contact one or two full-time individuals in a department and schedule an informal meeting (treat them to a cup of coffee) to talk about what is happening in a specific discipline or some of the challenges they face in teaching specific subject matter.

- Offer to serve on a departmental committee. When I was chair of my department, I sometimes invited people from the local community to join us for a meeting regarding a new initiative or directive. That "outside perspective" gave me some information important in structuring certain courses or an entire program.

- Connect with as many people in an academic department as possible. Volunteer to be a guest speaker in their classes, ask them for some assistance in a project you are working on, or inform them of documents or materials you have that you would be willing to share.

- Consider teaching a continuing education, career training, or personal enrichment course offered by the college. Even better: propose a new course that has never been offered before. This will help establish your credentials as an expert as well as give you valuable teaching experience that will enhance any future job openings in a specific department.

- If you are working in a local industry, consider partnering with a local college by offering students academic-based internships. Establish yourself as the "go-to" person for assisting students with career-related experiences at your place of employment. Many academic departments on campus also have career advisory boards on which you can volunteer to serve.

3. **Getting Your Act Together.** This is the time to do all those things necessary to securing a traditional job. Basically, you need to prepare your CV (curriculum vita), write a compelling cover letter, assemble a list of references, and bone up on your interviewing skills. Here are a few suggestions to consider:

- Unlike individuals who are applying for tenure-track positions, it is not necessary to focus on items such as books published, articles written, research conducted, or contributions to professional organizations. You will be considered for a teaching position and those doing the hiring are more interested in your competencies as an instructor than they are in your "formal" agenda. It is far better to emphasize your teaching experience and the credentials you have in your discipline than it is to try and impress with a long list of publications, for example.

- Begin formulating your cover letter. If you have a deficit of formal teaching experience, highlight your informal experiences: coaching, mentoring, leading workshops, designing programs, or volunteer work (see the sample cover letter earlier in this chapter). If you have some formal classroom experience, be sure to emphasize that early in the letter so that it catches the eye of the reader. There are many excellent internet resources on how to compose an outstanding cover letter, including:

    - www.resumegenius.com
    - www.uptowork.com/blog
    - www.livecareer.com
    - www.monster.com
    - www.themuse.com/advice
    - www.indeed.com

- In selecting your references, consider contacts who can attest to your ability to lead a group of people. While teaching experience is valuable, it is not the sole requisite for an adjunct teaching position. Consider listing references who can attest to your ability to conduct informative staff meetings, lead groups of people in activities as diverse as a weekend hike or a political campaign, work together to craft a new project or occupational document, or head up a volunteer group in the local community. Teaching college is about managing people and helping them obtain new skills or knowledge. Select references who can highlight those aspects of your job, volunteer activities, or service in your town or community.

- Much of the emphasis on getting an adjunct professor position will rest on the interview. This is the one chance you have to impress an administrator, department chair, or dean with your personality, teaching abilities, communication skills, and dedication to the education of college students. There are numerous resources, both in print and on the internet, available to help you put your best foot forward in any interview. Take the time to hone your interviewing skills, and you will be doing yourself a tremendous favor in securing an adjunct position. Here are a few outstanding and time-tested references for your consideration:

  - *101 Great Answers to the Toughest Interview Questions* by Ron Fry
  - *Ace Your Teacher Interview: 149 Fantastic Answers to Tough Interview Questions* by Anthony D. Fredericks
  - *Get That Job! The Quick and Complete Guide to a Winning Interview* by Thea Kelly
  - *How to Answer Interview Questions: 101 Tough Interview Questions* by Peggy McKee
  - *Knock 'em Dead Job Interview: How to Turn Job Interview into Job Offers* by Martin Yate
  - *What I Wish Every Job Candidate Knew: 15 Minutes to a Better Interview* by Russell Tuckerton

4. **Into the Fray.** In most cases, adjunct professor positions are not advertised. Since they come up at all times of the year, they become available (often on short notice) and are frequently filled because

"someone knows someone." The process is, at best informal, and frequently lacks all the pomp and circumstance of a standard full-time occupational opening. In many cases, a position opens up suddenly, a faculty member has a friend or is familiar with someone in the community, a quick interview is scheduled, and the position is filled. All this may take place in a matter of days, instead of the usual weeks and months associated with full-time positions.

How can you use this scenario to your advantage? Here are three suggestions that can go a long way to helping you out:

- Let everyone you know that you are looking for a part-time teaching position. Take advantage of social media and "advertise" the fact that you would enjoy teaching a course at the local college or university. Broadcast to all your friends and associates that you "are in the market" for an adjunct teaching position and ask them to share that with all their contacts, too. Keep this networking active and constant. Many adjunct positions are filled because of a social connection, more so than a professional one.

- Follow the suggestions above regarding the establishment and maintenance of contacts at the local college or university. Again, ask if you could do a guest lecture, work with a college intern, contribute to a committee assignment. Stay in touch with people in a specific department and when adjunct positions open up, you will likely be one of the first people contacted.

- Find out who is in charge of hiring adjuncts within a particular academic department. Pull up a department's website and locate the person in charge of hiring. It may be a dean, a department chair, or a full-time faculty member who has this assignment. If no one is listed, call the administrative assistant and ask who you might contact. Send an email or make a phone call and ask if you might stop by to drop off your CV and list of references. It would be critical to meet this individual in person so that she or he can put a face to a name. This is a wonderful opportunity to indicate that you are interested in working for the department. Since this is not a formal "interview" meeting, keep it short and sweet (say, ten minutes or less).

> **QUOTE**
>
> According to Jill Carroll, who runs the website www.adjunctsolutions.com, "Avoid human-resources departments if at all possible because of the likelihood that your application will get filed away or set aside or otherwise lost."

One of the best things you can do for yourself is to be consistent and constant. In other words, contact an individual or department on a regular basis (my suggestion: once a semester) and let them know of your interest and availability. These contacts can take the form of an email, short phone call, or quick personal visit. Of course, all of your contacts should be polite, cordial, and friendly (It is not necessary to "Friend" these individuals on Facebook.). Just let them know you are still available and still interested. By the same token, let them know you are also willing to contribute to the department via guest lectures or other volunteer work. These efforts will keep you "front and center" in the minds of department members, and when adjunct positions become available, you will, most likely, be the first one considered.

Often, getting an adjunct teaching position is a matter of "being in the right place at the right time." Waiting for a job to be advertised by the Human Resources Department at your local college or university may be counterproductive to actually getting a job. Success often depends on being a proactive agent for yourself. Let your community of friends and associates know of your interest, initiate and maintain contacts with a specific academic department, and be patient. You may discover, as I did and as many adjunct professors across the country have, that your success in getting a teaching position often boils down to what you do long before a position becomes available.

I wish you all the best in your venture!

APPENDIX A: PROFESSIONAL RESOURCES

BOOKS

If you are looking for additional books (other than this one) about becoming a successful adjunct professor, here are some possibilities. You will quickly note, however, that this list is quite short. Unfortunately, I discovered a dearth of available resources (one of the main reasons why I wrote this book) to assist people in succeeding as an adjunct instructor. However, these titles may offer you some additional perspectives.

- *A Handbook for Adjunct/Part-Time Faculty and Teachers of Adults,* Donald Greive & Patricia Lesko, Part Time Press.
- *Adjunct Teaching Online & On-Campus: How to Make Up To 6-Figures and More as an Adjunct Professor,* Howard Rubin and Daniel Hall, Create Space
- *Confessions of an Accidental Professor,* Lisa del Rosso, Serving House Books
- *Happy Professor: An Adjunct Instructor's Guide to Personal, Financial, and Student Success,* Erin Lovell Ebanks, Create Space
- *The Adjunct Professor's Guide to Success: Surviving and Thriving in the College Classroom,* Marcella L. Kysilka and George E. Pawlas, Allyn and Bacon

ORGANIZATIONS

There are a few professional organizations which can assist you in honing your skills as an adjunct professor. You are invited to check out these groups as a way of establishing some vital networks to support your teaching.

- Adjunct Nation: https://www.adjunctnation.com
- American Association of Adjunct Education: adjuncteducation.weebly.com
- Society of Certified Adjunct Faculty Educators: www.socafe.org

RESOURCES ON THE INTERNET

This list is a brief compilation of additional resources that can both inform and educate you on the dynamics of adjunct professors. You'll discover lots of valuable information and insightful tips.

- Adjunct Action:actionnetwork.org/groups/adjunct-action
- Burnt-out Adjunct: burntoutadjunct.wordpress.com
- Higher Ed Hub: www.higher-ed.org
- Professional Adjunct: proadjunct.com/blog
- The Adjunct Nation: www.adjunctnation.com/category/nation-blogs
- The Chronicle of Higher Education: www.chronicle.com/Blogs
- The Homeless Adjunct: junctrebellion.wordpress.com
- The Professor is In: theprofessorisin.com/category/adjunct-issues
- The Teaching Professor: www.magnapubs.com/newsletter/the-teaching-professor-2907-1.html

TWITTER RESOURCES

There are several Twitter resources that will provide you with up-to-the-minute information and data regarding adjunct teaching. Consider the following as part of your overall preparation for, and survival in, your role as an adjunct professor:

- Adjunct Twitter: @AdjunctAction
- Faculty Forward: @FacultyForward
- Guardian Higher Education Network: @GdnHigherEd
- New Faculty Majority: @ NewFacMajority

APPENDIX B: SAMPLE SYLLABI

A syllabus is the backbone of any college course. It details (for students) your responsibilities are as well as theirs. It clearly states your expectations and the methods students can employ to satisfactorily satisfy those standards. For that reason, syllabi should be clear, definitive, and precise.

What follows are several (slightly abbreviated) course syllabi from college teachers in a variety of disciplines. They are presented as outlines of what your syllabi can look like. You are encouraged to review them as examples of different designs, delivery systems, and course requirements.

HISTORY 200

The American Experience
Professor: Norma Leigh Lucid
Office: XXX
E-mail: XXX
Hours: XXX

HIST 200 fulfills the General Education requirement in Category I: Western Culture and Traditions, which is designed to "introduce students to the norms and patterns of civilizations associated with the Greco-Roman and European traditions and the legacy of those traditions in North America" and to "stress concepts, values, and events in Western history that have shaped contemporary American and European civilization." As we work to satisfy the intellectual and methodological requirements of this GE category, we hope to provide you with a useful perspective on the nation's past—a central feature of any solid liberal arts education, and, with the family history project, a historical perspective on your personal past.

I. Readings:
- Divine, Robert, et al. *The American Story*, 2nd Edition.
- Nash, Roderick and Graves, Gregory. *From These Beginnings*. Vol. I and II
- Periodic handouts of documents to be used in discussion sessions.
- II. Course Requirements:
- Three essay exams will be given—two in-term exams and a final exam.
- A research paper of 15+ pages on your family's personal history over the past few generations.
- All students are required to enroll and participate in one of the weekly discussion sections [led by Teaching Assistants].
- For those interested, credit for participation in the Joint Educational Project (JEP) is an option.
- Each requirement of the course will contribute to your final grade as follows: First Exam: 15%; Second Exam: 20%; Final Exam: 25%; Discussion Sections: 20%; Family History Project: 20%.

III. Tentative Lecture Schedule
1. Background and Beginnings
2. Patterns of Colonial Life
3. From Colonies to Provinces; Coming of Revolution
4. The Family History Project
5. The Revolution and Constitution
6. First Hour Exam
7. Launching and Stabilizing the Early Republic
8. The Antebellum North and West
9. The Antebellum South and Slavery
10. Drift to Disunion and Civil War
11. Contours of Postwar Society and Reaction
12. Second Hour Exam
13. Imperialism and the Great war
14. "Normalcy," Depression, and the New deal
15. War: Hot, Cold, and the "New World Order"
16. Civil and Other Rights
17. our Decades of Revolutions and Uncertainty
18. The Nineties and Into the Millennium
19. Final Exam

MARINE BIOLOGY

BIO 210
Professor: Sam Minella
Office: XXX
Phone: XXX
E-Mail: XXX
Website: XXX
Office Hours: XXX

Class Times and Locations
- Lecture: M-F 8:30-10:30 or 11:00-1:00 in A200
- Lab: Marine Science Consortium, Wallops Island, VA

Readings
- Readings will be placed on my website or on electronic reserve in the library.

Course Description and Objectives
Marine Biology is an introductory course designed to acquaint students with the diversity and ecology of marine organisms. The main objectives of this course are to understand:
- how scientists investigate questions in marine science
- which organisms are found in the ocean
- how marine organisms are adapted to the unique physical, chemical, and geological characteristics of various habitats in the ocean
- aspects of ecological theory as they apply to marine environments
- how human activities are impacting the ocean

Examinations
Lecture exams will contain a variety of questions including multiple choice, true/false, fill-in-the-blank, illustrations, short answer, essay, etc. Your exams may cover material from the lectures, readings, and field trip to the Marine Science Consortium.

Marine Science Consortium
The lab section of this course will include a multi-day field trip to the Marine Science Consortium in Wallops Island, VA. We will visit sand dunes, a high-energy beach, a low-energy beach, a salt marsh, and will participate on a boat trip to trawl in nearby channels. You will be asked to determine how physical, chemical, and geological features of the environment help to determine community structure.

Lab Report
While at Wallops Island, we will perform student-designed experiments. Over the semester, you will write up the experiments in scientific paper format, including an introduction, materials and methods, results, and discussion. A detailed description of this assignment is attached to this syllabus.

Evaluation
- Exams (2 x 150 points)   300
- Consortium Handout   100
- Lab Report   100
- Total   500 points

Grading Policy
4.0 = Excellent (90 – 100)
3.5 = Very Good (85 – 89)
3.0 = Good (80 – 84)
2.5 = Above Average (75 – 79)
2.0 = Average (70 – 74)
1.0 = Below Average (60 – 69)
0 = Failure (<60)

Attendance Policy
It is very important that students attend lectures. We will have several in-class activities, which will be important for the exams. [More]

Writing Standards
Students enrolled in Marine Biology are expected to use literate and effective English in their speech and in their writing. [More]

Academic Dishonesty
Academic dishonesty (including cheating, plagiarism, etc.) will not be tolerated under any circumstances. [More]

Maintaining Copies of Graded Assignments
It is the student's responsibility to save copies (hard copies or disk copies) of all assignments in the unlikely event that materials become lost, destroyed, or damaged while in my possession. [More]

Schedule
1. Introduction, Classifying living things
2. Phytoplankton
3. Invertebrates
4. Invertebrates/Introduction due
5. Fish
6. Test #1/Methods
7. Whales
8. Sea turtles/Birds
9. Marine Science Consortium
10. Coral Reefs
11. Deep Sea
12. Fishing
13. Final/Results and Discussion

DIVERSITY AND RACIAL CONFLICT

Sociology 142
Professor: Jerry Atrick
Office: XXX
Phone Number: XXX
E-Mail: XXX
PLEASE TURN OFF ALL CELLPHONES

An Overview of the Course
What is "race?" What is "racism?" Why does race continue to matter in contemporary society? This course emphasizes the past and present relations between the white majority and the "colonized" or "kidnapped" minorities (especially, African Americans, Latinos, Native Americans, and Asian Americans). White ethnic immigrants, and "mixed racial groups" are also discussed.

The focus is on power inequality as the most important dimension of a racial stratification order. For example, the colonized minorities not only entered into relations with whites by force and violence, but they experienced enduring systems of subordination such as the slavery institution and the control of tribal institutions by the Bureau of Indian Affairs.

I think you will find the class challenging and hopefully, provocative. Your class attendance and participation in lectures and discussion sections are mandatory and constitute an important portion of your final grade.

Required Readings:
1. *Course Reader for Sociology 142*, Ransford
2. Feagin, *Racist America*
3. Espiritu, A*sian American Women and Men*
4. Hayes-Bautista, *La Nueva California*

Course Grade:
5% quiz, 26% midterm, 26% empirical paper, 26% final, 10% participation and attendance in discussion sections and 7% attendance lectures. Attendance and participation in class discussions is important and the 17% allocated to A&P can make a substantial difference in your final grade. To receive full credit for attendance and participation, you must arrive to class and discussion sections on time.

The midterm and final emphasize essay questions with a preview set of questions handed out one week before the exam. For example, I will pass out seven or eight questions one week before the exam. On the day of the exam, I might call out three essays.

Schedule

1. Introduction to the course
2. Multiple Hierarchy Stratification
3. Colonized vs. Immigrant Minorities
4. Conquest of American Indians
5. Asian-Americans
6. Bureau of Indian Affairs
7. Paternalistic race relations
8. Video: Ethnic notions
9. Research methods
10. Later competitive relations
11. "Eyes on the Prize" video
12. Latinos
13. Midterm Review
14. The social construction of race/ethnicity
15. Interracial marriage and growth of multi-racial groups
16. "Color of Fear" video
17. Mexican Americans and education
18. Dual mobility patterns in Black America
19. Race, class, and health outcomes
20. Mexican immigration
21. Asian immigration
22. Final exam

Empirical paper
The empirical paper (about 10-12 pages) is a required observation paper. It must be a current (this semester) empirical paper dealing with some area of race/ethnicity. It must not be a library report or synthesis of existing research. It must involve direct observation or field work (e.g. questionnaire surveys, in-depth interviews, diary accounts of some situation, participant observation, or an analysis of stereotypes in the media books or magazines). You must do the paper to complete the course.

There are three options for the empirical paper;
1. Participation in the Joint Education Project.
2. Ethnic immersion in churches.
3. Research report on a race/ethnic topic

AMERICAN EDUCATION

Foundations of Education
Professor: I. Noah Lott
Phone: XXX
E-mail: XXX
Hours: XXX

Significance of the Course

This course—designed for both Education majors as well as non-majors—is structured to provide a basic understanding of the American education system. The primary emphasis in this course will be on standards, curriculum, instruction, materials and resources for instruction, fair assessments, and appropriate interventions. Students will learn about significant career foci and about institutions of education within our social, political, and economic systems. Students will also examine the big questions of education - working to know and understand the basic purposes and functions of our schools and school systems.

Required Text
Fredericks, Anthony D. *Ace Your First Year Teaching*. (Indianapolis, IN: Blue River Press, 2017).

Course Objectives
Students in this course will:
1. Develop, implement, assess and modify curriculum and lessons;
2. Apply principles in social competence, social withdrawal, and social role;
3. Create environments that are educationally-focused, respectful, supportive and challenging for all children;
4. Know and understand the multiple influences on development and learning;
5. Effectively apply the principles and theories of child development including developmentally appropriate practices, constructivism and socio-cultural theory;
6. Demonstrate understanding of the way in which classroom environments influence children's learning;
7. Plan, implement and adapt, for all children, developmentally, culturally and linguistically appropriate instructional practices and strategies;
8. Develop classrooms as communities of practice that are learner-oriented;

Course & College Expectations
Class attendance is both mandatory and necessary. Valuable information and ideas are presented and shared during each class session and it is to your benefit as well as the benefit of your colleagues to be both physically and mentally present for each and every class. In fact, it is your primary academic responsibility to attend all classes and to be mentally engaged in the dynamics of each and every lesson. Roll will be taken throughout the semester. Your final grade for the course will be affected as follows:

- 3 unexcused absences (physical or mental) = deduction of 1 full grade
- 4 unexcused absences (physical or mental) = deduction of 2 full grades
- 5 unexcused absences (physical or mental) = deduction of 3 full grades

Excused absences (for health or family emergencies) must be verified with a physician's note or a memo from the Student Affairs Office. Materials, assigned work, and information missed due to absence (physical or mental) are your responsibility and will need to be made up on your own time. Each student is responsible for making sure that all course requirements are completed and on time. The instructor is not responsible for reminding students of missing work.

Course Assignments
- GROUP QUIZZES (20%)
- DIGITAL DISTRICT PROFILE (10%)
  Due Date: February 23
- SCHOOL BOARD MEETING (10%)
  Due Date: April 27
- CLASSROOM VISIT (20%)
  Due Date: April 20
- TEACHER INTERVIEW (20%)
  Due Date: May 2
- MIDTERM EXAM (10%)
  Date: February 23
- FINAL EXAM (10%)
  Date: Thursday, May 11

TENTATIVE COURSE SCHEDULE

1. Introduction to course
2. Philosophy of teaching
3. Effective and successful teachers
4. Effective and successful teachers
5. Administration of schools
6. Administration of schools
7. History of education; standards
8. Diverse students; social problems
9. How students learn
10. Special needs
11. Motivation; discipline
12. Effective classrooms
13. Ethical/legal issues
14. Effective schools
15. Reforms

A

abstraction, 104
academic integrity, 7, 289–294
accountability, 206, 207, 317–320
accrediting agencies, 71
achievement of students, 208
active learning, 31–32
active listening, 228, 238
adjunct professors, 3–14
   active learning, 31–32
   benefits working as, 5
   cooperation among students, 29–31
   costs to institutions, 22
   diverse talents and ways of learning, 37–38
   expectations, 5–7
   high expectations, 35–36
   job descriptions, 15–23
   prompt feedback, 32–34
   salaries, 5, 18
   student-faculty contact, 28–29
   time management, 34–35
   tips for success, 7–9
   types of, 4
adult learners, 238, 239
advance organizers, providing, 129–130, 137
advance preparation, 335–336
advising students, 21
African Americans, 251
aggressive students, 225–228
American Association for Higher Education (AAHE), 27, 28, 29, 32, 34, 35, 37
Analysis
   errors, 104
   perspectives, 104
   questions, 175
anger, 225, 226, 227
anonymity, 163
anticipation guides, 270–273
application, significant learning, 45, 47
applying questions, 174–175
approachability, 92–94
assessments, 7
   evaluations, 268–279 (see also evaluations)
   protocols, 244
assignments, 6, 75, 159–160
   groups, 211
   late papers, 295–296
   outside reading, 243
   reading, 163–164
   unprepared students, 222, 223
attendance, 286–288
attention, maintaining, 126–127, 137
attention-seeking students, 229–230
audio-visual presentations, 132
authenticity of evaluations, 262
authoritarian climate, 231

B

background information, 334–335
background knowledge, 127–128, 137, 171
Bain, ken, 303
behaviors, 253
   discussions, 196–197
   models, 233, 284–285
   problem students, 231–232
beliefs, 79
best practices, 27–38
   active learning, 31–32
   cooperation among students, 29–31
   diverse talents and ways of learning, 37–38
   high expectations, 35–36
   prompt feedback, 32–34
   student-faculty contact, 28–29
   time on tasks, 34–35
Black Student Union, 251
blocking lectures, 144–145
brainstorming, 128
buzz sessions, 133, 166

C

case studies, 215–216
catalogs, 259
chapter logs, 211, 212
chapters. See also textbooks
   logs, 60, 61
   readings, 58–61
chapter summaries, 52
cheating, 73, 289–294
Chicanos, 251
chronological blocks, 144
clarification of questions, 182
classes
   concluding, 136–137
   conducting, 125–138
   developing student connections, 130–131
   large, 155–168 (see also large classes)
   lesson design, 126–127
   providing advance organizers, 129–130
   tapping into background knowledge, 127–128
classification, 104
class reaction forms, 167
classrooms
   building communities, 110–115
   building rapport, 115–122
   constructivism, 203, 204 (see also constructivism)
   designing, 193
   discussions (see discussions)
   dividing into groups, 114–115
   environments, 284
   first day of class, 109–123
   humanistic, 92
   management, 232–234
   meetings, 115
   tips, 122–123
cliffhangers, 136–137
collaboration, evaluations, 262
collaborative groups, 203–205
college enrollment, demographics of, 250

college policies, 76
college services, 259
Colorado State University, 250
color coding lectures, 143–144
commentaries, 52
communication
    departments, 319
    within departments, 285
    oral, 209
communication skills, 91
communication strategies, 245–247
communities
    building, 110–115
    creating, 222
    diversity and, 260
community, sense of, 208
comparing, 104, 182
complaints
    about teachers, 85
    about textbooks, 57
comprehending questions, 174
comprehensible presentations, 87–89
concreteness, 241
confidence, 246
conflicts of interest, 22
consensus building, 205
constructing support, 104
constructive controversies, 214
constructivism, 100–103, 107, 108, 190, 203, 204, 324–325
    groups, 216–217
    learning, 208
content, 48. See also topics
    designing courses, 41
    presentations, 216
continuing education, 336
contracts, 4, 5
controversial blocks, 144
controversial topics, discussions, 202
cooperation among students, 29–31
cooperative groups, 206–209, 285
costs to institutions, 22
counseling students, 21
courses, 125–138. See also classes; designing courses; lessons
    designing, 39–50
    diverse students, 255–259
    evaluations, 78, 258, 261–281, 308 (see also evaluations)
    introductions, 41–45
    nontraditional students, 241–243
    objectives, 70–71
    schedules, 223
    syllabi, 65–80 (see also syllabi)
    teaching, 4, 5
    what students want, 83–96
    without textbooks, 63–64
creating questions, 176
credibility, 226
criteria, evaluations, 267–268

criterion checks, 306–307
critical learning environments, 322–324
critical thinking skills, 209
culture, learning, 317–318
curriculum vita (CV), 335, 336–338
customizing rubrics, 270

D
debriefing, 135
deduction, 104
deficit models, 250
demographics of college enrollment, 250
demonstrations, 132
departments
    communication, 319
    diversity and, 259–260
DePaul University, 53
designing
    classrooms, 193
    courses, 39–50
    content, 41
        errors, 40
        introductions, 41–45
        significant learning, 45–48
        topics, 48–50
    elements, 69–79
    large classes, 168
    lessons, 126–127
    questions, 114, 119, 120
    syllabi, 65–80
differences, respecting, 253
differential treatment, 258
directions, clarity of, 207
discouraged students, 228–229
discrimination, 250, 255
discussions, 6, 189–202
    behavior, 196–197
    benefits of, 191
    controversial topics, 202
    groups, 166, 167
    monopolizers, 201
    panel, 213
    participation in, 200–201
    ping-pong effect, 198–199
    questions, 196
    stages of, 191, 192
        after the discussion, 199
        before the discussion, 192–197
        during the discussion, 197–199
    starting, 194
    stimulating, 195
    troubleshooting, 200–202
    unprepared students, 200
    visual organizers, 197–198
divergent viewpoints, 205, 251–255
diverse students, 37–38, 249–260
    courses, 255–259
    institutions, 259–260
divide and conquer strategy, 230
Draves, William, 238

Drew, Charles, 255
Dunno Syndrome, reducing, 182–185

E
elements
  of lessons, 131
  of a syllabus, 69–79
  of textbooks, 52–53
emotional characteristics of nontraditional students, 237–239
employment strategies, 327–342
  expectations, 328–329
  qualifications, 329–331
  searching for employment, 338–340
  sequence of planned activities, 334–340
  teaching experience, 331–334
encouragement, 107, 245
end-of-course ratings, 308
enthusiasm, 20, 94–96
environments
  critical learning, 322–324
  supportive, 89–96
errors
  analysis, 104
  course design, 40
essays (exams), 162
evaluations, 7
  anticipation guides, 270–273
  assessment tools, 268–279
  collaboration, 262
  courses, 78, 258
  criterion checks, 306–307
  end-of-course ratings, 308
  group quizzes, 273–279
  groups, 205
  instructors, 78
  journal entry sheets, 279
  learning, 264–267
  mid-term course, 307, 330
  peer, 309–312
  performance, 263–264
  progress, 171
  questions, 175–176
  rubrics, 269–270
  self evaluation, 312–313
  sheets, 166
  standards and criteria, 267–268
  student perceptions, 305–306
  student ratings, 303–305
  students, 18, 261–281, 302–303
  teaching, 301–313
  tests, 161–163
  textbooks, 55–58
Everybody In strategy, 185–187
exams. See tests
expanding questions, 179–181, 182
expectations, 35–36, 245, 253. See also syllabi
  of adjunct professors, 5–7
  approachability, 92–94
  comprehensible presentations, 87–89
  employment strategies, 328–329
  enthusiasm, 94–96
    vs. reality, 283–286
  real life experiences, 86–87
  respect, 92–94
  stating, 286
  supportive environments, 89–96
  what students want, 83–96
experience, 7
experimenting, 133
expository advance organizers, 129
extras, 76
extrinsic motivation, 105

F
facilitation of groups, 217
faculties, 22, 28–29. See also adjunct professors; teachers
fairness, 227, 230, 246
familiarity, 240
fears, 225
feedback, 32–34, 89, 90, 136, 230, 238
Filene, Peter, 41, 68, 301
final exams, 162
Fink, L. Dee, 45
first day of class, 109–123
  building communities, 110–115
  building rapport, 115–122
  tips, 122–123
fishbowls, 158
focus groups, 214, 223–224
follow-up lessons, 136
forms, class reaction, 167
foundational knowledge, 45, 47, 49
full-time positions, 22–23
Furio, Brian, 146

G
gender sensitivity, 257, 258
generalizations, avoiding, 253
glossaries, 53
goals, 36
  course introductions, 41–45
  groups, 206
  instructional, 231
  syllabi, 69
grading plans, 74–76
graphic organizers, 130, 133, 143
Gross, Barbara, 94
grouping practices, 251–255
groups
  accountability, 206, 207
  anonymity in, 163
  assignments, 211
  chapter logs, 211, 212
  collaborative, 203–205
  constructive controversies, 214
  constructivism, 216–217
  cooperative, 206–209, 285
  discussions, 166, 167

facilitation of, 217
focus, 214, 223–224
goals, 206
heterogeneous, 207
jigsaw, 213
numbered heads, 215
quizzes, 273–279
selection, 209–212
snowball, 166
STAD (Student Teams-Achievement Divisions), 213
strategies, 212–216
study, 167, 245
think-pair-share, 214
trial, 213
guest speakers, 78, 256–257
Guided Reading, 58

H
handouts, 158
Harvard University, 115
health care, 17
help, asking for, 21
heterogeneous groups, 207
hierarchical blocks, 144
high expectations, 35–36
Hispanics, 251
human dimension, 46, 47
humanistic classrooms, 92
humor, 90, 91, 239

I
identity (self-concept), 105
immediacy, 241
inappropriate comments, 254
inattentive students, 224–225
independent practice, 134
individual accountability, 317–320
induction, 104
information, obtaining, 182
information storage, 31
institutions, diverse students, 259–260
instructional goals, 231
instructions, clarity of, 207
instructors
    evaluations, 78
    teacher roles, 93
integration, learning, 46, 47
interdependence, 208
interviews, 132, 215, 336–338
intrinsic motivation, 105
introductions, 41–45, 52
invitational classrooms, 107
issues and concerns, 283–296
    academic integrity, 289–294
    attendance, 286–288
    expectations vs. reality, 283–286
    late papers, 295–296
    stating expectations, 286
    tardiness, 288–289

J
jigsaw groups, 213
job descriptions, 15–23
job security, 16
journal entry sheets, 279

K
key ideas, 52
key questions, 52
knowledge element of lessons, 131–132, 137–138
Koch, Ed, 94, 304

L
language, respect, 254
large classes
    active student involvement, 158–168
    designing, 168
    organization, 156–157
    teaching, 155–168
    tests, 161–163
late papers, 295–296
laws of learning, 99–100
    Law of Association, 100
    Law of Challenge, 100
    Law of Effect, 100
    Law of Emotions, 100
    Law of Expectations, 100
    Law of Feedback, 100
    Law of Intensity, 100
    Law of Involvement, 100
    Law of Readiness, 99–100
    Law of Relaxation, 100
    Law of Relevance, 100
learning
    active, 31–32
    adult, 238, 239
    application, 45, 47
    building communities, 110–115
    collaborative, 204–205
    constructivism, 100–103, 208
    diverse talents and ways of, 37–38
    emphasis on, 98–99
    evaluations, 264–267
    foundational knowledge, 45, 47
    how students learn, 97–108
    how to learn, 46, 47
    human dimension, 46, 47
    integration, 46, 47
    laws of, 99–100
    lectures, 139–153
    as lifelong process, 325–326
    objectives, 207
    psychology of, 97–98, 105–107
    questioning, 103–105
    significant, 45–48
    time to learn, 207
learning enhancement, 29
Learning Resources Network, 238

lectures, 6, 131–132, 139–153
    blocking, 144–145
    color coding, 143–144
    concluding, 149–150
    continuing, 146–149
    formats, 285
    graphic organizers, 143
    length of, 141
    notes for, 142–143, 157
    overview of, 140–142
    planning, 142–145
    processing breaks, 152
    research, 141
    starting, 145–146
    tips, 151–153
lessons, 125–138
    concluding, 136–137, 138
    designing, 126–127
    developing student connections, 30–131
    follow-up, 136
    plans, 16–17
    providing advance organizers, 129–130
    samples, 137–138
    tapping into background knowledge, 127–128
    teaching, 131–135, 137–138
LGBT students, 251, 252, 255
life insurance, 17
listening
    active, 228, 238
    skills, 227
lists
    goals, 43
    outcomes, 44
logs, chapters, 60, 61

M
Management
    classrooms, 232–234
    time, 34–35
marginal notes, 52
mass punishment, 231
McAdams, Kay, 105
McGlynn, Angela, 193
meetings
    classrooms, 115
    students, 254
memory, remembering questions, 173
mentors, 319–320
Middle East, 255
mid-term course evaluations, 307, 330
minor events, ignoring, 285
models
    behavior, 233, 284–285
    deficit, 250
monopolizers, discussions, 201
motivation, 105
motivational characteristics of nontraditional students, 239–240
multiple colleges, teaching at, 4, 5

multiple courses, teaching, 4, 5

N
narrative advance organizers, 129
national licensing boards, 71
negativity, 231
Nolan, Jessica, 157
nontraditional students, 235–247. See also students
    communication strategies, 245–247
    courses, 241–243
    emotional characteristics, 237–239
    motivational characteristics, 239–240
    personal characteristics, 240–241
    planning, 241
    social characteristics, 236–237
    teaching considerations, 243–245
notes for lectures, 142–143
numbered heads groups, 215

O
Objectives
    courses, 70–71
    learning, 207
observation, 132, 177
observers, 78
One-Minute Paper, 160
One Page Only, 160
One Question Quiz, 223
open door policies, 227
opening lessons, 126–127, 137
opinions, expressing, 227
opportunity for success, groups, 206
oral communication, 209
orientation, student, 320–322
outcomes, course introductions, 41–45
outlines, 66. See also syllabi
outside readings assignments, 243
overreacting, 231

P
panel discussions, 213
participation in discussions, 200–201
pausing, lectures, 152
peer evaluations, 309–312
perceptions, students, 305–306
performance
    element of lessons, 134–135, 138
    evaluations, 171, 263–264
permanent positions, 22–23
permission forms, 79
personal characteristics of nontraditional students, 240–241
personal development plans, 326
perspectives, 104, 240–241
ping-pong effect (discussions), 198–199
planning
    lectures, 142–145
    lesson plans, 16–17
    nontraditional students, 241

points, reading, 196
point systems, 75
pop quizzes, 161
positive feedback, 89, 90, 238
positive interdependence, 206–207
poster sessions, 159
post-reading activities, 60
PowerPoint presentations, 157
predictions, 128
prejudices, 246, 250
presentations, 87–89
    blocks, 159
    content, 216
privacy, 78
probing questions, 182
problem-solving, 133, 240
problem students, 221–234. See also issues and concerns
    aggressive students, 225–228
    attention-seeking students, 229–230
    behaviors, 231–232
    classroom management tips, 232–234
    discouraged students, 228–229
    inattentive students, 224–225
    unprepared students, 222–224
processes, 48
processing breaks, 152
professional resources, 341
progress, evaluations, 171
progressive blocks, 144
prompt feedback, 32–34
prompting questions, 181–182
protocols
    assessments, 244
psychology of learning, 97–98, 105–107

Q
qualifications, employment, 329–331
questions, 136, 158, 169–187
    analysis, 175
    applying, 174–175
    clarification, 182
    comparing, 182
    comprehending, 174
    creating, 176
    designing, 114, 119, 120
    discussions, 196
    evaluations, 175–176
    expanding, 182
    how to teach students, 9–14
    learning, 103–105
    obtaining information, 182
    question blocks, 145
    reasons for asking, 171–172
    remembering, 173
    self, 196
    self-questioning, 128
    strategies, 177–187
        Everybody In, 185–187
        expanding, 179–181
        probing, 182
        prompting, 181–182
        reducing Dunno Syndrome, 182–185
        wait time, 177–179
    taxonomy of, 172–176
quizzes, 161
    cheating, 292, 293
    groups, 273–279
    One Question Quiz, 223
quotations, 52

R
racial discrimination, 255
Ransford, Ed, 37, 286
rapport, building, 115–122
ratings
    end-of-course, 308
    students, 303–305 (see also evaluations)
reader's roundtables, 215
reading
    assignments, 163–164
    chapters, 59
    importance of, 196
    information, 132
    points, 196
reality, expectations vs., 283–286
real life experiences, 86–87
reasons for asking questions, 171–172
reducing Dunno Syndrome, 182–185
reflective inquiry, 135
relationships, 28–29, 38
    developing student connections, 130–131
    students, 137, 208
remembering questions, 173
research, lectures, 141
resources
    colleges, 259
    handbooks, 53
respect, 92–94, 245
    differences, 253
    language, 254
    for students, 208
responsibilities, 5–7, 15–23
resumes, 333. See also employment strategies
retirement, 17
reviewing understood material, 231–232
reviews, three-minute, 215
Richardson, Steven, 284
role playing, 135
Rotenberg, Robert, 53
roundtables, 115
rubrics, 269–270

S
salaries, 5, 18
samples
    lectures, 150–151
    lessons, 137–138
    syllabi, 342–345
schedules, 17, 223

searching for employment, 338–340
seating charts, 165
Seip, Terry, 305
selecting groups, 209–212
self-esteem, 209, 237
self evaluation, 312–313
self-fulfilling prophecies, 252
self questions, 128, 196
self reflection, 312–313
self-worth, 237
semantic webbing, 134
seminars, 167
sessions
   buzz, 166
   poster, 159
significant learning, 45–48
simplicity, 241
simulations, 135
skimming advance organizers, 130
small group discussions, 133
snowball groups, 166
social characteristics of nontraditional students, 236–237
social context of learning, 106
social skills, 209
STAD (Student Teams-Achievement Divisions), 213
stages of discussions, 191, 192
   after the discussion, 199
   before the discussion, 192–197
   during the discussion, 197–199
standards, 71, 267–268
starting discussions, 194
stimulating discussions, 195
strategies. See also best practices
   constructivism, 100–103
   divide and conquer, 230
   employment, 327–342
   evaluations, 266
   feedback, 32–34
   groups, 212–216
   interviews, 336–338
   lesson plans, 16–17
   problem students, 221–234
   questions, 177–187
      Everybody In, 185–187
      expanding, 179–181
      probing, 182
      prompting, 181–182
      reducing Dunno Syndrome, 182–185
      wait time, 177–179
   reader interaction, 59–60
   reading chapters, 59
   syllabi design, 67
   teaching, 9–14, 94
student-faculty contact, 28–29
Student Observation Form, 304
Students
   achievement, 208
   active involvement (lectures), 58–168
   active learning, 31–32
   activities, 52
   advising, 21
   aggressive, 225–228
   approachability, 92–94
   attention-seeking, 229–230
   blame of, 19
   cheating, 289–294
   classroom management tips, 232–234
   communication strategies, 245–247
   comprehensible presentations, 87–89
   constructivism, 100–103
   conversations with, 21–22
   cooperation among, 29–31
   developing connections, 130–131
   discouraged, 228–229
   discussions, 200
   diverse, 249–260
   diversity of, 37–38
   enthusiasm, 94–96
   evaluations, 18, 261–281, 302–303 (see also evaluations)
   expectations vs. reality, 283–286
   feedback, 32–34
   how students learn, 97–108
   inattentive, 224–225
   involvement, 171
   laws of learning, 99–100
   LGBTQ, 251, 252
   meetings, 254
   nontraditional, 235–247
   orientation, 320–322
   participation in discussions, 200–201
   perceptions, 305–306
   problem, 221–234 (see also problem students)
   psychology of learning, 97–98, 105–107
   ratings, 303–305
   real life experiences, 86–87
   relationships, 137, 208
   respect, 92–94
   respect for, 208
   stimulating to ask questions, 171–172
   summaries, 136, 138
   supportive environments, 89–96
   surveys, 84, 85
   unprepared, 222–224
   what students want, 83–96
study groups, 167, 245
study guides, 157
Study of Social Change, 250
study sheets, 78–79
success, 315–326
   adjunct professors, 7–9
   in the classroom, 122–123
   constructivism, 324–325
   critical learning environments, 322–324
   groups, 206
   individual accountability, 317–320
   learning as lifelong process, 325–326
   student orientation, 320–322

suggestions for, 78
suggested readings and resources, 52
Suinn, Richard, 250
summaries
   students, 136, 138
   teachers, 136, 138
support, constructing, 104
supportive environments, 89–96
support services, 79
surveys, 57, 84, 85
syllabi, 6, 35, 41
   academic dishonesty, 73
   additional materials, 72
   class participation, 73
   course description, 70
   course information, 69
   course objectives, 70–71
   course procedures, 72–73
   course schedules, 76–77
   designing, 65–80
   elements, 69–79
   grading plans, 74–76
   instructor information, 69–70
   miscellaneous, 77–79
   mixed assignments/exams, 73
   overview of, 65–69
   required textbook(s), 72
   safety rules, 73
   samples, 342–345
   supplementary readings, 72
synthesis element of lessons, 132–134, 138, 205

T
tardiness, 288–289
taxonomy
   of questions, 172–176
   of significant learning, 45–48
      application, 45, 47
      foundational knowledge, 45, 47
      human dimension, 46, 47
      integration, 46, 47
      learning how to learn, 46, 47
teachers
   roles, 93, 205
   summaries, 136, 138
teaching
   development of skills, 19–20
   evaluations, 301–313
   experience, 331–334
   large classes, 155–168
   lessons, 131–135, 137–138
   nontraditional students, 243–245
   strategies, 9–14, 94
teamwork, 216–217. See also groups
temporary job security, 16
terminal degrees, 23
tests
   cheating, 292, 293
   diverse students, 256
   large classes, 161–163

textbooks
   courses without, 63–64
   effective use of, 58–61
   elements of, 52–53
   evaluations, 55–58
   selecting, 51–64
   as tools, 62
texting, 224
think-pair-share groups, 214
Thirty Percent Rule, 160
three-minute reviews, 215
three-step interviews, 215
time management, 34–35
time to learn, 207
tools
   anticipation guides, 270–273
   assessment, 268–279
   evaluations, 262 (see also evaluations)
   group quizzes, 273–279
   journal entry sheets, 279
   rubrics, 269–270
topics
   blocks, 144
   controversial (discussions), 202
   designing courses, 48–50
Totenberg, Robert, 225
trial groups, 213
troubleshooting
   discussions, 200–202
   problem students, 221–234
trust, establishing, 257, 284

U
understood material, reviewing, 231–232
University of California, Berkeley, 94
University of North Carolina at Chapel Hill, 41, 68, 301
University of Southern California, 22, 37
US Department of Education, 236

V
validation of student contributions, 93
vignettes, 52
visual organizers, 197–198

W
wait time, 177–179
web support, 53
West, Kim, 22
Winona (MN) State University, 284
writing course introductions, 41–45

About the Author

Anthony D. Fredericks, Ed.D is a nationally recognized educator well known for his practical teacher materials and stimulating and engaging conference presentations. A retired professor of education at York College of Pennsylvania, he is an award-winning and best-selling author of more than 150 books, including teacher resource materials, children's, and adult non-fiction titles. His extensive background includes experience as a classroom teacher, reading specialist, professional storyteller, curriculum coordinator, educational consultant, and staff developer.